The Philadelphia Inquirer

WEEKEND JOURNEYS

52 trips

*A destination for
every weekend of the year*

THE MIDDLE ATLANTIC PRESS
Wilmington, Delaware

WEEKEND JOURNEYS

A MIDDLE ATLANTIC PRESS BOOK

First Middle Atlantic Press printing, 1988

ISBN: 0-912608-59-5

The Middle Atlantic Press, Inc.
848 Church Street
Wilmington, Delaware 19899

Distributed by:
National Book Network, Inc.
4720 A Boston Way
Lanham, Maryland 20706

WEEKEND JOURNEYS

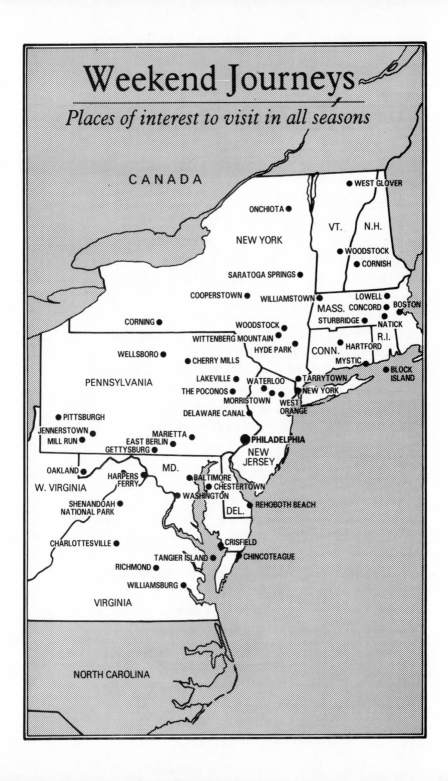

Weekend Journeys

Places of interest to visit in all seasons

Weekend Journeys

Spring

Summer

Fall

Winter

Preface

The trouble with newspapers is that you throw them away. This usually means that by the time you're ready for a weekend getaway, the story you meant to clip about canoeing in the Adirondacks is long gone. At The Philadelphia Inquirer, however, we save just about everything, so we have that canoeing story as well as hundreds of others that have appeared under the Weekend Journey heading in the Travel section of the Sunday paper.

Over the years, the Weekend Journey column has managed to cover most of the Eastern seaboard in trips of two to four days. For this book, we have selected 52 of the best stories — one for every weekend of the year — from our recent files. The destinations range from Vermont to Virginia and include 12 states and Washington, D.C., proving that you have a lot of choice when your starting point is Philadelphia. Although some of these stories are a few years old, that doesn't mean that they are out of date; all prices and hours of operation have been checked and updated as of the fall of 1987.

The destinations are divided by season. Deciding which trip should be made in which season was sometimes simply a matter of common sense. Unless you like tramping about in the cold, winter is not the time to tackle the sites along Boston's historic Freedom Trail. On the other hand, winter is a good time to visit Colonial Williamsburg, which comes alive with special Christmas programs in December, or to tour Thomas Jefferson's Monticello,

where the crowds are smaller in the off-season and you'll probably get a more extensive tour.

But some places are ideal destinations for a Weekend Journey no matter what the weather, so assigning them to a season was sometimes a rather arbitrary decision. Therefore, if you're reading this in July, don't confine yourself to the summer pages. Browse through some of the other seasons because many stories mention festivals or special events that take place throughout the year.

For example, you'll find Chestertown, Md., in the winter section. A charming town in any season, it is particularly interesting in the colder months when its inlets and creeks are filled with thousands of swans and other migratory birds that have arrived for the winter. Yet the story also mentions that it's worth the two-hour trip in September for a candle-light tour of the town's Federal, Georgian and Victorian homes and that its summer delights include boating, picnicking and catching blue crabs.

We have tried to include some small towns that you may not have heard of as well as the major cities. When it came to choosing stories about Washington, D.C., Baltimore and New York City, we found that we couldn't capture the essence of any of them in a single story. So you will find one story devoted to the major museums along the mall in Washington, D.C., and another on the city's little museums; one story on the old-fashioned romantic things to do in New York City and another on the

i

newest of the new in the art world of SoHo; one story on the aquarium and Inner Harbor in Baltimore and another on the museums, theaters and other aspects of the cultural side of the town as well as a story on four Maryland railroad museums that starts at the magnificent roundhouse of the Baltimore & Ohio Railroad.

Sometimes you know how many hours you want to spend getting to your destination, but not exactly where you want to end up. In that case, consult the distance index at the end of the book, which groups the trips according to driving time. This index can also help you decide whether you want to drive or whether it might make more sense to fly all or part of the way.

Like the writers who traveled with their children in tow, we have tried to keep everyone happy with a variety of activities. All of the stories are indexed by activity including those that just seem to defy categorization such as the weekend in the "land of love," where the Jacuzzi in your room is a seven-foot-tall champagne glass. And what about candlepin bowling? We admit you wouldn't head to New England just to go bowling (at least not the first time), but you might want to check out the local version of the game the next time you're in Massachusetts.

There are stories on hiking, biking, skiing and canoeing for the athletically inclined. If you and your traveling companion have different ideas of what constitutes outdoor activity, be sure to read the story about Shenandoah National Park in Virginia to see how one couple has solved the problem — without resorting to divorce.

If you're more at home in museums than on the trail, there are plenty of places for you to visit including Fallingwater, the stunning, dramatic house that Frank Lloyd Wright built over a waterfall in Mill Run, Pa., and Morristown, N.J., one of the Revolutionary War encampments for George Washington and his troops. While you're in Morristown, don't forget to check out the fine restaurants, antiques stores and craft galleries. (There are also hiking trails nearby — for those who get itchy in museums.)

Indeed you may find that some places offer almost too much to do. Says the writer of the Chestertown, Md., story, "Although it would be quite possible to spend a weekend doing absolutely nothing taxing in Chestertown, it's also quite possible to find the sun setting Sunday before you have gotten halfway through your activities list." And that, she suggests, may be the sign of a perfect Weekend Journey.

•

This book was edited by Martha Hewson with assistance from Lisa Karoly. The stories originally appeared in the Travel section of The Philadelphia Inquirer, which is edited by Mike Shoup, travel editor, and Jack Severson, executive travel editor. Roger Hasler of The Inquirer's editorial art department provided the maps.

A painter works at the North Bridge in
Concord, Mass., where "the shot heard round
the world" was fired on April 19, 1775.

Baltimore, Md.

How to have a whale of a time at the aquarium and Inner Harbor

By Mike Shoup
Inquirer Travel Editor

Take a few thousand fish of striking sizes and colors — from vicious-looking, 10-foot-long, gray sand tiger sharks down to dainty powder-blue surgeonfish that measure a few inches, nose to tailfin.

Put the fish in gargantuan tanks of filtered saltwater, where it's possible for mere humans to meet them practically face to face.

Construct an eye-catching building, with color panels on the walls, soaring glass pyramids on top and a long scribble of blue neon on the side that tells the night of the aquarium's flamboyant form and dramatic harborside location.

Open the doors and, presto, what do you get? For the visitor, a delightful time exploring the denizens of the deep and the best introduction to a weekend along Baltimore's revivified waterfront that money can buy. And, for the City of Baltimore, one of the major success stories of urban tourism today.

It's amazing what just a few fish can do.

Of course, the story of Baltimore's emergence in the 1980s as a top tourist destination is not just a fishy tale. It is a story of steady leadership at the top and of enthusiastic corporate and public cooperation below. The National Aquarium and surrounding Inner Harbor attractions also have those three salient qualities that cause real estate moguls to salivate in their sleep: location, location and location.

Beyond the Inner Harbor, Baltimore has, in the last decade, opened new museums and upgraded old ones. First-class hotels have sprung up at the waterfront periphery, and new retail and office construction spirals back from there. The Rouse Co. is involved in a major way here. In addition to its Harborplace shops and restaurants, the largest single investment in the Inner Harbor's history is currently rising not far back from the water's edge. It's the Gallery at Harborplace, a complex that will include offices, more than 100 shops and restaurants and a 622-room hotel.

But it is the aquarium that anchors a visit to the Inner Harbor. When it opened in August 1981, the projected annual attendance was somewhere between 600,000 and 700,000; the average since has been double that. A major expansion, which will feature a 1,300-seat amphitheater for dolphin and whale shows, is about to be built on the adjacent Pier 4.

It's difficult to be anything other than enthusiastic about the aquarium. Visitors follow escalators, walkways and moving ramps on a tour through different aquatic environments, ranging from an Appalachian pond in Maryland to a Pacific coral reef teeming with fish of bright colors and startling shapes. There is an immense amount to absorb and learn here, and although the average visit takes two hours, the curious may spend half a day among the tanks.

The long lines that used to form at the aquarium have been pretty much eliminated by advance ticket sales for entry at a specific time. While they're waiting, visitors can wander about the adjacent retail shops of Harborplace, board a submarine or several other dockside ships, stop in at the Maryland Science Center nearby or just watch feedings of the harbor seals and gray seals that frolic in the aquarium's outdoor pool.

Once inside, visitors are drawn to the marine mammal pool and two beluga whales named Anore and Illamar, which inhabit the 260,000-gallon pool. Divers enter the water five times daily to feed the whales and frolic with them, and they can be seen from practically all levels of the aquarium. The whales were captured in a Canadian river near Churchill, a Hudson Bay community known primarily for its fall invasion of polar bears.

Watching the excitement of children who press their noses to the glass here is almost as interesting as watching the fish.

At the tanks where sharks prowl the deep: "Oh, oh. Look at that. Wow!" "Ah, he's cute." "Look at that huge one." Or, screaming, "Eeeeeee! Look at those teeth!"

Or at the Pacific Coral Reef, where you'll find all the incredible fish you always wanted to see while diving or snorkeling, but never did: "OK, I'm looking for the yellow-face angelfish." "Wow! Wow! Mine's that one, the red one." "OK, that one's mine; the yellow one's mine."

(Those who don't appreciate grade-school classes of enthusiastic children — and it can get awfully loud — should avoid Friday mornings, the most likely time for school visits.)

Smaller children are especially drawn to a children's cove, where guides help them touch and examine crabs, sea urchins and anemones. Somewhere along the way, visitors encounter everything from electric eels and piranhas to "poison arrow" frogs that secrete a toxin used by natives of the Amazon to poison the tips of their arrows.

Eventually, the upward route ends in a humid South American tropical rain forest — in the glass pyramid that, from the exterior, gives the aquarium its unique trapezoidal look. There are dozens of tropical birds here, and you don't have to search much for some of them, such as the bright-red scarlet ibis and the brilliant green Amazon parrots. There are also two thoroughly repulsive sloths, named Charlie and Rapunzel, lurking in the trees and moving very slowly, as sloths are wont to do. Perhaps they will remind you of somebody in your office.

The best is last: The huge, ring-shaped tank containing Atlantic coral reef fish, and, below this tank, another that holds the aquarium's collection of sharks (nurse, lemon, sand tiger and sandbar), rays and game fish. Together, these two tanks contain well over a half-million gallons of water.

Visitors descend ramps through the center and are surrounded, first, on the upper level, by hundreds of parrot, angel, butterfly and damsel fish and other exotic reef creatures, then by the sharks and game fish on the darker lower level. Divers descend into the upper tank several times a day to feed the fish; the lower tank is off-limits, as one glance at its inhabitants will tell.

After this dramatic conclusion, lunch or dinner is probably in order, and a good number of tourists head for the nearby Taverna Athena for Greek dishes, or Phillips Harborplace, a huge seafood house. Both are located in separate pavilions that make up Rouse's Harborplace dining and shopping areas — one of those retail developments typical of waterfront revivals in other parts of the country — and both serve meals that seem above average, considering the location and tourist clientele.

For lighter, faster fare or sweets, there are several raw bars and various fast-food establishments, plus the usual shops vending ice cream, cookies, fudge etc. Harborplace is full of these places, and all seem more than a cut above the average in appearance, merchandise and that intangible quality one might simply call attitude. Certainly, Harborplace is superior to its New York equivalent, the South Street Seaport.

Those still intent on following a watery theme will enjoy visits to the USS Torsk, a World War II submarine moored beside the aquarium, and the Chesapeake lightship, which spent many years at the mouth of Chesapeake Bay before it was replaced by a light tower in September 1965. (A tour of both costs $2.50.)

Nearby, its prow overhanging the awnings of the Taverna Athena, is the frigate Constellation, launched Sept. 7, 1797, and now "the world's oldest ship continuously afloat." (Touring its four decks costs $1.75.)

The mere fact that this beautiful ship is still around in one piece is nothing short of astounding. It participated in the Barbary Coast wars off Tripoli in the early 1800s, and was back in Norfolk, Va., in 1813, firing at the British. Later, it was used in efforts to eliminate pirates in the West Indies and sailed around the world as part of a squadron seeking to open trade with China. It was not until 1955 that the Constellation was decommissioned.

Back on the ground, you can get a good view of the harbor and surrounding area by taking the elevator to the 27th-floor observation platform of the World Trade Center, which is also right at harborside.

The Maryland Science Center is nearby, and if you have children, it's probably worth the $5 entrance fee to let them tinker with the many hands-on displays and computer-keyboard games.

Nightclubbers flock to the Power Plant, once the source of power for Baltimore's streetcars and now home to several clubs and entertainment centers. The huge brick building looms a bit gloomily over the aquarium, but at night, it's more cheerful, outlined in bright yellow lights like Philadelphia's Boathouse Row.

For dining, Baltimore's Little Italy is practically behind the Power Plant, just a little farther east on Pratt Street, and within easy walking distance of the Inner Harbor. On the way over, you'll pass Connolly's, a small, casual seafood restaurant that's packed on weekends, or the more pretentious Chart House.

Perhaps the greatest thing about the Inner Harbor, beyond the aquarium, is not any one of its attractions and institutions, but rather the sum of its more subtle parts: the click of heels on brick promenades; the murmur of voices on a warm spring evening; the sight of lovers embracing on a harborside bench; the bright lights reflecting and shimmering off the harbor; the rhythm of Dixieland jazz echoing from a terrace bar, or simply the smell of the sea wafting up against urban America.

H. L. Mencken, a native son, once complained that the rotting wharves and warehouses and the fetid atmosphere of Baltimore's harbor "smelled like a million polecats." He'd hardly know the place today.

•

Admission to the National Aquarium is $6.75 for adults, $5 for children 12 to 18, $3.75 for ages 3 to 11 and free for those under 3. During the summer, it is open Monday to Thursday 9 a.m. to 5 p.m., Friday to Sunday 9 a.m. to 8 p.m. The rest of the year it's open daily 9 a.m. to 5 p.m. except Friday, when it stays open until 8 p.m.

There is another world of museums and history just beyond the Inner Harbor. For more information, contact the Baltimore Office of Promotion and Tourism, 34 Market Place, Suite 310, Baltimore, Md. 21202. Phone 301-837-4636.

Baltimore, Md.

A *harbor for the arts that's alive with plays, concerts, exhibits*

By Stephan Salisbury
Inquirer Staff Writer

This is a town that's well-known for what used to be here — football, for instance, or Poe, or Mencken.

It's a town that used to have a gritty waterfront but now sports a pristine shopping mall instead, and a concrete bunker filled with fish swimming in circles. That's called progress.

But there is more to Baltimore than jokes and nostalgia and the Inner Harbor. Over the last several years, a lively cultural scene has developed here, anchored by a couple of theaters, some musical organizations and the two principal art museums.

On any given weekend, the revivified and cozy downtown is alive with plays, concerts, art exhibitions and performances of all kinds. What's more, virtually everything is within easy walking distance.

For people used to making cultural treks to New York City and Washington, Baltimore represents not only a welcome change, but a real surprise. During the course of a recent leisurely weekend, a friend and I took in two challenging theatrical productions — at the Center Stage and the Theater Project — and paid lengthy visits to the Walters Art Gallery and the Baltimore Museum of Art.

And we still had an opportunity to spend a morning sitting in a cafe on the waterfront and visiting some of this city's excellent bookstores — like Louie's on Charles Street.

Our base of operations was a real find, the red brick Shirley Guest House, 205 W. Madison St. (301-728-6550), an absolutely charming 17-room Victorian inn, just two blocks west of Charles Street and a stone's throw from the Meyerhoff Symphony Hall, the Lyric Opera House, the Walters Art Gallery and numerous other cultural institutions. (The Shirley offers a special package of rooms and tickets with the innovative Theater Project; call for details.)

After a two-hour Friday afternoon drive, the Shirley proved a true haven. We had time to savor some complimentary sherry and relax a bit before strolling over to the Center Stage, no more than five minutes away, at 700 N. Calvert St. (301-332-0033), for its production of Christopher Durang's *The Marriage of Bette and Boo.*

The Center Stage is hardly a new kid on the block. It is the leading regional theater in these parts and has been in its current home, a converted Jesuit school building, since 1975. In recent years, it has even served as a stop on the pre-Broadway circuit.

A work by Christopher Durang,

5

then, is not unusual for this stage. But given Baltimore's Catholic traditions and the previous incarnation of the theater itself, something like *Bette and Boo* takes on particular tang. Most of Durang's wit here, as in *Sister Mary Ignatius Explains It All for You*, is aimed at the alternately soft and brittle heart of American Catholic life.

After the theater, there are any number of diverse restaurants to choose from in the area for a late dinner. We settled on Akbar, a small and quite elegant Indian spot at 823 N. Charles St. It couldn't have been much better — reasonably priced curries, delicious breads and creditable, though uninspired, desserts.

After a continental breakfast in the Shirley's comfortable parlor on Saturday morning, we decided to stroll down to the Inner Harbor. Sipping coffee and reading the paper in the warm air of early spring, we watched hundreds of people milling around the National Aquarium.

We headed for the Walters Art Gallery, 600 N. Charles St. The collections in this museum were assembled by William Walters and his son Henry, and are housed in three connected buildings, two of which were undergoing renovation when we were there. As a result, many wonderful paintings by Raphael, Veronese and other old masters, and a large proportion of the Asian collections, could not be seen.

What was on view was of more than passing interest. During our visit, the major special exhibition consisted of glasswork made by Frederick Carder, a founder of the Steuben Glass Works in Corning, N.Y.

More intriguing and idiosyncratic was a fine small exhibit of Dutch and Northern European art drawn from the museum's holdings. Here was a brilliant portrait by Hugo van der Goes (1440-1482) and a grim rendering by Josse Lieferinxe of St. Sebastian interceding for the sick during a Roman plague. This latter panel, done in the late 15th century, probably belongs to the same Marseille

altarpiece as four panels in the collections of the Philadelphia Museum of Art.

Elsewhere during this visit, the Walters offered two very small and very fine manuscript displays. One consisted of illuminated European musical texts from the 12th through the 16th centuries; the other contained half a dozen Islamic miniatures and manuscript leaves from the 17th through the 19th centuries.

These exhibitions are drawn on a rotating basis from the Walters collection, which, in this country, is second only to the Morgan Library in New York City in the depth and quality of its illuminated-manuscript holdings.

Saturday night, we headed off to Philip Arnoult's Theater Project, 45 W. Preston St. (301-752-8558), which is only a short walk from the rosy pink and dark mahogany of the Shirley, but is light-years away in sensibility. If the Center Stage represents the city's leading regional theatrical space, the Theater Project is its leading theatrical adventurer.

Founder and director Arnoult spends huge amounts of time traveling around the world — contracts in suitcase — seeking out the unusual and provocative, the best experimental theater. At the time of our visit, for instance, he was poking around in the Soviet Union, looking for companies to present here.

Argentina's Teatro del Sur had just left town after its U.S. debut, and TMU-NA, a performance troupe from Tel Aviv, moved in soon after. We saw TMU-NA's production *5 Screams*, a dance/theater piece that is very loosely based on Milan Kundera's novel *The Unbearable Lightness of Being*.

This visually stunning work consisted of a skein of tableaux and movements that explore relationships between freedom and order, escape and imprisonment, sexuality and banality, red carnations and dust. It is a work, in short, that adheres to a high level of abstraction.

A light meal, at the very solid and

concrete Great American Melting Pot (better known as GAMPY'S), 904 N. Charles, seemed the ticket after *5 Screams*. Broiled swordfish. No surprises.

On Sunday, after a leisurely breakfast, we headed for the Baltimore Museum of Art, the only place that wasn't within an easy walk. The museum had a number of special exhibitions, including the Frederick R. Wiseman Collection of trendy recent work.

At this point, somewhere in the midst of a small exhibit of Danny Lyons' photographs of Texas prison life, "Conversations with the Dead," we reached critical mass and decided to skip a concert of the Pro Musica Rara in the museum auditorium.

Music could well be the anchor for another weekend. We did not hear anything at the Meyerhoff, which was only offering pop concerts the weekend we were in town. Nor did we go to the Lyric Opera House. The Baltimore Opera Company, back from the brink of dissolution a couple of seasons ago, was in rehearsals for *Turandot*, so we missed that too.

We also decided to skip *Cats* at the Morris A. Mechanic Theater, Baltimore's Broadway road theater.

Cultural Baltimore is clearly more than one weekend.

Concord, Mass.

A town endowed with a rich legacy of American history and literature

By Janet Ruth Falon
Special to The Inquirer

This is where "the shot heard round the world" was fired on April 19, 1775, igniting the Revolutionary War.

This is where such heavyweight literary lights as Ralph Waldo Emerson (who wrote the above line), Nathaniel Hawthorne, Louisa May Alcott, and Henry David Thoreau lived, worked and shared ideas during the next century. Right out of town is the site of the pacific Walden Pond, where Thoreau lived a hermitic intellectual existence for two years, in a 10-by-15-foot cabin.

Although Concord is only a 20-minute drive from Boston and, as a manageable commute, could certainly be considered a suburb of the Hub city, it stubbornly and proudly retains a strong sense of its own separate identity as a New England town, buttressed by a literary and historic tradition of overwhelming proportions.

Great books and important dates aside, wine fanciers (Manischewitz in particular) will want to know the

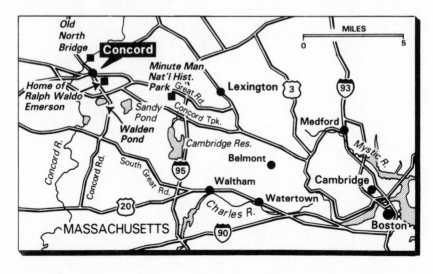

most obvious but least known fact about this town: that it is, really, the home of the lush Concord grape.

The original grapevines still stand in the yard of a private home, the result of one Ephraim Wales Bull's planting the seeds of a wild grape found growing on the hillside of his property. With a bit of experimentation, the indigenous variety became, in 1849, the Concord grape.

Concord is a town for all seasons. The downtown is a typical sweet New England town, with a central square — the rectangular Monument Square — and war memorials dedicated to soldiers of the Revolutionary and World Wars. There is a flagpole and a working water fountain when the weather's warm, and a view of the multitude of church steeples that watch over the town and emit an hourly serenade.

The commercial streets — including Walden and Thoreau Streets, and the requisite small-town Main Street — are a blend of utilitarian and unobtrusive upscale-touristy, the latter trading on the town's rich legacy. There are, for instance, several bookstores specializing in Concord authors.

Concord Center is also the site of the Old Hill Burying Grounds, a cemetery with unusual tombstones: Many of the graves of Concord's original settlers lean into, or away from, the slope that rises steeply from the street.

The Pallett Barrett DAR House, built in 1658, is the oldest home in Concord and is also in Concord Center. When Cambridge was besieged during the Revolution, Harvard College moved to Concord and used this building as a makeshift library and faculty quarters.

Across the street, the Wright Tavern served as headquarters for the British commanders on April 19, 1775. It is now the Tri-Con Gift Shop, selling genteel curios as well as yardstick-long 60-hour candles and those delightfully kitschy pens that show a moving scene — here, the Minutemen crossing North Bridge — when you lift them to write.

Meander the side streets near Concord Center and you'll see upstanding New England homes, many proudly bearing the year in which they were built. It is a no-nonsense town that still manages to keep from becoming too ponderous, thanks to whimsical touches like the silhouettes of militiamen carved into the shutters of the local telephone company building.

But Concord Center itself is not where the bulk of attractions is situated. It is only the geographic core from which to depart for the literary and historic sites, none more than a few miles away. You might, in fact, want to organize your trip here into historic and literary portions. A good place to start your visit and unify your overview of the town would be the Concord Antiquarian Museum, which has exhibits bridging both the historic and literary themes.

The museum consists of 15 period rooms that chronicle the history of Concord through the domestic artifacts and decorative arts from 1640 to 1860. The rooms also contain a huge collection of Thoreau-related objects, some used at Walden Pond, and the contents of Emerson's study. The museum, in fact, sits on land that was Emerson's apple orchard. His home is right across the street.

A large portion of the museum's collection consists of the Concord-related curios collected by local eccentric Cummings "Little" Davis. Davis amassed many of his pieces during the Industrial Revolution era when people were "modernizing" and collecting wasn't chic. His diverse collection includes a samurai sword, the Alcott family teakettle, an hourglass for timing three-hour sermons and more. These, and the sequence of period interiors, can all be seen on one-hour tours.

Be sure to look for the fife that was played at the battle in Lexington, the lantern that was hung from the steeple of the Old North Church on the night of Paul Revere's ride, and muskets impressive for their very long barrels.

For more information, write to the Concord Antiquarian Museum, Box 146, Concord, Mass. 01742, or call 617-369-9609. The museum is open 10 a.m. to 4 p.m. Monday through Saturday and 1 to 4 p.m. Sunday.

•

Anyone who has studied or will ever study the basics of the Revolutionary War will want to visit the North Bridge, one of many sites between Lexington and Concord that make up the Minute Man National Historical Park, operated by the National Park Service. All sites commemorate events associated with the armed conflict of April 19, 1775, marking the beginning of the Revolution.

The wood bridge, which has been reconstructed to look as it did in 1775, spans the quiet waters of the Concord River. If it were not for the endless procession of tourists — mothers who snap photographs of their kids wearing tricorner hats, artists who paint the patriotic scene, American history buffs who can smell the residue of real-life drama in the air — the area would probably not feel a whole lot different from the way it did when the 400 early revolutionaries followed Maj. John Buttrick's advice to "Fire, fellow soldiers, for God's sake, fire!"

Park rangers posted at the bridge will fill you in on the details of history that you've probably buried way back in your mind, and periodic re-enactments re-create the battle.

In brief, an early pre-Revolutionary committee decided that arms and supplies were to be stored in relatively isolated Concord in case of a war with England. On April 18, 1775, British Gen. Thomas Gage, military governor of Massachusetts, sent his troops marching from Boston on a "special duty," and Patriots assumed he intended to destroy the Concord supplies.

Of three warning riders, including Paul Revere, only Dr. Samuel Prescott made it past British patrols into Concord. (The others were held up at Lexington by a British patrol, but Prescott himself eluded capture.) After a skirmish at Lexington, when eight Americans died and 10 were wounded, the British moved on toward Concord.

When they reached the town, the British took possession of the town center — headquartered at the time at Wright Tavern. British Maj. John Pitcairn sent patrols out to find the hidden supplies. Although their search was fruitless, they burned cannon carriages in the town square and started a fire in a store. The Patriots, watching from nearby Punkatasset Hill, saw the smoke and assumed the British had set Concord on fire. It was then that Joseph Hosmer asked the question, "Will you let them burn the town down?"

The British and Patriots met at North Bridge. The British fired warning shots at the Patriots and then attacked. The fight was on — and over, quickly, with the Patriots driving the outnumbered British out of town.

But it was just the beginning of the war.

The frequently photographed statue of a minuteman stands by North Bridge, with Emerson's inscription:

By the rude bridge that arched the flood
Their flag to April's breeze unfurled
Here once the embattled farmers stood
and fired the shot heard round the world.

(Speaking of poetry, your guide at the Concord Antiquarian Museum will tell you that Henry Wadsworth Longfellow took poetic license with his "Paul Revere's Ride." It was Sam Prescott, not the Boston silversmith hero, who said "The British are coming," — but "Listen, my children, and you shall hear" rhymes much better with "Revere" than "Prescott.")

Graves of British soldiers, the field where the militiamen mustered and other vivid spots all help make the North Bridge site a lively piece of

American history. There's also an accompanying museum with uniforms and war paraphernalia. (Check out the "housewife" in a typical minuteman's haversack. To any feminist's dismay, it is a sewing kit.)

•

Another Concord attraction that elicits a feeling of history is Thoreau's cabin site, tucked into the wooded Walden Pond State Preservation. It was Emerson who permitted his friend Thoreau to build the one-room, 10-by-15-foot cabin on his land, but it was Thoreau, pondering his stint at Walden from July 4, 1845, to Sept. 6, 1847, who wrote the unforgettable words: "I went to the woods because I wished to live deliberately, to front only the essential facts of life, and see if I could not learn what it had to teach me and not, when I come to die, discover that I had not lived."

Stones mark the outline of the cabin site, as well as the woodshed that was almost as large as the cabin. (The cabin no longer stands.) The pile of stones, or cairn, memorializing Thoreau's achievement as a writer, philosopher and naturalist, is just as moving — particularly since visitors have been adding their reverent pebbles to the pile since 1872. There's an indisputably ghostlike presence here, consisting of Thoreau's spirit as well as the presence of countless visitors who've tramped through the woods to pay homage. The cabin site is about 30 yards uphill from the 62-acre pond, which is known to be extraordinarily deep.

The cabin site is also quite a distance in from the road, away from the traffic and a trailer park. As you hike into the woods, the noise of the modern world recedes and the sounds of birds, rustling leaves, crackling pine cones and twigs underfoot take over.

Thoreau wasn't Concord's only famous philosopher-writer. The philosophy of the founder of American Transcendentalism — Ralph Waldo Emerson — espoused a turning away from materialism and finding a personal God and nature through introspection, contemplation and dreams. Emerson was the center of Concord's literary circle.

Emerson and his second wife lived in Concord, and their home attracted famous people who traveled to, or through, Concord. The large home, filled with fine creature comforts and objects that recall many famous philosophers and writers, is now run by one of his great-grandchildren.

Emerson and his wife lived in the Old Manse. (Manse is an English and Scottish word for a minister's home.) It was their temporary dwelling, after a fire destroyed the roof of their own home. The Old Manse, down the road from Concord Center, was built by Emerson's grandfather and is the home that young Ralph Waldo visited and where he learned to love Concord. The elder Emerson, a patriotic minister, opened the Manse as a refuge for Concordians seeking safety during the battle of April 19, 1775.

Nathaniel Hawthorne and his wife, Sophia, lived in the Old Manse for 3½ years. *Mosses From an Old Manse* came from this period.

Louisa May Alcott, with her parents and sisters, lived in Concord's Orchard House, also down the block from Concord Center. They moved in after years of rambling, poverty and an unsuccessful attempt at communal living. It was here that her father, A. Bronson Alcott, founded the School of Philosophy, a summer school for adults. A Transcendentalist who philosophized with Emerson, Thoreau and Hawthorne, he was also a vegetarian, journal-keeper and radical school-reformer.

Louisa, who was born in Philadelphia's Germantown section, wrote *Little Women* while living at Orchard House. Her sisters — Anna, an actress, and May, an artist — produced some of their best work in Concord, too. (Elizabeth, a musician, died before the family moved here.)

Some of the more delightful touches in Orchard House include Louisa's "mood pillow," which she stood on its end only when she was in a good mood, and May's painting of an owl in her writer-sister's room, because she called Louisa a "wise old owl."

The Alcotts also lived for a while, in the pre-Orchard House days, at the nearby Wayside, and the family produced Louisa's early plays in the Wayside's barn. They lived here after the failure of the communal experiment, but Bronson Alcott enlarged the existing Wayside house — just in case they might need room for guests for a second try at communalism.

The Hawthornes, now with three children, purchased the Wayside from the Alcotts and also added to it. It was the only house that the reclusive Hawthorne, who customarily dressed in black, ever owned.

Margaret Sidney and her husband, publisher Daniel Lothrop, later owned the Wayside and used it as a summer home. Admirers of Hawthorne, they preserved the house and study and opened it to scholars and travelers. The couple also bought Orchard House and the Grapevine Cottage, home of Ephraim Wales Bull, both for preservation — another example of the "cross-polli-nation" of Concord's literary greats. In addition, many of Concord's writers are buried at Sleepy Hollow Cemetery in Concord.

The Orchard House is open from April 1 to October 31, Monday to Saturday, 10 a.m. to 4:30 p.m.; Sunday and holidays, 1 p.m. to 4:30 p.m. and by appointment during the winter. Admission is $2.75 for adults, $2 for senior citizens, $1.50 for children ages 6 to 16, free for those under 6.

The Wayside House is open from April to October, Friday to Tuesday, 10 a.m. to 5:30 p.m.

From June 1 to October 31, the Old Manse is open Monday, Thursday, Friday and Saturday, 10 a.m. to 4:30 p.m and is closed holidays. From mid-April to May 31, it is open weekends only 1 p.m. to 4:30 p.m. Admission: adults $2.75, senior citizens $2 and children ages 6 to 16 $1.50.

And the Emerson House is open mid-April to mid-October Thursday to Saturday 10 a.m. to 4:30 p.m., Sunday 2 p.m. to 4:30 p.m. Admission is $2.50 for adults and $1 for children ages 6 to 17.

Write to the Concord Chamber of Commerce, ½ Main St., Concord, Mass. 01742 for more information.

Cooperstown, N.Y.

Remembering the best of times at the Baseball Hall of Fame

By Terry Bitman
Inquirer Staff Writer

Shoeless Joe Jackson wore shoes. They're about size 8½, medium width, black, slightly scuffed. They're here, enshrined in the National Baseball Hall of Fame and Museum, mecca of America's sport (excuse me, football fanatics).

The shoes — and much more — are on display for anyone in search of great moments from the glory days of ballplayers, whose likenesses, uniforms, gloves, bats and helmets are forever immortalized on bronze plaques, on black and white action photos, in glass cases and in precise basswood carvings.

Vince Coleman's shoes are here, too. Bright red. Shiny. Befitting the speedster who set the base paths ablaze as a rookie with the St. Louis Cardinals.

Shoes have come a long way since the days of Shoeless Joe, a stellar player for a team that will always live in infamy, the 1919 White Sox (a.k.a. the Black Sox). But then, so have the gloves, bats, hats and uniforms. And so have the ballparks.

Just stroll around the blown-up replicas of stadiums past, like Ebbets Field or Connie Mack, and gaze at photos of the superboxes from a stadium today, like the Astrodome, and you see just how much comfort has become a part of the game.

Need more reinforcement? Sit a minute in the faded, pinkish gray wooden seats from Connie Mack Stadium. They're here, too.

But don't sit too long. The memories of that old park are too painful. And they drift back so rapidly. A flu-stricken Johnny Callison striking out amid the Phillies' seasonal collapse in 1964. A huffing, puffing Robin Roberts pitching valiantly to preserve whatever thin lead he was lucky to get. A gritty Richie Ashburn, hands choked high on the bat, slashing a single the opposite way, the ideal lead-off man save that his team so rarely took advantage of his knack for getting on base.

Such was Connie Mack Stadium. But it felt good to see one of the last remaining parts of it again.

This nostalgia has no impact, however, on a 14-year-old son for whom Connie Mack Stadium is some wistful fantasy that his father too often speaks of. He wonders, if the teams that played there two and three decades ago were so terrible, why his father would want to remember the place at all.

So personal nostalgia gives way to a larger one. That's one of the nice things about the Hall of Fame. You can marvel at the feats of the greats of the game like Babe Ruth, Lou Gehrig, Ty Cobb, Cy Young, Roberto Clemente and Casey Stengel. Or recall the brief shining moments of players like Harvey Haddix, whose 12-inning perfect game was lost in the 13th. It was a game that one remembers struggling as a child to stay awake and hear from a bedside radio, with the broadcast static sometimes louder than the voices emanating out of Pittsburgh. Or — sigh! — even the '80 Phillies, who fulfilled a life's dream, raised hopes once again, and made the pain of Connie Mack Stadium easier to cope with.

Yes indeed, the national shrine to the national pastime is a wonder to behold. The typical tour (there are no guides, you are on your own, save for a small, slick brochure that tells you where everything is) begins quite appropriately in front of a likeness of Babe Ruth, bat cocked, awaiting for all eternity another fastball to swat into the upper decks of some forgotten stadium.

If any one player dominates the hall, it is Ruth, who has a section all to himself on the top floor to display memorabilia, including one of his lockers. Surrounding the Ruth statue in the vestibule are photos of contemporary stars and near-stars.

My son first notices a prominently located photo of White Sox slugger Harold Baines hanging down from the ceiling. Baines also is a member of our team in a Strato-matic league, Strato-matic being one of several intricate board games in which players' statistics and the roll of the dice determine the outcome of each hitting, pitching and fielding situation. Baines has been one of the stalwarts of our team, and his enlarged countenance there in the lobby starts off my son's day on just the right note.

He stops, takes a photo of Baines' photo, then continues to scan above him, looking for other members of our Strato team. Several of them he finds quite easily, such as Tigers shortstop Alan Trammell and Pirates catcher Tony Pena. Then he spots his favorite non-Phillies, non-Strato player — Rod Carew. The eyes light up even more. The camera clicks again.

As for me, I'm still admiring the Bambino's stance, wondering what it might have been like to have seen him play, imagining what fun announcer Harry Kalas might have had yelling "It's outta here" for more than 700 blasts by Babe Ruth.

Though the Bambino rules the entranceway, it is the hall, where plaques of 199 inductees line the walls, that dominates the rest of the floor. (This is technically the Hall of Fame. The rest of the Colonial-style structure is considered the museum.)

We scan the plaques, pausing at familiar names like Ruth, Gehrig, Joe DiMaggio, Jackie Robinson and, of course, Robin Roberts. I try to explain to my teenager who some of these folks were. Not having seen many of them play myself, I realize I am passing on sketchy lore. My friend is having an even tougher time explaining these things to his 10-year-old son.

Baseball, they say, is a boy's game best played by men. The hall, I would suggest, is a boy's paradise best enjoyed by men.

The tour of the first floor is completed with visits to the Cooperstown Room — where the origins of the game and development of the museum are highlighted — and the Great Moments Room, with its 9-foot blowups of modern stars and a collection of original baseball art. The large gift shop, located near the main stairwell and calling sirenlike to the boys, is bypassed, left to be the dessert at tour's end.

The second floor provides even more of a history lesson. More than 1,000 artifacts and photographs recount the game's story. There is a large display area dedicated to black baseball, poignantly showing the stars of the old Negro Leagues, all too belatedly immortalized.

It is on this level that you observe the development of equipment over the years. One questions how players like Joe Tinker or Johnny Evers or Frank Chance ever caught anything with gloves that appear no larger than those some of us wear for warmth in the winter. No wonder Cobb and Honus Wagner had such great batting averages. Even an infielder with the greatest of range lacked the large webbing to get ground balls an arm's length away.

The second floor also is Casey Stengel's floor. Memorabilia from the Old Professor's playing and managing days gets about triple the space of anyone else in the museum save Ruth. Even his Mets uniform is there.

The third and top floor is a child's joy. A unique collection of baseball cards through the ages, without the gum and tobacco many of them came with, is as impressive as anything in the hall.

There also is a section on the evolution of uniforms, which makes you wonder why early players didn't die of heatstroke. The uniforms of those days were heavy wool, not double-knit polyester, and the teams played mostly day games and sat in hot dugouts and changed in locker rooms that were not air conditioned. (And when, by the way, did we stop calling them "locker rooms" and begin calling them by the more trendy name of "clubhouses"?)

The ballparks are displayed on the upper level, too. Stand in a re-creation of the modern White Sox dugout and look out over Comiskey Park, which takes form in a huge one-dimensional blowup. Send your pinch-hitter to the bat rack. But don't have him try too hard to grab either bat or helmet. They won't come loose from their casings.

Go through the the World Series section and recall the men of October. Reggie Jackson, of course, in the late '70s. Sandy Koufax in the mid-'60s. Yogi Berra and Mickey Mantle in the late '50s. And, lest we ever forget, Michael Jack Schmidt and Edwin "Tug" McGraw in 1980.

Then, inhale all that was the Bambino. If there ever was any doubt who was the greatest of the greats, the curators of the hall have none. Sure, Cobb is prominent. So are Hank Aaron, Willie Mays and Koufax. So, even, is Pete Rose. But if Yankee Stadium was the house that Ruth built, then the Hall of Fame is the museum where he lives.

The trophies, uniforms, photographs are imposing. There is even a brief film about the life and legend. And, of course, there is the ball and bat from the famous 60th home run in 1927, the year he hit his record number of home runs.

Catch your breath a minute, but don't forget to go back down the stairs all the way to the basement. There we find the uniforms from all 26 teams today, displays on how balls and bats are made, and a records room that, though imposing in its detail, is a bit disappointing in its lack of timeliness. Unlike an enclosed case out front that provides the scores for the day's previous games through hand-placed lettering, the records room lags behind.

Less obstrusively displayed are various board games. Strato-matic, the game my son and I play so fervently, is enclosed in glass. So is the All-Star Game, a less sophisticated board game that involves disks placed on spinners to determine the outcome of batter vs. pitcher — a game that I long ago forgot I had ever enjoyed.

What is lacking, however, is any explanation of these games. If you're not familiar with Strato-matic or any of the others there, you would likely bypass them.

Which just points out that as attractive and exciting as the hall is, it is also, like the sport you come here to worship, not perfect.

The current teams' section, for example, had not yet been updated for the season, which at the time of our visit late in April seemed understandable.

But my son noticed that the 1985 Phillies team photo was out of date before that season even started; it was a spring training group shot that didn't reflect later roster cuts and trades. (But whose fault is that? The Phillies' or the hall's?)

In the gift shop, the emphasis is on T-shirts, sweat shirts and facsimilies of uniforms. There are no baseball cards for sale. The stock of statistical reference books was outdated, many of them still last season's editions. Though the season had just begun, we'd already seen current editions back home.

We browse through the shop, but do most of our buying a few doors up the street at a rather disheveled place called F. R. Woods House of Souvenirs. There, my son purchases an entire set of baseball cards and a large pennant inscribed with the names of all hall inductees.

The hall does not provide any eating facilities, but that's all right. When you pay your admission ($5 adults, $2 children age 7-15), your hand is stamped so that you can come and go throughout the day. We took time for lunch at a little restaurant down the street called the Shortstop, which seemed an appropriate name until my son, the budding critic, noted that none of the current players whose pictures lined the walls were shortstops.

There are two other stops that can be made on the visit. Adjacent to the hall is the National Baseball Library, which boasts the world's largest collection of written and visual baseball reference materials. And a block and a half away is Doubleday Field, where, since 1940, an annual Hall of Fame exhibition game has been played each summer between two major-league teams, usually before capacity crowds of 10,000, and where, it is alleged, Abner Doubleday organized the first game in 1839 in a pasture.

The hall sits without fanfare along, appropriately, Main Street, across from the police station and next to a Newberry's, similar to a Woolworth's, only a few blocks from picturesque Otsego Lake. The hall was built in 1939 to commemorate the centennial of Doubleday's game.

There are several ways of getting to Cooperstown, depending on how scenic a drive you want. Heading for Albany first, we went via the New Jersey Turnpike to the Garden State Parkway, into New York state and then up the Thruway, which is Interstate 87 until it veers west at Albany and becomes Interstate 90 as it heads toward Syracuse and Buffalo. Exit 29 will put you on state Route 80 south, and within 20 minutes you'll be in Cooperstown.

A more leisurely drive would take you through northeast Pennsylvania, past Binghamton, N.Y., onto Interstate 88 and north to state Route 28, then slightly northeast on Route 80.

The hall is open daily from 9 a.m. to 9 p.m., May 1 to Oct. 31 and from 9 a.m. to 5 p.m. Nov. 1 to April 30. Information can be obtained from the National Baseball Hall of Fame and Museum, Cooperstown, N.Y. 13326. The phone number is 607-547-9988.

Harpers Ferry, W. Va.

A peaceful town holds turbulent memories

By Bob Allen
Special to The Inquirer

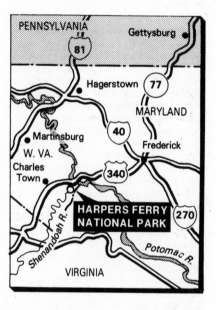

A t first glance, as a visitor leaves busy West Virginia Route 340 and enters the narrow stone and asphalt streets of Harpers Ferry by automobile, there is little about the sleepy riverfork town that hints of its rich and turbulent past.

The small downtown, with its stone sidewalks and squat-looking, restored early 19th-century brick and stone buildings, appears as if it had been carved out of the granite and limestone formations of this tiny "peninsula" of northeastern West Virginia.

Three states meet here — Maryland and Virginia are the other two — and the Blue Ridge foothills taper down dramatically to the majestic juncture of the Potomac and Shenandoah Rivers. In the warmer months, when the thick forested hillsides are in full foliage, the steep winding streets — particularly when viewed from one of the high cliffs just across the river — seem submerged in a vivid sea of green.

But, as a weekend journey will reveal, Harpers Ferry's idyllic slumber is a bit misleading. As the town's numerous historical exhibits and several museums attest, this small riverside settlement, a leisurely 3½-hour drive from Philadelphia (through Baltimore) and a mere 40 miles from Washington, has repeatedly found itself at the crossroads of American history.

Time and time again, it has played host — sometimes reluctantly, and even unwillingly — to events that have shaped the course of our nation.

It was here in 1859 that the fiery abolitionist John Brown launched his ill-fated slave insurrection and briefly captured the federal arsenal, the ruins of which can be seen in the town's riverside square. When Brown was tried for treason and hanged a few months later, in nearby Charles Town, repercussions of his actions — and his swift execution — echoed from one end of the country to the other.

A mere 15 miles, as the crow flies, from the bloody Civil War battleground of Antietam, Harpers Ferry was the scene of much Civil War activity. Because of its importance as a railroad and munitions-manufacturing center, its streets were raked by small-arms fire and bombarded by artillery (from the nearby cliffs) as it was repeatedly captured and abandoned by the Confederate and Union forces. It was finally taken by the Union in 1863.

The largest and most dramatic raid was made by "Stonewall" Jackson, who paused in September 1862, on his way to the Battle of Antietam, and forced the surrender of the 12,700 Union troops who were garrisoned at the arsenal. By the end of the war, much of the town had been destroyed by the repeated shellings. But for more than a century before the Civil War, Harpers Ferry had been known as the gateway to the lush Shenandoah Valley for westward-bound pioneers. On their westward expedition, Lewis and Clark paused there to procure firearms. George Washington, who prompted development of the settlement as the major munitions-manufacturing center it would become by 1850, and Thomas Jefferson made cameo appearances.

Jefferson was, in fact, one of the very first tourists (nearly a million a year pass through these days) to go on record with his rather vivid impressions of Harpers Ferry's rugged wilderness charm.

Today the National Park Service maintains and oversees the town and surroundings as a National Historical Park. This enables the weekend traveler to readily experience Harpers Ferry's rich historical heritage and rustic natural setting (virtually unchanged since the days of John Brown and little changed even since Jefferson's 1783 visit).

Though it may seem a world away, Harpers Ferry can also be visited as a brief side trip from Washington, only about an hour away by automobile or train.

Don Campbell, head of the local division of the National Park Service, calls Harpers Ferry "one of the great restored towns of the country." But those who visit can balance the pleasures of historical enrichment with other leisure-time activities, such as canoeing, white-water rafting, fishing, hiking or thoroughbred-horse racing (at the Charles Town Turf Club, just a few miles south on Route 340).

Visitors can leisurely take in the town in much the same way Jefferson did when he was a guest at founding father Robert Harper's stone tavern. They can climb the steep stone steps (carved out of the rock in the early 19th century) and footpaths that lead from High Street, near the town's center (the village has only two through streets), to the high promontory now called Jefferson's Rock. They, as Jefferson did, can gaze out across the wide rivers, the hazy Blue Ridge foothills and the craggy, forested cliffs on the far shores, and take in that very same breathtakingly evocative view, which he hailed as "stupendous" and "well worth a trip across the Atlantic."

Today, a restored, 19th-century brick-and-stone stagecoach inn (one of the first buildings on the left as you enter the town on Shenandoah Street from Route 340) serves as Harpers Ferry's visitors center. A short orientation film is shown here, and during the warmer months, the park service offers one-hour tours on themes ranging from John Brown's raid and the Civil War to the town's past as a milling and munitions center, where more than a half-million firearms were produced in the years preceding the war.

The small but comprehensive museums, one on Brown and one on the involvement in the Civil War — located side by side on Shenandoah near the intersection with High Street, just a block or so from the visitors center — are a good place to begin. Dozens of other walk-through exhibits, in the many restored buildings along Shenandoah, High and Potomac Streets, are within a half-block of the museums.

One walk-through exhibit is the Harper House (up the stone steps that lead to Jefferson's Rock), where Jefferson most likely stayed during his visit. Built between 1775 and 1782, it is the oldest surviving structure in the town. Its interior has been restored as a tenant house of the town's 1850s industrial era.

Other walk-through exhibits include a restored blacksmith shop, a dry-goods store, provost office, master armorer's house, an armory worker's quarters, a tavern, a post office, a confectionery and a pharmacy. All have been restored to capture the flavor and detail of Harpers Ferry in the mid-1800s.

The fire engine house, where John Brown and his ragtag army sought refuge after their failed attempt to capture the arsenal, can also be visited. It's just across the street from the John Brown Museum, amid the ruins of the old federal arsenal buildings. Some of these buildings were built as early as 1799, and most were burned by retreating Union forces in 1861.

The armory, like practically all structures in Harpers Ferry, has been ravaged more than once over the years by war or flooding, but has been painstakingly restored. Well-tended footpaths, festooned with informative markers, lead through the grassy ruins of the original arsenal buildings and on to the river overlook at the Point, which was the town's center.

Other well-worn paths traverse the cool, tree-shrouded banks of the Potomac and Shenandoah, offering opportunities for hikers and picnickers to watch trout fishermen, canoers and rafters, who frequent the shallow but treacherously swift waters.

The old stone steps lead not only to Jefferson's Rock but also to the old Harper Cemetery, where Robert Harper and other civic pioneers were buried. They also lead to the 150-year-old St. Peter's Catholic Church (which maintained neutrality, and avoided destruction, in the Civil War by flying the Union Jack), and to the ruins of St. John's Episcopal Church.

Well-marked woodland trails lead farther afield to the foundations and remnants of the old millworks and munitions factories on tiny Virginius Island in the Shenandoah.

The Appalachian Trail also runs through Harpers Ferry. The Appalachian Trail Council, the national organization charged with the preservation and maintenance of this 2,100-mile, Maine-to-Georgia footpath, is also based here, and offers guidebooks, maps and information (phone: 304-535-6331). The trail crosses the Potomac by a recently opened pedestrian bridge; there are additional hiking and browsing opportunities on the Maryland side of the river.

Just across the footbridge, by the river overlook near where Shenandoah and Potomac Streets intersect and come to a dead end, are the ruins of the Chesapeake & Ohio Barge Canal. This extensive, 184-mile canal system, with its hand-dug channel and intricate locks, took 22 years to build (1828-1850). During its heyday, it carried a continuous stream of mule-towed barges (bearing mostly coal) between Cumberland, Md., and Washington.

It has been more than 60 years since the last barge passed through, and floods and erosion have since taken their toll. But today, more than 77 miles of the original canal system are preserved as a historic park. The old mule towpath gets heavy use as a convenient hiking and biking path from Washington. (For more information, call the C&O National Park's visitors center in Hancock, Md., at 301-678-5463.)

Farther north on the Maryland riverbank, about a half-mile or so up the old C&O towpath, is the entrance to the Grant Conway Trail. (This can be reached even more easily by car — take Route 340 back across the two river bridges, into Maryland. Exit on Route 180 and proceed to Sandy Hood Road, turn right, and go 1.1 miles to the trail.) This forest pathway leads to high overlooks, as well as various Civil War fortifications, gun batteries and monuments along Maryland Heights.

At 247 feet above sea level, Harpers Ferry is not only West Virginia's easternmost point but also its lowest. Small wonder that early settlers, from around the time of Peter Stephens, a trader who established an outpost there in 1733, simply called it "The Hole."

It was in 1747 that Pennsylvania millwright Robert Harper came to the then-remote locale and began eking out a living by running an irregular ferry service across the river.

The first two cabins that Harper built were destroyed in floods, but Harper hung on, undeterred. It was the last residence he built — a stone tavern completed in 1782, the year he died — that Jefferson visited.

Washington visited the still-tiny settlement in 1785 and prompted the War Department to acquire land for an armory and musket factory. By 1801, the first flintlocks were being made, and production quickly rose to 10,000 a year.

In the late 1820s, Harpers Ferry was envisioned as a gateway to the West by the builders of the Baltimore & Ohio Railroad and the Chesapeake & Ohio Canal. The two companies became locked in a bitter race to see which could be first to claim this portal of commerce.

The canal builders reached Harpers Ferry first — in 1833, with the B&O arriving a year later. The railroad and canal opened up Harpers Ferry for its golden era of prosperity. By the 1850s, as munitions, carriage-building, saw- and flour-milling, and other related industries thrived, the town's population swelled to 4,000 (many times its present full-time population of 350).

With all this in full swing, no one took particular notice in the summer of 1859 when a bushy-bearded man rented a farm in the nearby Maryland countryside.

But that October, when John Brown led his ill-fated raid on the federal arsenal, the entire nation seemed to rise.

Brown's uprising was quickly quelled by a contingent of Marines led by Col. Robert E. Lee and Lt. J.E.B. Stuart. The abolitionist was tried and hanged that December in the Jefferson County Courthouse at Washington and George Streets in Charles Town. The courthouse is now open to visitors Monday through Thursday 9 a.m. to 5 p.m. and Friday 9 a.m. to 7 p.m. (phone: 304-725-9762).

John Wilkes Booth regaled the crowd at the execution with Shakespearian oration, and "Stonewall" Jackson led the small contingent of troops that kept order. Brown's gun, the wagon that carried him to his death and other artifacts relating to his life, as well as the area's involvement in the Civil War, can be seen at the Jefferson County Museum at 200 E. Washington St. in Charles Town.

It's open Monday to Saturday, April through October 10 a.m. to 4 p.m. (phone 304-725-8628).

The farm that served as Brown's staging headquarters is a National Historic Landmark and is open to the public year-round on weekends. It's in Maryland, on Chestnut Grove Road, just off Route 340 north (phone 301-791-3130).

After having been burned and shelled during the Civil War, the town fell victim to a series of disastrous floods in the late 1800s. Gradually, its industry and its populace fled for higher ground, and its prosperity faded. By the turn of this century, it had begun to take on the aura of rural slumber that characterizes its quiet streets today.

Marietta, Pa.

Finding a quieter America in western Lancaster County

By James Asher
Inquirer Staff Writer

Head out toward the rolling fields of Amish Country and then past the quaint gentlefolk with their 19th-century ways.

Go beyond the plentiful tourists they attract, the ersatz bargain outlets, "authentic" Amish farms and the traffic.

Follow my family and me to an out-of-the-way corner of western Lancaster County that has its roots in the colonial period and whose residents are not German Amish or Mennonite but predominantly proud Scotch and Irish. Come to a place still wrapped in the mystique of the Susquehanna River trade that fueled America's westward expansion before the railroad barons gave the doctrine of "Manifest Destiny" its most powerful push.

Welcome to the towns of Marietta and Mount Joy, Columbia and Maytown, Bainbridge and Elizabethtown.

Each of these communities has a vital character of its own. Each is attractive to anyone with a sense of history, an eye for architecture, an interest in good food and a thirst for a quieter, less hectic America.

Soon after arriving in this section of Pennsylvania on a Saturday, we stumbled onto a community celebration — the boys' basketball team of Columbia had just won the state Double-A championship.

In what was to become a full-scale municipal pep rally, the whole town came alive with excitement about 4:30 p.m. as news of the victory spread.

From the homes on North Third Street, already festooned with red and yellow balloons and "Crimson Tide" streamers, fans spontaneously began cheering and waving at the honking automobiles that passed. The scene on North Third, one of Columbia's main thoroughfares, was repeated on Maple and Poplar streets, on Chestnut and Locust, Walnut and Cherry.

One of the community's fire trucks, cruising local streets with intermittent siren blasts, was sporting a placard bearing the corrupted Caesarean quote: "We came. We saw. We conquered."

Even a Columbia Borough police car was bedecked with a "Crimson Tide" streamer.

By 9 p.m., the cheering had stopped and the caravan of cars that had filled local streets had wound its way home.

This celebration had all the stuff of a sketch by Norman Rockwell and was, in a way, a fitting beginning for our weekend visit. For what we found in this part of Pennsylvania was a sense of place romantically familiar to anyone who was raised in or fantasizes about small-town America.

For those from the fast-paced city, western Lancaster County offers a chance to wind down, to reflect, to see how we once were.

Our journey to the Susquehanna River towns actually began several years ago when I toured that area, researching a story on the multiple farming tragedies resulting from the avian flu epidemic. Millions of chickens and turkeys perished, either from the disease itself or under the government slaughtering program designed to contain and ultimately halt its spread.

The assignment took me on a madcap dash from town to town in search of the poultry farms affected. As the settlements passed by me in a blur, I resolved to retrace my steps one day in search of the quaintness that work was forcing me to miss.

On our tour of Marietta, I noted several changes and improvements made since my first quick visit in 1984.

Much has been renovated. Even Philadelphia's premier historic resuscitator, Historic Landmarks for Living, has restored a 19th-century silk mill into apartments and townhouses.

Marietta's restoration, which actually began in the mid-1960s, ultimately received a boost from the near-depression that kept the town stagnant during the first half of this century.

During those hard times, residents had little extra cash to "improve" or modernize their homes. As a result, virtually all of the housing stock reflected its former glory, making Marietta ripe for the tax-break-abetted historic restorations of the last two decades.

The pace of historic rehabilitation reached such a level in the early 1980s that 48 percent of Marietta was placed on the National Historic Register, and the slick Colonial Homes magazine published a cover article on the borough in its May-June 1984 issue.

The 27-page article featured photographs of five homes as well as several scenic shots of the community. Colonial Homes described the borough this way: "Few small country towns in America can claim to have preserved as much of a record of their early history as Marietta. ... Today architectural history buffs touring Market Street can find anything from an old log cabin to later Federal and Victorian homes built during the town's halcyon days."

Town fathers are proud of such a heritage. A call or letter to the Borough Hall at 111 E. Market St. produces a map of the community with a brief history and some advertisements by local antique shops and restaurants.

In Marietta's historic business district, two buildings struck my fancy as we toured the town on our first day. The First National Bank of Marietta at 100 W. Market St., now a branch of a Lancaster bank, was established in 1863 as the 25th national bank in the United States and the first federally chartered bank in Lancaster County. Its striking Victorian architecture is worth a close inspection.

The other building that caught my eye, not nearly as old, is the Marietta Theater at 130 W. Market St., built in 1914. As the oldest movie house in Lancaster County, it's a real gem.

We ended our day in Marietta with dinner at the Colonial Inn, 324 W. Market St. The restaurant bills itself as serving "gourmet foods in a colonial setting at moderate prices." Dinner was quite good with most full dinners priced between $8 and $10, near bargain rates. Among the wines available are those from the nearby Nissley Winery.

Friends steered us toward the Colonial Inn and away from the more elegant Railroad House Hotel Ltd. The Railroad House is regarded as Marietta's best restaurant, but the proprietors discourage young children.

In fact, if you are searching for overnight accommodations with some character in this corner of Lancaster County, you won't find any that accept children willingly. Some outright ban them.

Our first choice for rooms was the Cameron Estate Inn in Mount Joy, a well-restored 1805 estate set on 15 acres and surrounded by tulip poplars and black walnut trees. A Betty Groff enterprise, the inn boasts 18 rooms, French and American country cuisine and no children under the age of 12. Rooms range from $50 to $95 a night. Another choice, the Three Center Square Inn, which from all outward signs was as quaint and pleasant as the community of Maytown in which it is located, was slightly more liberal. They prohibited only children under 10 years old. At this inn, rooms are priced between $69 and $79.

Not wanting to be forced into a roadside motel, of which there are a number in the area, we opted for a stay at a working farm.

For our older son, Alexander, who is 5½, the stay was an experience. Byron, our toddler, was pretty excited as well.

We chose Rocky Acre Farm, located between Mount Joy and Marietta. (There is another nearby working farm that also accommodates guests — the Brenneman Farm Bed and Breakfast. A room is $45, or $65 with a private bath.)

With a couple of horses to ride, scores of cows to watch and even milk, and a multitude of cats (all kept outdoors), Rocky Acre Farm was the highlight of our children's weekend. Dressed in his cowboy boots and chaps and mounted on a horse with a farm girl, Alexander headed off. Later he would recount nearly every gallop his mighty steed took and how the wind in his face felt as they hurtled along.

Rooms at Rocky Acre are nicely furnished and our rate with tax and without a private bath was $42.40 a night, including a country breakfast every morning. (Breakfast on Sunday is not included although the Saturday-night rate is no lower.) Ac-

commodations with private baths are available at a slightly higher rate.

On Sunday, we reset our compass and headed for some new adventures.

And here, a word of warning: Some of the guide books and pamphlets we received from the Lancaster County Chamber of Commerce or that we picked up at various attractions were not entirely accurate.

We had planned to have a nice Sunday luncheon at Betty Groff's well-known Groff Farm Restaurant, which was just around the corner from the farm. While the pamphlet said we could enjoy a "Sunday Lunch in the Country," the Sunday we were there the restaurant was closed. So if your heart is set on some place in particular, call ahead when planning your itinerary.

Disappointed, we headed back to Columbia for a fast, but refreshing lunch at Hinkle's Pharmacy Restaurant. Hinkle's has been serving ice cream sodas and meals since 1893. A relatively recent modernization detracts from any charm it might have had, but Hinkle's is a popular meeting place and offers some pretty passable food in immaculate surroundings.

The place mat at Hinkle's noted that, in the 18th century, Columbia had been considered as the site of the nation's new capital. Columbia was also the site of the northernmost advance of the Confederate army when, in 1863, a contingent of J.E.B. Stuart's cavalry burned the covered bridge connecting Columbia and Wrightsville.

After lunch, we decided to visit the Susquehanna Glass Co.'s factory store. We bet on the inaccuracy of our brochure on Columbia — which said the store was closed on Sunday — and came up winners. It wasn't. We found all kinds of glassware and crystal, much of it of interesting and unusual design.

Columbia is also home to the Wilton Co., makers of Armetale dinnerware and cookware. At the Wilton Co. factory outlet, there is a large selection with seconds selling for about one-third off.

A particularly fascinating attraction in Columbia is the National Association of Watch & Clock Collectors Museum, which we had visited on Saturday. One could spend hours inspecting all manner of clocks and watches, ranging from a 19th-century calendar clock to a German Black Forest Organ clock sporting 94 pipes.

The clock museum is a natural, since the region has a history of clock- and watch-making that stretches back more than 200 years. One museum exhibit notes that, in 1750, there were 48 clockmakers in Columbia, Marietta and Lancaster. The Hamilton Watch Co. was founded in Lancaster and is still going strong, although it has since been purchased by a Swiss firm.

From Columbia, we headed northwest to the Nissley Vineyards & Winery Estate. The winery is near Bainbridge on 300 acres of farmland and woods. While there are no winery tours on Sunday, we did have the opportunity to sample several wines and then purchase our favorites.

On Saturday evenings in the summer, Nissley offers Big-Band concerts, and regularly Nissley sponsors special events, including an annual harvest festival in September on the second weekend after Labor Day.

But just about any time throughout the congenial months, picnics seem to be in order around here.

A Nissley pamphlet advises visitors: "Sun-dappled meadows, a well groomed lawn, a rushing brook, shady woods and a bottle of chilled wine are all available for your picnicking pleasure."

All too quickly, our stay in western Lancaster County was ending. Dusk was coming and our little brood was tuckered out from a full weekend.

As we headed back to the Philadelphia suburbs, we gave this region our highest compliment: We'll return.

•

Although it is impossible to visit all the interesting sites in the area in a single weekend, some which should be considered include:

Wright's Ferry Mansion, Second and Cherry Streets, Columbia: A 1738 mansion that belonged to Susanna Wright, regarded as an intellectual of the period. She was proficient in Latin, French and Italian, and studied local Indian languages. The mansion, restored by the Louise Steinman von Hess Foundation, contains an impressive collection of 18th-century antiques, textiles, English ceramics and glass. The house is open from May through October on Tuesdays, Wednesdays, Fridays and Saturdays from 10 a.m. to 3 p.m.

Columbia Market House & Dungeon, Third and Locust Streets: One of the oldest continuously operated markets in Pennsylvania. Built in 1869, the structure contains a lockup for miscreants. A farmers' market offers the usual array of produce, baked goods and crafts. The market is open Friday from 8 a.m. to 5 p.m. and on Saturday from 8 a.m. to noon.

Bube's Brewery & Catacombs, 102 N. Market St., Mount Joy: Described as the only intact, pre-Prohibition brewery in the United States, Bube's is now a museum and it is also listed on the National Register of Historic Places. A restaurant occupies the subterranean part that once housed some of the brewery operations. Tours are offered from Memorial Day to Labor Day. Tours are also given as a complimentary addition to dinner. Dinner is served seven nights a week. Reservations suggested; phone 717-653-2160.

Historic Donegal Presbyterian Church on Donegal Springs Road in Mount Joy — Site of various historic markers commemorating events in the nation's past. The church was founded before 1721. It is the location of the Witness Tree, a large white oak where, legend has it, Revolutionary War patriots joined hands around the tree in 1777 to pledge allegiance to the new union.

New York, N.Y.

A guide to the most romantic places in the fanciest city in the land

By Margot Hornblower
Special to The Inquirer

New York City seemed to me, as a child, both feverish and serene. Just to gaze out the window at the skyscrapers, glittering honeycombs against the black night, was to drink in a sense of mystery and madness. So many towers and spires and so many people. The sirens and the distant surge of traffic never ceased. The city was awesome, yet inviting.

Moving back to Manhattan after 20 years, I find myself still dizzied by the lights, with childlike wonder undiminished. The city looms as big and bad, as mystical and seductive as ever, even as it has become more crowded and manic.

"The city is like poetry," wrote E. B. White in an essay on New York, "it compresses all life, all races and breeds, into a small island and adds music and the accompaniment of internal engines. The island of Manhattan is without any doubt the greatest human concentrate on earth, the poem whose magic is comprehensible to millions of permanent residents but whose full meaning will always remain elusive."

So here is a prescription for romance, from an unembarrassed Gothamite. This list of New York pleasures is random: Some are obvious, some less so; some are expensive, some free; some are newfangled, but most are old-fashioned ways to savor the biggest, fanciest, craziest city in the land.

To begin, New York should be seen from on high. The view can be had for free. Bring your Nikes and walk the Brooklyn Bridge at sunset. The pedestrian passage extends for a mile and a quarter suspended far above the traffic and the waves. The Statue of Liberty salutes in the distance and the lights twinkle on around the city. Once in Brooklyn, stroll along the shoreline promenade, one of the city's gentlest spots, tucked against the brownstones of Brooklyn Heights, a cozy neighborhood of historic townhouses. Joggers, lovers and children riding bicycles pass each other with few collisions, and the water muffles the noise of the city.

Nearby, at the River Cafe, 1 Water St. you can dine on American specialties on a barge anchored by the shore. Crowded with tourists, natives, families and hand-holding couples, and festooned with flowers, it looks out on the glorious skyline across the water. On a summer day, sailboats and tugboats ply the harbor.

Meanwhile, gorgeous views can be had in other Manhattan establishments. A cheerful Indian restaurant at 30 Central Park South, Nirvana, looks down onto the lighted city surrounding the park. It is a cozy room, tentlike with red and silver fabric hanging from the walls and ceilings. A chicken and rice dish with pistachios and raisins was delicious, accompanied by fresh yogurt and warm poori, the light, puffy Indian bread.

At the top of Columbia University's Butler Hall, 400 W. 119th St., the peaceful Terrace, an expensive French restaurant, has a magical quality with its night windows on the Hudson. Candlelight reflects off the mirrored walls. With classical guitar music in the background, a red rose on each table and a menu of exquisite fish dishes and sumptuous desserts, it is arguably the most romantic restaurant in the city.

By day, discover the city's parks. Hokey as it sounds, that old chestnut, a ride in a horse-and-carriage from Central Park South (or 59th Street), is not to be scorned. On weekends and holidays, motor traffic is banned from Central Park's drives, and, for $17 a half-hour and $5 for each additional fifteeen minutes, a couple of lovebirds (even with kids in tow) can imagine themselves transported back to New York of the Gay Nineties. Lulled by the rhythm of the carriage, one can absorb the beauty of the city in slow motion.

Our driver, ruddy-cheeked and top-hatted, was Marty L'Herault, an actor who had come to the city after graduating from the University of Wisconsin in theater. Even Jordan, the horse hitched up to our 75-year-old carriage, was in show business: He posed as a race horse on a TV soap opera, *Another World*.

On day rides, L'Herault gives a cheerful guided tour on request, pointing out, among the graceful buildings that line the park, the green roof of the Dakota, where Yoko Ono lives. We passed the carousel, over 100 years old, and the Central Park Zoo, which was started, he said, when wealthy New Yorkers in the mid-1800s had no place to put the wild pets they brought back from African safaris. Joggers, roller-skaters with Walkmans, fathers with baby carriages throng the walkways.

On night rides, passengers snuggle under the carriage blanket and "the less you talk and turn around, the better," L'Herault said.

Another way of capturing the spirit of old New York is to hire a couple of horses from the Claremont Riding Academy at 89th Street and Amsterdam Avenue. For $25 an hour, experienced riders can borrow a hard hat and guide their own steeds along the bridle paths surrounding the Central Park reservoir. Ducks, squirrels and other wildlife play around the water. The moist air smells of the forest, though the skyscrapers rise through a distant mist. Lessons are also available. Hours are 6:30 a.m. to 10 p.m. on weekdays and 6:30 a.m. to 5 p.m. on weekends. Reservations are required on the weekends: 212-724-5100.

For an intimate picnic, one of the prettiest, little-known corners of Central Park is the Conservatory Garden at 104th Street and Fifth Avenue, with fountains, formal flower beds, statues and benches under a canopy of trees. Across the street is the Museum of the City of New York, an uncrowded collection of lovely paintings, Duncan Phyfe furniture, Tiffany silver and delightful antique toys and dollhouses. A multi-screened movie evokes the sights and sounds of New York from the days of the Dutch to the great migrations through Ellis Island and the upheavals of the modern city. The museum, located at 103d and 5th Ave., is open Tuesday through Saturday 10 a.m. to 5 p.m. and Sunday 1 to 5 p.m. The grandiose Metropolitan Museum of Art is an easy walk or bus ride down to 84th and Fifth.

A more private corner of the city, where tourists seldom venture, is Riverside Park, Frederick Law Olmsted's undulating stretch of hills, rocks and walkways along the Hudson River from 72d Street to 158th Street. To bicycle up the park, with the historic Beaux Arts townhouses and curved apartment buildings of

Riverside Drive like a wedding cake above you, gives a sense of Paris or London in the '30s.

The West Side is home to many of the world's best-known actors and musicians. On Riverside Drive, one catches a glimpse of Itzhak Perlman in blue jeans and Sherrill Milnes in a work shirt. Nearby, between 94th and 95th Streets just west of Broadway, one can pause at Pomander Walk, a charming little British-style lane and one of the city's architectural curiosities. Heralded with a painted rooster over the south entrance, its two-story homes were built in the 1920s on the model of the New York set of a London play, *Pomander Walk*.

Another delightful stop is the Rockefellers' Riverside Church at 120th Street on the edge of the park. The 74-bell carillon can be heard in full glory at noon Saturdays and at 12:15 and 3 p.m. Sundays. The church tower, with its view of the soaring cliffs of New Jersey's Palisades, is open to the public.

Whether on Fifth Avenue or Riverside Drive, wherever one walks in New York the streets seem to vibrate. "There is some electric influence in the air and sun here that we don't experience on our side of the globe," wrote William Makepeace Thackeray on a visit in 1855. Every New Yorker has his special passions — the chestnut vendors at Rockefeller Center on a cold winter day, the street mimes and breakdancers along Columbus Avenue on a hot summer night.

Threading through the crowds along Fifth Avenue, one can't help gawking — the fashions are more outrageous, more alien than anywhere in the country. For respite, one flees into Scribner's at 48th Street, surely the most romantic bookstore in New York.

Shoulder to shoulder across 50th Street, Saks Fifth Avenue, with glittering windows, each a work of art, and St. Patrick's Cathedral, with burnished pews and sculptured chapels, offer their separate visions of beauty in the city.

New York, N.Y.

You'll find art everywhere you look in SoHo

By Janet Ruth Falon
Special to The Inquirer

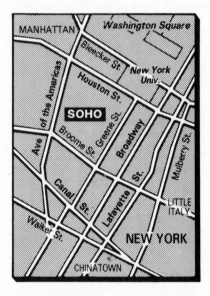

The omnipresent graffiti. The minimalist store window displays featuring mannequins with surrealistic posture. The "statement" designs on the boutiques' shopping bags.

You could call it art. Nearly everybody else does.

So it goes in SoHo, the Manhattan neighborhood where everything you see in the streets tends to look like potential art or art-in-the-making. Then again, maybe it only seems that way. After all, artiness is what we've come to expect from this indisputably hip slice of New York City.

SoHo can make the most in-the-know Philadelphian feel utterly out of it. Visitors don't easily blend into the scene, especially those toting cameras — unless you dress funky or have on a piece of what is called "wearable art," in which case your camera is magically transformed into a tool for artistic expression.

Even the street posters that disregard the "post no bills" warnings reek of an underground coolness: "To see UFOs in Utah is not considered extraordinary." "Leave home without it." Or, next to a photo, "This is my Mom. I like Mom."

And then there's the enormous graffito on a wall at Broome Street and West Broadway, with the words "I am the best artist," signed "Rene."

That is one huge claim, considering that SoHo (which has nothing to do with Soho in London) supposedly has superseded all other places as the cutting edge of the art world, with the possible exception of the East Village, just a few blocks north.

It was art that, in the late 1960s, rescued SoHo — formerly a light manufacturing district, turning out furs, silks, millinery, etc. — from total decline and decay, and turned it into a chic counterculture neighborhood in which working artists and more than 100 galleries coexist with interesting little shops and eccentric characters.

The art that originally brought people into SoHo is, for some people, second in appeal to SoHo's magnificent cast-iron architecture, featuring the largest remaining group of cast-iron buildings in the world.

The discovery of SoHo's cast-iron architecture is often a shock, albeit a delightful one, to visitors who only know of the neighborhood because of the art scene. Late in the 19th century, from about 1860 to 1890, the use of cast iron in commercial building, for structural as well as ornamental pieces, reached its apex in this area of New York. Lighter and cheaper than stone, it was sometimes painted to look like that material. Cast iron could be mass-produced from standardized molds that could be put together in any architectural style.

Many of those facades are hard for visitors to penetrate, both literally and figuratively. Maybe it's because SoHo's buildings were constructed for manufacturing and thus aren't as open and accessible as structures consciously made to invite passers-by. Or maybe it's because of the artsy mind-set that feels so exclusive. But to a first-time visitor, SoHo feels out of reach, as if there are things going on behind its doors that a visitor will never know.

The Haughwout Building, at 490 Broadway, is the most famous of the cast-iron structures. Originally a five-story emporium for china, silver and glass, it was built in 1856 in the style of a Venetian palace. The basic design motif, windows set in arches flanked by Corinthian columns, is rhythmically repeated on each level. Installation of the first Otis passenger elevator in this building led to the development of the skyscraper.

Greene Street, block after block, contains the most interesting variety of cast-iron structures, and on many of them, you can spot the foundry marks. It is the most unchanged of all SoHo streets. The Gunther Building, at Greene and Broome Streets, is a good example of cast iron that was meant to simulate stone. It also features unusual curved glass windows.

Some of the cast-iron buildings are dirty and beginning to deteriorate, and it requires a positive vision, in some cases, to see beyond the filth to the magnificence of the structures. You'll hear yourself saying, over and over again, "If that building were cleaned up . . . "

The exterior fire escapes, which visually intrude upon the facades of the cast-iron structures, were not part of the original designs. They were added after the 1911 Triangle Shirtwaist Co. fire, in which 146 deaths — mostly of young women — were attributed largely to locked exit doors and a lack of fire escapes.

The history of particular buildings provides a commentary about SoHo's development. For instance, 591 Broadway, near Houston Street, was until recently a place in which dress trimmings and parts of belts were manufactured. Only the basement still is used for manufacturing; the upper floors have been rented out for galleries and other endeavors of SoHo's new incarnation. Across the street, 568 Broadway has been similarly transformed and now houses 10 galleries.

G.W. Einstein, a gallery featuring contemporary artists, moved from posh Madison Avenue into 591 Broadway in 1986. Although the SoHo rents have increased to the point where many struggling artists have had to move elsewhere, relocated galleries like Einstein are saving a lot of money by freeing themselves from Midtown rental costs.

As SoHo rents go up (almost all of SoHo has gone co-op, and only once in a while do you see a sign announcing a loft for rent), a lot of those fringe artists have moved a bit north to the East Village — now considered the real cutting edge of the art world. SoHo, to those in the know, is now regarded as home to the more traditional avant-garde art.

Where one neighborhood ends and the next begins is always fluid in Manhattan. Not surprisingly, the boundaries of SoHo are changing all the time, with the biggest push now moving its eastern border from the traditional Broadway (mostly Hispanic, with lots of vendors) two streets over, to Lafayette Street. To the west, SoHo's boundary is the Avenue of the Americas (Sixth Avenue), where it has evolved into a more purely residential neighborhood. To the south, it's Canal Street. The northernmost boundary, Houston Street is where the area gets its name. SoHo stands for "south of Houston" (New Yorkers pronounce that HOW-stun).

SoHo, in its different sizes and shapes, has had a varied past. In the 17th century, SoHo was the city's first black district. In the early 1800s, it became a fashionable residential district, and John Jacob Astor developed many of the area's small Federal houses. SoHo changed in the mid-19th-century, becoming an elegant commercial district and the location of the city's fine hotels and theaters. The cast-iron era followed, with construction spurred by the need for new factories and warehouses. The hotels and theaters eventually withered away.

Today, in an effort to preserve its heritage as a manufacturing center, there is a conscious move to keep SoHo from becoming too residential. A ruling mandates that every building must have some commercial venture on its first floor. Traces of light manufacturing continue as well.

Also, because SoHo is a nationally regulated historic district, the shells of its cast-iron structures must remain intact.

Not surprisingly, SoHo restaurants are decorated with indigenous art. Sit in one of these restaurants and get yourself a window view for an unobtrusive peek at the natives. Many people sport the anorexic artiste appearance, sort of pasty and Yoko Ono-ish. And everyone dresses in that go-go New York style, each with his or her own gimmick: a dramatic cropped haircut, a flat-top French schoolgirl hat, sunglasses so out that they're in, a plastic pocketbook, whatever.

One Friday, a man sitting across from me at a natural-foods restaurant wore tuxedo pants, a lime green T-shirt, a Yankees basball cap and running shoes without socks. Compared to the goings-on outside, he looked tame. He was reading a computer printout and tearing at a Caesar salad as pulsating avant-garde music blared from unseen speakers. Absolutely anything goes.

West Broadway is the main shopping and gallery street cutting through SoHo. The whimsical nature of many of the boutiques makes for fun browsing, but be prepared to shell out big bucks if you want to make the move from browsing to buying. The high prices are not surprising when you consider that the shopkeepers are paying as much as $100 per square foot for rent each month.

Some of the most unusual shops include: Think Big, selling outrageously enormous decorative toothbrushes, diaper pins, crayons and candy dots; Harriet Love, with vintage jewelry and clothing; Urban Archaeology, with actual city artifacts for sale, such as building ornaments, ornate sinks, old bars and soda fountains etc.; La Rue des Reves, where you have to look closely to see who's a mannequin and who's flesh, with free-flying birds and roaming dogs and wearable goods for sale that can create Halloween in July; See, featuring high-tech Spanish and Italian furniture; Miso, an eclectic clothes and toy store for adults and children, where the line between the different age groups is purposefully blurred, and Dean & Deluca, one of the most beautiful, and expensive, gourmet food stores, where you can find luscious spices, cheeses and other edibles.

There are stores that sell art deco hammers and screwdrivers, shops that sell fluorescent snakeskin shoes and boutiques that sell miniature working jukeboxes that play "Rock Around the Clock" on minuscule cassettes.

Artisans in shops and flea-market stalls offer jewelry that ranges from subtly individualistic to the type that Cher might wear on her less tasteful days.

Monday is the only true "dead" day in SoHo. Some galleries and shops also are closed on Sundays.

Artists create the need for art galleries, and art galleries often lead to the development of restaurants and bars to quench the thirsts and appetites of creators and potential purchasers. Fanelli's was the first to open for this clientele. Another favorite is Broome Street Bar at 363 W. Broadway.

There are no hotels in SoHo anymore, so you'll have to find lodgings farther downtown or uptown.

Other places to visit here include the New Museum of Contemporary Art, at 583 Broadway, and the Museum of Holography, at 11 Mercer St.

•

If you reach your tolerance limit of SoHo's "avant" appearances and trendy boutiques, you're within walking distance of two of Manhattan's most interesting ethnic neighborhoods: Chinatown, which experienced such a boom that you can't buy even the most ordinary building for less than $1 million, and the adjacent Little Italy, which is fighting to maintain its ethnic identity.

Chinatown, like SoHo, is only one-fourth of a mile square. But that small space is crammed with people. "Old" Chinatown, roughly bordered by the Bowery, Canal Street and Broadway, is inhabited by about 33,000 people. But a thriving "new" Chinatown — now numbering about 100,000 — has expanded into turf that was traditionally Little Italy, creating a population base of about 133,000.

The first wave of Chinese people to come here were Cantonese who, spurred by racial struggles, left the West Coast in 1875. This migration to Manhattan continued until 1882, when Congress passed exclusion acts that tightly limited the flow of Asian-Americans.

The neighborhood that was to become the old Chinatown first developed after the Revolutionary War, as the boundaries of Lower Manhattan nudged farther north. Vestiges of those earlier years still can be seen. For example, the Edward Mooney House, at 18 Broadway, was built in 1789 and is the oldest rowhouse in Manhattan. The house's many windows — a sure sign of wealth, based on the cost of glass — show that Mooney, a butcher, was a prosperous man.

The Bowery, well-known as a Skid Row artery a few blocks away, runs right through Chinatown. During the 19th century, the Bowery was the heart of New York's theater district, and it was here that Stephen Foster worked for a while and died an alcoholic.

Confucius Plaza, at the Bowery and Division Streets, was erected during China's Cultural Revolution. It was a controversial project because it went against the revolutionary mindset by paying homage to a symbol of traditional Chinese culture.

The oldest Jewish cemetery in New York, Shearith Israel, is nearby, on St. James Place near Chatham Square. It dates from the mid-17th century. Nearby is the elaborate Chinese facade of the Manhattan Savings Bank. It looks schmaltzy, as if it were designed with a too-conscious desire to fit into the neighborhood. But the building is authentic, having been brought over from China and constructed here.

Mott Street is the main drag of Chinatown, with restaurants, grocery stores, gift shops and a game arcade. At 7 Mott St., in 1911, Sun Yat-sen organized support for the revolution against the Manchu dynasty.

Canal Street is the traditional boundary line between Chinatown and Little Italy, but the line is less rigid now as Chinatown expands. Still, the crowds thin out tremendously when you cross Canal Street into Little Italy, and the street banners displaying the Italian national colors demonstrate an unflagging ethnic pride. The many street cafes, too, are a giveaway that you've moved from Asia to Western Europe.

There are about 14,000 Americans of Italian descent in Little Italy. But as more and more of them have moved to other New York neighborhoods, the Italian population has declined proportionately; it now makes up only 60 percent of Little Italy's population. Neighborhoods such as Brooklyn's Bensonhurst are regarded as a step up, and out, of the first-stop Italian "ghetto."

This is, however, still the place to come for pizza (which also qualifies as Little Italy's perfume), ice cream and, especially at Ferrara, extraordinary cannoli.

Also, Little Italy's saints' celebrations are famous for their food and pageantry, and attract many visitors. Among them: San Gennaro (celebrated in mid-September) and St. Anthony of Padua (mid-June).

Observers of the city haven't given up on the future of Little Italy, however. The emergence of Morsa, an architectural firm consisting of Little Italy natives who are transforming some of the indigenous tenement buildings into highly fashionable Milan-style structures, is seen as a sign of hope.

Richmond, Va.

Appreciating the old and the new in the capital of the Confederacy

By Carol Horner
Inquirer Staff Writer

As a Southerner who has lived in the North for 14 years, I have repeatedly suffered certain indignities at the hands of Yankees.

Two examples: They hear my accent and want to know where it's from. I say "Richmond, Va., where I grew up," and they proclaim disdainfully, "That's not the South."

Or, they ask where I'm from and, when I tell them, they mumble something about having passed through there once on the way to Florida or Williamsburg or, God forbid, North Carolina. The implication is, usually, that of course there's nothing worth stopping for in Richmond.

In my bones I've known with certainty that they were wrong, wrong, wrong in the first matter. How could the capital of the Old Confederacy not be the South? The South is a history and a cultural style, not a latitude.

But I've been less certain about the second issue, the question of what there might be in my old home town to make it worth a stop — or a trip all its own.

Which is why I was delighted when a virgin Yankee, one who had never been to the South (the Atlanta airport doesn't count), said he wanted to visit Richmond with me sometime. As a born and bred New

Yorker, now a Philadelphian, he felt it would be a cross-cultural experience. I felt it would be a chance for me to see home through new eyes.

So off we went in mid-March, a few weeks before the azaleas and dogwoods, admittedly, but in time to savor the demise of winter in 50ish afternoon temperatures.

I decided to make the weekend a blend of the Old and New Richmonds, having learned on visits to my family over the years that a New Richmond did indeed exist, with different manifestations of it materializing almost by the month.

And with less than two full days to spend in the city, I decided to give my friend a taste of a lot of Richmond experiences, expecting that he would be provoked to return on his own to explore more deeply the parts of the city that interested him most. What resulted was a busy weekend that smacked heavily of history but that included its share of trendy modernity (faddishness, Old Richmond would say).

The 250-mile drive down Interstate 95 took just over five hours, with a brief stop in Maryland for hamburgers. My friend and I preferred to bypass the more convenient gasoline-restaurant stops built along the interstate — three between Philadelphia and Washington, none between Washington and Richmond — choosing instead to look for a fast-food chain near one of the exits along the highway. Breaking the trip almost as soon as we got hungry was no problem.

We could have cut the trip to about an hour by flying, but that would have cost more. Besides, then I would have been deprived of the visceral pleasure of loudly playing Joan Baez's "The Night They Drove Old Dixie Down" on my car tape deck as we hit Virginia soil, accompanying it lustily in an accusatory tone.

The Yankee slunk in the passenger seat. "I was on vacation that week," he muttered.

If you're arriving in Richmond cold, you might want to begin at the Metro Richmond Visitors Center at 1700 Robin Hood Rd. (exit 14 off I-95/64), open 9 a.m. to 7 p.m. Monday through Saturday. There you can collect maps, pamphlets and tips to ease your way. I had called (804-358-5511) and had material mailed to me, so we were already well-prepared.

Time was when I could come up with only a couple of hotel names in the unlikely event that someone asked me about a place to stay in Richmond — maybe the John Marshall in midtown or the old Jefferson Hotel a bit west of center. Now there's a multitude of choices in many price ranges.

The stately John Marshall is still there, touting its proximity to the sloping greens of Capitol Square, to newly invigorated downtown shopping and to Shockoe Slip, the renovated warehouse development of trendy restaurants and shops that is the focus of the city's downtown night life.

And the Jefferson Hotel, built in 1895, is now the Jefferson-Sheraton. A massive white brick structure that blends Louis XVI and Colonial Renaissance architecture, the Jefferson was closed for three years for restoration and its reopening in March 1986 was anticipated eagerly. If my Yankee friend's reaction upon stepping into the lobby — "I'm dazzled!" — is any indication, the restoration

was a success. (Note, however, that a recent edition of Style, a Richmond weekly, awarded first prize in its "You are very Richmond if ... " contest to the entrant who finished the sentence " ... you apologize to out-of-town guests for what they've done to the Jefferson.")

From an upper lobby whose centerpiece is an imposing statue of Thomas Jefferson, the visitor descends a grand staircase — by a shaky but longstanding legend, the model for the famous *Gone With the Wind* staircase — into a breathtaking expanse of Italian marble flooring, ornate imitation marble columns and plush carpeting covered far overhead by a huge Tiffany stained-glass skylight. The effect is indeed dazzling, making the lobby worth a walk-through at the very least.

Other new hotels adding sparkle to downtown are the Marriott, adjacent to the major downtown shopping area, and the Richmond Ramada Renaissance, which serves brunch in its dining room overlooking the Kanawha Canal and, beyond that, the James River.

A visitors bureau representative also called my attention to the small newly renovated Commonwealth Park, which faces Capitol Square and offers suites furnished with antiques and reproductions; the moderately priced Days Inn Marketplace, and the "real, real jazzy" Omni, which was scheduled to open soon after our visit.

The bureau also has information about the array of chain motels throughout the metropolitan area and about a few bed-and-breakfast-type accommodations. We had our own personal version of the latter with members of my family.

Our touring was done somewhat in keeping with the truism that Richmond is a city of museums, churches and graveyards. That might sound dull, but it isn't. Certainly no visitor should miss the White House of the Confederacy. (Yes, America, there was one — Jefferson Davis lived in it from 1861 to 1865.) Displays in the adjacent Museum of the Confederacy describe the social and economic origins of the war; delineate the roles of women, blacks, merchants and aristocrats, and display memorabilia of the Confederate leaders. In one display, the visitor can see the coat and sword Robert E. Lee wore at the surrender at Appomattox, as well as the gold pen he used to sign the articles of surrender.

Four blocks away from the White House of the Confederacy is another Richmond treasure, the Valentine Museum. Devoted to the city's history, the Valentine was showing an exhibit titled "Jackson Ward: A Century of Community" when we were there. Jackson Ward is a graceful old black neighborhood now designated a National Historic District.

By the way, Bill "Bojangles" Robinson, the world-reknowned tap dancer, was born in Jackson Ward and today is honored by a statue there. Also worth seeing in Jackson Ward is the Maggie L. Walker National Historic Site, a brick house that was the home of Maggie Walker, daughter of a former slave who became a bank president and advocate of black women's rights.

In Richmond, one is never far from history, and thus never far from reminders of the enforced racial separation that marked the city as recently as my girlhood. But I find it thrilling to see how far the city has come on matters of race, and even to find it outstripping Northern cities in racial harmony.

The most visible symbol of the New Richmond is also a symbol of that racial harmony. It's a bridge that is a segment of the Sixth Street Marketplace that spans Broad Street, the main downtown shopping street. The Marketplace, which opened in September 1985, is a two-level complex of specialty shops, restaurants and food stalls that joins the city's two biggest department stores, Miller & Rhoads and Thalhimers, and extends almost three north-south blocks.

The bridge — once considered the official name of the marketplace mall — is significant in the history of Richmond race relations because several decades ago there was an informal racial division on Broad Street. The less well-off north side, which bordered Jackson Ward, was frequented mainly by blacks, while the better-off south side of the street was considered primarily the preserve of whites.

Many people in Richmond, which at the time of our visit had a black majority on its City Council, a black mayor and a black city manager, were proud to hail the bridge, and the entire Marketplace, as a dramatic symbol of racial unity and cooperation between the predominantly black political leadership and the predominantly white business leadership.

We meandered from the Valentine Museum through lovely Capitol Square to the Sixth Street Marketplace early on a Saturday evening.

If we had had time, we could have hopped on a 25-cent trolley to take us 10 blocks east to another new shopping area, the restored Main Street Station. The 1901 station and its voluminous shed have been converted into a complex of specialty shops, outlets and international food stalls. Since our visit, a large restaurant and jazz club, Palm Court, has opened. In this unusual mall, the shopper can see the original exposed steel beams of the old train shed.

We did interrupt our museum and shopping day downtown with a quick trip west to the Virginia Museum of Fine Arts. There we visited the new 90,000-square-foot West Wing, which houses, among other things, a fascinating collection of contemporary art from Sydney and Frances Lewis of Richmond. The founders of Best Products, the Lewises are the best-known local art patrons.

In the museum's lobby, I ran into a network news reporter of my acquaintance who said that she and her sister had come down from Washington for the day just to visit the museum's West Wing. This was unimaginable in the old days. Someone would actually drive 100 miles from Washington to see something in Richmond? I was amazed and pleased.

Actually, the museum provided one of my more startling moments. At lunch in the members' dining room, I was stunned to find on the menu something called "Baked Brie Soup." I ordered it to see how far Richmond had fallen, and, sigh, it was very good. Although you can get into the members' dining room only with a museum member, the museum has a cheerful cafeteria, which in good weather spills out to a sunny patio.

On the matter of food: I did not try to make our visit a gourmet excursion, although it would be possible to do that now. After years of culinary lethargy, Richmond now has a number of new, chic restaurants.

But I was more interested in exposing the Yankee to certain ambiances. We had a New Richmond Saturday night dinner at DeFazio's on 17th Street, where a high ceiling, leaded glass wall and tile floors created an art deco atmosphere.

We followed that with a decidedly Old Richmond Sunday midday dinner at the Chesterfield Tea Room, where dark rosewood, flowered wallpaper and an older, genteel clientele created an atmosphere reminiscent of the 1940s or earlier. The $7 price of the meal was also old-fashioned.

Day two was devoted largely to trenches and graves. With my brother-in-law, a history teacher, as guide, we visited trenches dug on the city's outskirts for defense against the Yankees. We drove through Church Hill, and, in a brief foray back to Revolutionary times, viewed from outside St. John's Church, the small, white frame Episcopal church where Patrick Henry made his famous "liberty or death" speech.

Then, skipping forward once more to the Civil War, we stopped at the headquarters of the Richmond National Battlefield Park, where the National Park Service provides audio-visual presentations on the nu-merous battles fought in the Richmond area as the Yankees struggled to take the city. Color-coded maps for a driving tour of battlefields in surrounding counties are available.

On Sunday afternoon, we drove through Hollywood Cemetery, where Jefferson Davis, Gen. J.E.B. Stuart and two U.S. presidents, James Monroe and John Tyler, are buried. We saw a tall pyramid of unmortared stones, laid to honor the 18,000 Confederate dead buried there. Legend has it that the small, numbered "CSA" stones marking the graves of the Confederate unknowns were designed with pointed tops so that no Yankee could sit on them. The one with me didn't try.

By the end of our 42 hours in Richmond, we had hit most of the high spots, if only briefly. We had seen some of the museums and some of the shops. We had cruised wide Monument Avenue, with its majestic statues of Confederate generals, and driven through the Fan District, pausing to appreciate its renovated turn-of-the-century townhouses. We had even briefly visited Shockoe Slip with intentions of sampling the night life, though in the end we decided against plunging into the fashionable Saturday night crowds.

We had done all that, and there was still so much we didn't see or do. We didn't get to the Science Museum or its Universe Theater. We didn't tour the John Marshall House or the Edgar Allan Poe Museum. Nor did we visit any of the plantations within a half-hour's drive of the city. I felt frustrated, but I certainly had wiped away any lingering uncertainty I had had about whether there was anything to do in my old home town.

But I was anxious to find out what conclusion my Yankee companion would come to on the other matter — whether Richmond was indeed the South. I got my answer. Over and over he kept saying, "Toto, I have a feeling we're not in Kansas anymore."

Shenandoah National Park, Va.

A good vacation outdoors for those who prefer to remain indoors

By David R. Boldt
Inquirer Staff Writer

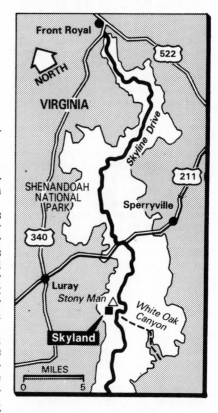

Perhaps it would be best to begin this story by disclosing a secret about my marriage.

Every relationship, of course, is made up of compromises, and my wife and I have been able to hammer out mutually acceptable agreements on a number of issues: where to send our child to school; which wallpaper to put up in the bathroom, and what should be the general parameters for resuming strategic arms limitation talks.

But one subject remains, uh, well — sensitive. And the point of this story is that we have found a solution that we wish to share with those of you who may face a similar dilemma. As for the rest of you, well, you are welcome to read on in a spirit of untrammeled voyeurism.

Simply stated, the problem is a difference of opinion as to what constitutes outdoor recreation. I think it would be fair to say (I've even asked her if it would be fair to say) that my wife's idea of rigorous outdoor recreation would be sipping an aperitif in a sidewalk cafe, preferably in a European capital to which she had just been flown first-class.

I'm no fanatic on the subject, but

for some reason, I've grown up to enjoy a somewhat different idea of how to commune with nature. I like to set off on a mountain path, carrying everything I need for the foreseeable future (until, say, dinner time) in a pack on my back, reveling in the feeling that the life force that animates me also flows through the panoply of nature around me.

We both like trees, and, in the larger sense, forests. But the intoxicating inspiration of the silence of a forest has been something we've found difficult to share. Somehow, whenever we go wandering along a mountain path, my wife can't shake a feeling that we are being stalked by a large predator, most likely a bear. Or, failing that, she is filled with a premonition (not always unsupported by the available evidence) that we will shortly be nibbled to death by gnats. And besides, she figures, if God had actually wanted us to walk up hills, why did He permit the invention of the internal combustion engine?

None of this is to say that my wife has no appreciation of natural splendor. It's all right with her, even pleasurable, as long as she doesn't have to run any risk of being eaten alive and doesn't have to walk very far uphill to see it.

One of the best solutions we've come upon is Skyland Lodge in Shenandoah National Park. It has worked for us, and perhaps it can work for you.

•

Skyland is at the highest point of the Skyline Drive, which runs through the park along the top of the Blue Ridge Mountains, as does a portion of the Appalachian Trail. Ten minutes of serious hiking along the Appalachian Trail, or any one of the dozens of other trails that lace the ridge and reach out to adjacent promontories, can take you out of earshot of the steel-belted radials humming along the asphalt of the drive.

In surprisingly short order, you are immersed in the allure of the outdoors. But at the same time, the illusion of having left civilization behind can be only as complete as one wishes. If my wife chooses to keep uppermost in her mind the fact that most of the amenities of the modern world, including beds, bathtubs, strawberry daiquiris, restaurants and gift shops, are no more than a few miles of unrigorous trail to the rear, well, that's her business.

There are other places, we have found over the last two decades, that also fill many or all of the aforementioned criteria. I once talked my wife into taking the cog railway up Mount Washington and then walking down.

Happily, most of the trails around Skyland either go down, as in the case of our favorite, White Oak Canyon Trail, or are at a fairly constant elevation. True, coming back up at the end of the day can provoke some complaints, but it has to be done.

Besides, the falls on the White Oak Canyon Trail are bewitchingly delicate cascades, a spectacle well worth the trip. And the water runs cold — just the right temperature to revive aching feet for the ascent to Skyland.

In Acadia National Park in Maine, we've worked out a system whereby my wife can drive to the Jordan Pond House and ransack the gift shop while others in our party hike to the same destination. The same tactic can be employed at Skyland, with the hikers (or bicyclists) in the group setting out along the trail (or Skyline Drive) and either looping back or being picked up at a designated rendezvous later in the day. Those who wish to soak in the bucolic splendor in more sedentary fashion are then free to sit at ease or look over the Appalachian handicrafts in the Skyland gift shop.

And there is still another Skyland option that allows everyone to get out on the trail, while threatening none with the dangers of working up a heavy sweat: letting horses do the walking. Trail rides leave several times a day from the stables at Skyland and head at a leisurely pace down White Oak Canyon or up to the

38

rocky summit of Stony Man, where riders dismount and look out over the valley from the top of the sheer cliffs that form the western face of the mountains.

•

Skyland is about 42 miles south of Front Royal Va., northern terminus of the Skyline Drive and about 10 miles south of the drive's interchange with U.S. Route 211. It is about 240 miles from Philadelphia.

The Route 211 approach is my favorite because there is a rise over which the Blue Ridge is suddenly revealed in the distance. There's something magical about this nearly mile-high ridge of mountains appearing in the blue haze above the gently rolling hills. The peaks are the highest in the Alleghenies south of New York. John Lederer, who explored the area in the 1670s, reported that his Indian guides fell to their knees on sighting the ridge and chanted, "Okee Paeze," which Lederer was led to believe meant that the Great Spirit was near.

When dedicating Shenandoah National Park in 1936, Franklin D. Roosevelt invoked Greek mythology: "There is merit for all of us," Roosevelt said, "in the ancient tale of the giant Antaeus, who, every time he touched his mother Earth, arose with strength increased a hundredfold." Shenandoah, he implied, would be an ideal place for Antaeus, or anyone else, to touch down.

For myself, the view of the haze-shrouded ridge gives meaning to the otherwise mysterious biblical injunction to look unto the hills, whence cometh one's strength.

Another reason for going via Route 211 is that it's only a short 10-mile drive down the Skyline Drive to Skyland. There's a lot to be said, and much of it has already been said, about the wonders of the drive itself, with its numerous scenic overlooks and the fact that, if you continue driving on it far enough, you can go all the way down into the Great Smoky Mountains National Park.

However, our experience has been that, after a time, if you've seen one scenic overlook, you've seen them all. In fact, the days I like best in Skyland, or on the drive, are the days when clouds have moved in at lower elevations, leaving you to believe, if you choose, that you are on a forested island in a sea of clouds — alone in the universe. Our goal now, after many years of visiting the park, is to get to Skyland as quickly as possible, unpack — and unwind.

Skyland itself is a mixture of old guest cabins and vaguely rustic but otherwise unremarkable motel units that have been built much more recently. Some of the cabins date to the time when Skyland was a private resort called Stony Man Camp, which was started in 1889 by George Freeman Pollock, a 20-year-old entrepreneur. (Pollock was later one of the principal figures in getting the Blue Ridge made into a national park.)

A walking tour of "Old Skyland" takes you past the wood-and-stone Massanutten Lodge, where Pollock and his wife presided over the multitudinous activities of the resort. These included mock cowboy-and-Indian battles and the enjoyment of spirits, which, according to legend, were kept during Prohibition in a Massanutten attic that could be reached only through a secret entrance behind a wall panel.

One of the cabins, called "Byrd's Nest" and once owned by the father of U.S. Sen. Harry F. Byrd Sr., was built in 1906, and a number of the other still-existing cabins were constructed in the decade before World War I. A path leads down past the remains of earlier cabins and a garden of plants and trees a couple took to Shenandoah from all over the world.

The old cabins usually seem to be reserved before the motel rooms, even though many of them lack the view out over the valley that nearly all of the motel unit rooms offer. Instead, the cabins, which accommodate one or two family groups, offer more privacy and rustic comfort. Many have back porches with rocking chairs, perfect for a long summer's evening, with your feet up on the porch rail and a glass of bourbon and branch water in your hand.

From the porch of the cabin at which we once stayed, you couldn't see the forest for the aspen, flowering rhododendron, four-leaf milkweed, downy false foxglove, dogtooth violets, dandelions and daisies. John Bartram, Philadelphia-based botanist, thought that the beauty and diversity of plant life in the Shenandoah Valley was such a floral gold mine that he declined initially to identify it as the source of many of the species he gathered for shipment to Europe in the 1700s.

Birds are also abundant; more than 200 species have been sighted there, according to National Park Service literature. The park also abounds in deer, some of which come right up to your porch rail.

The real trick to getting into Skyland's guest accommodations is to get your request in early. Skyland is often filled three or more weeks in advance, though it is sometimes possible to call on a Wednesday or Thursday and pick up a reservation for the coming weekend as a result of a cancellation. If you make reservations in advance, a deposit is required. Room rates vary from $43.50 to $49 a night (the lower-priced rooms do not have views). The number for reservations is 703-999-2211. All of Skyland is operated by a subsidiary of ARA Services Inc. of Philadelphia.

Even when Skyland is booked, it is often still possible to get a room at Big Meadows, a newer center on the Skyline Drive about 10 miles farther south, or at Lewis Mountain Lodge near the southern end of the park. Big Meadows is not without its charms, including a nature trail that points up the remains of the farms of the 450 families who lived in the region before it became a park in 1935. But it lacks the scenic splendor, sense of history and woodsy charm that make Skyland such a special place.

The quickest route to Skyland is to go down Interstate 95 to Washington, then around the Beltway to I-66, which heads west to Front Royal. A somewhat more scenic variation on this route is to get off I-66 at Gainesville, Va., and follow U.S. 29 to U.S. Route 211 in Warrenton. A still longer, but again somewhat more pastoral option, is to take the Pennsylvania Turnpike west to I-81, then continue south down the Shenandoah Valley, turning off for the Skyline Drive at the exit to Front Royal or the exit to Luray.

On any route, most families, especially those traveling with children, probably will be looking for spots to break the trip. An ideal one is Luray, the site of caverns discovered by two men looking for a limestone cavern that they could turn into a tourist attraction — and, sure enough, they succeeded.

By going through Washington and stopping off at the Bull Run battlefield, then coming home by way of Gettysburg, you can make your excursion to Skyland into a short course on the Civil War. Signs on the overlooks along the Skyline Drive often deal with the military action that took place in the Shenandoah Valley during the Civil War.

History buffs with a knack for map-reading may wish to approach the Skyline Drive and Skyland by way of Harpers Ferry, W. Va., where abolitionist John Brown made his stand. We've stopped for the night at nearly all of those places, most of which offer the usual assortment of motels, country inns and other hostelries. Our family's favorite place to stop on the way to Skyland, for the record, is the Dulles Airport Marriott.

After we check in and watch a few jets take off, we drive a couple of exits down the airport-access road, get off at Reston and go to the outdoor restaurant at the Lake Ann Center called 11 Cigno, where my wife sips an aperitif or two. It may not be the Boulevard St. Germain, Syntagma Square or the Via Veneto, but, as I was saying, this trip offers something for everyone.

Waterloo, N.J.

Taking a step back in time
at historic Waterloo Village

By George Anastasia
Inquirer Staff Writer

A burly blacksmith, a bright red bandana wrapped around his head, a broad leather apron covering his chest, pounds a glowing piece of iron into the shape of a horseshoe, explaining that the trick is to make sure the iron is hot enough to bend, but not soft enough to mold.

In a barn across the village green, two women in bright floor-length dresses sit behind looms and pedal away as strands of colored wool magically intertwine. Around them hang the fruits of their labor, woven blankets, rugs, vests and dresses.

Outdoors there's the lyrical sound of a flute coming from just beyond a little knoll and the bleating of sheep from behind the barn. Off in the distance someone is strumming a guitar and picking at a fiddle.

This is Waterloo Village, a national historic site in Allamuchy State Park, tucked into New Jersey's northwest corner. Waterloo is a working historic village, complete with houses, shops and barns and a group of artisans dressed in the attire of early settlers. It's all designed to take you back 200 years, when life was slower and time was spent doing instead of watching and making instead of buying.

"It's a walk back in time," said Eugenia Pagano of the nonprofit Waterloo Foundation for the Arts, the organization that, since the early 1950s, has directed the restoration of the village.

"It's a restored village, not a reconstructed village. Everything was rebuilt on its original foundations. We go from the colonial times through the federal period to the Victorian era."

Every year close to 200,000 visitors come to the village, which features craft and antique exhibits in the spring and a summer-long music festival. But the prize attraction is the village itself, nestled beside Waterloo Lake, the Musconetcong River and the Morris Canal on 1,100 largely unspoiled acres in a pristine area of the Garden State unfamiliar to many tourists who think of the state only in terms of the shore, casinos and race tracks.

Parts of Morris County, where the village is located, are more New England than New Jersey and quickly call to mind the state's historic past. Rolling hills, horse farms and restored colonial inns and residences dot Route 206 as it winds its way from Princeton to Waterloo about 45 miles north. The ride seems light years removed from the belching smokestacks and pollution of the turnpike oil refineries and the sand, surf and honky-tonk of the Jersey shore.

The "walk back in time" begins once you pull your car off the two-lane asphalt road that leads from Route 206 into Allamuchy State Park and set out on foot for the village.

There you'll find a mix of architecture and characters blending together to tell the story of the village's past.

A Victorian church. A colonial tavern. An apothecary from the turn of the century.

A unicyclist in leather cap. A guitar-strumming troubadour in plumes. A buckskin-suited rifleman. The tour guides are dressed in costumes representing different periods in the village's existence, explained Pagano.

The first homesteaders are said to have arrived in the area in the 1740s, and in their wake came merchants, miners and adventurers seeking to cash in on the water power, timber and ore in the Allamuchy Mountains to the north. By 1760, a four-fire, two-hammer forge, grist and saw mill formed the foundation upon which the village grew.

The forge became the major source of armaments for the colonial army during the Revolutionary War and the industrial magnet for the development of the village.

By the 1800s, the Waterloo Foundry and the Morris Canal, which ran through the village on its 102-mile course from Phillipsburg to Jersey City, had brought a boom time to the area and turned the village "into a bustling inland port," according to a thumbnail historical sketch provided by the Waterloo Foundation.

Later in the century a train depot and the Mountain Ice Co., which operated a 30,000-ton commercial ice-house on the lake, kept industry and commerce alive and the village growing.

It is against that historic backdrop that the village has been painstakingly restored and its artisans set to work.

There are approximately 18 buildings open to the public at any one time, along with several private residences. Two other structures — a library and the original forge — are being restored.

The Methodist church, its white steeple poking up through a clump of trees along Old Public Road at the entrance to the village, was built in 1859 at a cost of $2,300, and has been the site of religious services ever since.

The General Store, beside the Morris Canal, was built in 1831 and today is a central gathering place for visitors interested in village artifacts and crafts ranging from brooms, pottery and hand-dipped candles to wrought-iron objects and hand-woven clothing.

In the center of the store is a huge wooden support post that extends from floor to ceiling. Near its base the post is worn away on one side to about half its two-foot diameter — the legacy, a sign explains, of the canal boatmen who would spend hours leaning their booted feet against the post as they sat back in chairs shooting the breeze and exchanging the latest gossip in the store each day.

Directly below the store is the Towpath Tavern, where light snacks, beer and wine are available. In cooler months the tavern also boasts "hearty, home-made soup" from the blazing hearth.

The apothecary with its herb drying room, the pottery shed, the blacksmith shop, the weaving barn and the broom and cabinet shop — all operational and manned by artisans — offer glimpses into the village's commercial past.

Several colonial and Victorian homes, restored and maintained, are open for inspection along with the Canal Museum, the grist and saw mills and the Stagecoach Inn and Tavern, circa 1760.

The surroundings are virtually unspoiled and unchanged from the days when the village was first established. Wooden foot bridges cross the streams and small canals. Rolling lawns lead down to the lake and river. Horses romp in a large corral.

Sheep and goats meander in a fenced-in area behind the village barn. And the green water of the Morris Canal rolls by while a cool breeze blows down from the Allamuchy Mountains through the trees.

When "people think of New Jersey, they think of the cities and they think of the shore," said Pagano. "Here it's different. It's just very quiet, tranquil, peaceful. ... You walk into the village and it's like time has stood still."

•

The most direct way to get from Philadelphia to Waterloo Village is to take Interstate 95 north into New Jersey and then Route 206 north through Princeton. Route 206 offers a scenic but at times frustrating drive. The signs are confusing, particularly where Route 206 crosses Interstates 80 and 287. Stay on Route 206 north, however, and eventually there will be signs directing you from the town of Netcong to Waterloo Village.

The village is open Tuesday through Sunday, April through December. Admission on weekends is $7.50 for adults, $5 for senior citizens and $3 for children 6 to 12. Children under 6 are admitted free. During the week, admission is $6, $4.50 and $3, respectively. Phone: 201-347-0900.

Refreshments, including hamburgers, hot dogs and beverages, are sold in the village, and there is a picnic pavilion seating 200, where you can buy refreshments or bring your own, near the village Meeting House.

Lodging is available at several quaint inns and motels in the immediate area, including Feher's Country Inn in Andover and the Publick House in Chester, both within a 20-minute drive of the village. Several small motels are also in the vicinity.

Wellsboro, Pa.

A romantic hike along the local Grand Canyon

By Jane M. Von Bergen
Inquirer Staff Writer

Something romantic happened on the Western Rim trail that runs for 30 miles on the ridge above Pine Creek gorge in north-central Pennsylvania.

After a thunderous downpour, the sun had turned a green meadow into a mass of diamonds that glinted on every blade of grass. Blue, yellow and red wildflowers punctuated the slender birches that ringed the clearing under a now-clear blue sky. At the far edge of the clearing, a stream ran by, and it, too, caught and reflected the sunlight.

Wearing our backpacks and blisters, George and I turned to each other and smiled. And that's about all the detail I'll offer about the romantic moment.

But suffice it to say that the Western Rim trail is packed with places for romantic moments. There are broad vistas with mountains backing up against one another in giant rolls. There are miles of tranquil forest where ferns cover the forest floor and everything seems as soft as the curls on a baby's head.

At one point, we hiked up to a vista with a long view of the Pine Creek gorge. When we looked to our right, we saw a couple of canoes moving

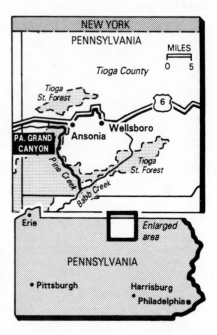

like ant boats on the river far below. When we looked to our left, we could see nothing because we had buried our noses in a sweet-smelling white mountain laurel bush.

Such are some of the many charms of the Western Rim trail, located on the Pine Creek gorge about 10 miles west of town. In a fit of hyperbole, an enthusiastic promoter once billed the gorge as Pennsylvania's Grand Canyon, and the name stuck.

The Grand Canyon begins just south of Ansonia near U.S. Route 6 and continues 47 miles along the creek. It's a short drive from Wells-

44

boro, a cute small town with gracious homes, a movie theater and a couple of restaurants. Figure, however, on a five- to six-hour drive from Philadelphia to Wellsboro.

Anyone who has seen the sun set on the dappled pastel rocks in Arizona's majestic canyon knows that there is little comparison, but Pennsylvania's version is impressive nonetheless.

From our vantage point along the ridge, we could see the clean cut made by the river through the mountain, even when we could not see the river itself. And unlike the canyon in Arizona, where ridge watchers must take on faith the presence of the Colorado River far below, canyon vistas in Pennsylvania offer frequent glimpses of Pine Creek.

Other than the Laurel Highland trail near Pittsburgh, where the trail's charms include pit toilets and pumped water, few trails in the Keystone state can beat the 30-mile Western Rim trail, which runs along the perimeter of the canyon, for pure hiker comfort.

Unlike a hotel resort, where vacationers define luxury in terms of plug-in coffeemakers, infrared bathroom lights and color televisions, trail luxury means reliable streams, good views and easy walking. We found all of that along the trail, making it an excellent spot for a beginning backpacker.

There are plenty of places where unpaved but accessible roads cross the trail, allowing a hike to be short or long. The trail runs primarily along a ridge so that there are few precipitous, heart-pounding climbs and equally few precipitous, knee-shattering drops.

Two state parks, one on each side of the canyon, offer vantage points of the gorge at its deepest — 800 feet. Both the parks, Leonard Harrison and Colson Point, have camping facilities, playgrounds for the kids and lookout points with hiking trails. Leonard Harrison Park also has a display that explains the area's history, wildlife and geography.

Pine Creek, which flows down the center of the canyon, used to flow northeasterly until the glaciers covered much of northern Pennsylvania with ice and silt. When the glaciers retreated, they left a dam of gravel, sand and clay that blocked Pine Creek's northeasterly flow. So Pine Creek changed course and flowed south, carving out the canyon in the process.

We began our hike near the Bradley Wales picnic facility on the edge of Pine Creek — near a boating entrance, about 15 miles from the trail's end. We parked our car in a dirt lot there, and Susan Dillon gave us a lift to a spot where the trail crossed a dusty back road.

She and her husband, Chuck, who both hold regular, white-collar jobs in Philadelphia during the week, run canoe and rafting trips in the spring and summer through their company, the Pine Creek Outfitters. They dream of someday leaving the city and expanding their business to include bicycle trips and regular services to hikers. They can be reached at 717-724-3003.

We waved goodbye to Susan, hefted our packs, watched her car drive away and began walking. Minutes later, we dropped our packs, dazzled by the first of the half-dozen or so magnificent views we would encounter on our trek.

We pulled out our books and began reading. Dedicated hikers who don't stop to read by every stream and leave their cameras at home probably could hike the entire 30-mile stretch in two or three days with little problem.

As it was, we followed the orange-blazed trail at the rate of about a mile an hour, stopping early and often. We passed plenty of places to camp, both near streams, in meadows, in pine-needled forest groves and in breaks in the trees with wide views of the gorge.

For some reason, we never can get organized enough to get that brisk early start we have read about in hiking books. So we didn't finish our first day's hike until about 6 p.m.

The last stretch before we stopped for the night was along what appeared to be an old lumbering road. The trail was soft, grassy and wide enough for us to hold hands and walk side by side — a pleasant change from the usual view of the other person's pack.

We came to a clearing with a view of the canyon. About a mile before that, we had passed a good flowing tributary where we could have replenished our water supply if necessary.

We always pitch the tent first, figuring that if it rains, at least we have someplace to go. Next, we rigged up a rope on a tree a city block or so from the campsite, where we could hoist our food after dinner to protect it — and us — from raccoons, skunks and bears.

By then, it was time to light up our stove and dig into some freeze-dried chili, cookies and hot chocolate. After we cleaned up the dishes and hoisted the food, we sipped a little Sambuca over a fire and watched the moon rise over the clearing.

The next morning, under graying skies, we packed up our gear and set off down the trail. During the first day, the trail had taken us primarily along the ridge. But the second day, the trail had to circle around, back from the rim to allow us to cross a tributary.

The trail moved through meadows and forests. The two were nicely alternated, so that in the meadows, just when the sun seemed too hot to bear, the cool forest appeared. And in the forest, when things seemed a little too dark, the welcome lightness of a meadow could be seen at a turn.

On this trip, we startled a few squirrels and watched a turkey buzzard turn lazy circles in the sky.

The trail turned onto a dusty back road at the worst possible time — right when a sudden downpour made us reach for our ponchos. In a forest, it takes a lot of rain to make things uncomfortable because the trees often reduce the average rainfall to a drizzle made bearable by wearing a hat.

We waited under a tree for the rain to stop, and then we set off. No sooner had we reached the forest when, sure enough, the rain slowed and stopped.

By that time, my blisters really hurt and we had gotten very thirsty, with purified water in short supply. Even with all that, the beauty of the trail made it possible to forget blisters and thirst for miles at a time. Still, when the trail began to descend toward Pine Creek, we began to look forward to the end of the trip.

And it was odd how, even when mountain vistas beckoned and streams glimmered in the light, our beat-up red Pinto with clean socks in the trunk seemed about as beautiful a sight as I could have imagined.

For more information on the Grand Canyon and the Wellsboro area, contact the Wellsboro Area Chamber of Commerce, Box 733, Wellsboro, Pa. 16901. Phone: 717-724-1926.

Woodstock, N.Y.

Great food and conversation in the heart of the Catskills

By Regina Schrambling
Special to The Inquirer

Drop the Catskills into a word-association game and the most common responses might be Rip Van Winkle and the Borscht Belt.

But there's another side of this rolling region of New York state beyond sleepy legends and frenetic entertainment. Ulster County, in the heart of the mountains, is afflicted with neither extreme. On a weekend journey here, you can be as active or as vegetative as you like.

The county might not ring many bells of recognition, but for one long weekend nearly 20 years ago, one of its towns wound up on the national map when hordes descended on a farm near Bethel for an extended rock concert.

The concert, of course, went down in history as Woodstock, the name of the town where it was originally supposed to be held. And today, that town is a mix of 19th-century architecture and 1960s attitude. Boutiques bear names such as Dharmaware; the clapboard hardware store stocks 20-pound bags of National Audubon Society birdseed on its front porch, and the pharmacy displays Levon Helm's copy of Bob Dylan's gold record for *Planet Waves* on a wall alongside a marble soda fountain.

Woodstock is only the most obvious part of this corner of the Catskills. Most people head for these hills in other seasons, but spring is the best time for exploring. In fall, Ulster County is overrun with hunters. Winter is when the skiers flood in, thronging to Hunter Mountain and the Belleayre and High Mount resorts. And summer is crowd season everywhere.

This time of year, the Catskills are turning green again. The weather is still cool enough to invite wandering on foot, and traffic on the winding roads is light enough to encourage leisurely drives through the purple-tinged mountains.

From Philadelphia, Ulster County is a painless drive of five hours or so, straight up the New Jersey Turnpike to the New York State Thruway, then left at Kingston.

In any season, weekend visitors have a range of accommodations, from rough country inns with the bathroom down the hall to lodges straight out of Architectural Digest.

As for food, count on indulging in some of the most sophisticated fare outside Manhattan. Thanks to an influx of French chefs who were originally looking for weekend homes, Ulster County harbors a surprising number of high-quality restaurants with decidedly reasonable prices.

Our first weekend there, we chanced across a rambling inn

called La Duchesse Anne, sitting alongside a bubbling stream and below an imposing Zen monastery on Miller Road just off Route 212 in Mount Tremper.

As we drove up, a man in a red jacket was nailing the inn's weathered sign back up after a storm. At the front door, a huge, menacing black dog was barking wildly.

Both were tip-offs that this was no ordinary motel. The "repairman" was the chef, and the dog had no teeth. Inside, next to a dimly lit bar with signs offering "fromage et saucisson," we found the owner, Martine Garbaud, a striking woman with an almost abrupt attitude. Her rooms are $25 for a double; she told us to take the one at the top of the stairs on the right.

Up those creaking stairs, we found a stripped-down room filled with not much more than an iron bedstead and warm late-afternoon sunshine. A painting by a local artist hung on one wall, a sink sat in one corner, cracked linoleum lined the bare floor. And on the bed, a sleek gray cat sprawled possessively, lazily giving itself a bath. We decided to stay.

Downstairs, the owner conceded that she told all comers, "If you like it, have it. If you don't, leave."

Over the next couple of days, we met other innkeepers with a more conventional welcome and lodgings. But La Duchesse Anne turned out to be an adventure in itself.

We spent our first afternoon listening to Martine's stories of France, where her family ran restaurants, and of Africa, where she and her husband take safaris each year. In the next room, her sister pressed linen tablecloths for dinner with the sizzle and hiss of iron against starch. As the sun faded, Martine stood looking out her front door and explained, almost wistfully, that she and so many other French immigrants chose to settle in this valley because it reminded them of the south of France. Then, abruptly, she turned away and ran out, calling behind her: "Excuse me, I've got to get my goat out of the rosebushes."

That night, we stopped into the bar again for a nightcap and thought we'd stepped out of the country. Conversations in French and English were raging. We indulged in a little Calvados and a bit of eavesdropping on tall tales in two languages. Before heading upstairs, we stopped to get towels and soap from the bartender's 83-year-old father, who doled them out of an antique armoire.

In the morning, we awoke to geese chattering and the sound of an ax against firewood. Downstairs, Martine was cooking crepes to order on two round cast-iron griddles in the cafe. Cats and dogs and kids wandered among the tables.

From a list of fillings that ranged from jam to sausages, we ordered one crepe with tomatoes and another with chestnut cream. Martine said crepes were made this way — folded square — in her native Breton. Each filled an entire plate. And for the chestnut version, Martine demanded freshly whipped cream from the kitchen. We decided we would be back for dinner.

But that was a few hours away, and so we went exploring. By sticking to the main road, Route 28, it's hard to get lost and easy to find most big sights. Just before finding Woodstock, we stopped at pristine Ashokan Reservoir for the view. With a permit, you can fish from the water New Yorkers are destined to drink.

In the village, Tinker Street, winding along and over streams and stunted waterfalls, is the center for shopping and gallery-hopping. As might be expected in a '60s-holdover town, crafts are everywhere: leather bags, pottery bowls, stained glass and endless earrings. The Woodstock Guild, at 34 Tinker St., is a cut above the average, its airy bi-level shop stocking work by members of a group organized in 1940 to promote arts, crafts and literature.

A small sandwich shop opens into the gallery, and right next door is the Kleinert Arts Center, where performances have included traditional musicians playing hammered dulcimer, fiddle and cello. (For a schedule, write the guild at 34 Tinker St., Woodstock, N.Y. 12498, or call 914-679-2079.)

The village is even more culture-oriented in summer; the Woodstock Playhouse says it is the state's longest-running professional stock theater. A copy of the Woodstock Times is the best bet for finding tips on shows and performances.

Away from the central district is the Colonial Pharmacy, a mini-shrine to Bob Dylan's days here. Photographs of The Band and other musicians line one wall in what would otherwise be a small-town drugstore, although one with a fully stocked ice cream parlor. Next door, the Sunflower Health Food shop is busier than the Grand Union across the highway.

When it comes to restaurant food, Woodstock seems to be more a dinner than a lunch town. Most places open after 5 p.m. Pizza, burritos and Middle Eastern-inspired foods are sold along Tinker Street in daylight.

Outside of Woodstock, Ulster County is not heavily developed. Villages such as Shandaken and Mount Tremper and Big Indian are listed on the map but difficult to spot even as you drive through them. Down in the valleys and along the side roads are innumerable antiques shops. Antiques auctions are scheduled most weekends; listings are in the paper.

Ulster County is also home to 14 wineries, many of them open for tastings and tours, especially on weekends. Woodstock Winery is closest to town, just a few miles beyond the reservoir, in West Shokan; it gives tours by appointment only (914-657-2018).

Farther east and south are other fairly well-known wineries, including Windsor Vineyards, Cagnasso, Brimstone Hill and the kosher Royal Kedem. For those not averse to exercise, Ulster County offers some of the state's best outdoor activities. Slide Mountain, the highest peak in the Catskills, is just south of Big Indian.

Nature trails are everywhere, and billboards advertise summer tubing on Esopus Creek. There are also campgrounds here, and horseback trails (including the Circle Tee Stables in Woodstock).

As we found in our exploring, though, most people seem content to come to Ulster County and do nothing more strenuous than talk and eat. One afternoon, we stumbled across the Shandaken Inn and blundered into what seemed to be an almost exclusive resort for paying friends of the owners, Albert and Giselle Pollack. Pollack said that they came just to get away, to eat his wife's French cooking and relax in a sumptuous home. The Inn is open only on weekends and closed December and April. Rooms are $165 a night for two, which includes dinner and breakfast (914-688-5100).

Another morning we rang the bell at the Mount Tremper Inn, across from La Duchesse Anne, after noting its Victorian architecture, fresh green trim and wide verandas from the road. The owners, Lou Caselli and Peter LaScala, welcomed us.

Two guests were putting away an elaborate and aromatic breakfast at a long dining table in the parlor as classical music played in the background. Red velvet and dark wood predominated. Caselli explained that he and his partner collected antiques for eight years before finding this place, a hunting lodge that had been converted into an orphanage.

Here, too, guests seemed happy just to sit out on the front porch or settle indoors with a book, although the inn has shuffleboard and badminton courts. Rooms with shared bath are $55 a night; with private bath, $70. That includes an impressive breakfast, sherry at dusk and a chocolate on the pillow. (For reservations, call 914-688-9938 or write Box 51, Mount Tremper, N.Y. 12457.)

Another night we stopped in at Val d'Isere, a few miles out Route 28 in Big Indian, a town with not much more than a gas station and a weathered country store complete with a video rental counter. Serge and Marguerite Bertrand, two more French refugees from Manhattan, opened this immaculate place two years ago.

Bertrand, an avid skier who had cooked for French officials and for wealthy families in New York, named it after the home town of Jean Claude Killy, whose picture hangs at the front door.

Here you enter to a warm smile from Marguerite Bertrand and the aroma of hot French bread. From a menu of French classics, we tried country pate and a creamy lentil soup, then tender veal filets with mushroom-and-brandy sauce and crispy, almond-coated boneless trout.

Like most restaurateurs here, the Bertrands realized they would have to supply rooms as well as food to guests coming from New York for the weekend. Upstairs, they rent a handful of clean and comfortable rooms with a shared bath. (Rates are $40 a night, including a continental breakfast; for reservations, call 914-254-4646 or write Val d'Isere, Route 28, Big Indian, N.Y. 12410.)

On our last night in Ulster County, we went back to La Duchesse Anne for dinner and found the place transformed. Obviously, food is the real focus of this unorthodox inn; reservations on weekends are essential (914-688-5260). Virtually every table was taken in the candelit dining room.

Feeling lucky to be seated, we started off with duck rillettes, the rich, fatty preserved meat spread over good bread, and eggs Breton, poached, then baked with cream under a crisp layer of Swiss cheese. For main courses, we tried salmon with lobster sauce and tender roast pork with apples, mushrooms and Calvados. Finally, we found room for chocolate-drizzled profiteroles and creme caramel, figuring the long drive home would burn off the calories. We're thinking about going back to Ulster County, just for the taste of it.

•

To get to Ulster County, take the New Jersey Turnpike north to 287/87, the New York State Thruway, on to Kingston and west at Exit 19 to Route 28.

For more information, write the Ulster County Public Information Office, Box 1800, Kingston, N.Y. 12401; 914-331-9300.

Special to The Inquirer / FAWN VRAZO

Tangier Island is a less-than-five-mile speck in Chesapeake Bay, where time seems to have stopped in the 18th century.

Baltimore, Md.

With four railroad museums, Maryland is the train buff's Mecca

By Tom Belden
Inquirer Staff Writer

For railroad-history buffs and the legions of fans who just love looking at or riding old trains, a trip south to Maryland is a bit like a trek to Mecca or the Vatican.

America's first railroad, the Baltimore & Ohio, started in Baltimore in 1830. And since the early 1950s, the memory of the B&O has been lovingly enshrined there in a beautiful, domed, cathedral-like building that was the main B&O roundhouse.

The roundhouse is connected to America's first passenger station, which abounds with railroad artifacts and model trains, and is side by side with a huge collection of 20th-century passenger rail cars and locomotives.

As if that weren't enough, the other end of the original B&O rail line is only 13 miles to the west, in the handsomely restored 19th-century mill town of Ellicott City. There, a group of dedicated volunteers has preserved the little station that was the first terminus of the B&O 157 years ago.

That's still not all. On a weekend journey of only two days, in fact, it is possible to see no fewer than four museums, either in Baltimore or within an hour's drive, that are

dedicated to the preservation and memory of the Iron Horse.

Other rail museums are hardpressed to match the authentic atmosphere of the B&O Museum, which also happens to have been one of the earliest large-scale efforts to preserve an entire complex of railroading. The museum was opened in 1953 by the B&O Railroad itself, and it has been operated since by the company's successor, the Chessie System, owned by CSX Corp.

Although the museum is showing its age, with its displays not quite as slick as the newer, highly acclaimed, state-sponsored museums in Pennsylvania and California, the B&O still has much to brag about. The collection of original railroad cars and locomotives is probably unmatched in this country, in size and significance.

You start your tour of the museum in the original passenger depot, Mount Clare Station, amid display cases that tell of the earliest efforts to establish railroads in America and the success that came to a group of Baltimore entrepreneurs. In addition to its role in railroading, the building was the place where Samuel Morse strung the first wires for his telegraph.

There are not just a few scattered railroad artifacts here. This is a

52

treasure house of memorabilia, case after case on two floors of early photographs, timetables, tickets, hardware, sturdy and elaborately decorated Centennial china once used in B&O dining cars, a beautiful array of clocks that hung in stations and offices, telegraph equipment and early telephones, and even a complex set of models to show the pioneering work that the railroad did on bridges.

Taking up much of the room on the second floor is the favorite attraction of many visitors, a sprawling O-gauge model railroad, with tracks lacing through valleys and towns and among mountains. Nearby, hundreds of model train cars of all gauges are on display.

But the highlight is through a short passageway from the first floor. The magnificent soaring roundhouse, put up in 1884, is where the B&O built and repaired thousands of cars and locomotives over the years. The building was built round so that the engines and cars could be brought onto its huge turning table in the center, then moved into position to be shunted onto the short pieces of track that surround the center while they were being worked on. The oak turning table now is polished and gleaming.

The 22 stalls that circle the turning table are home to original engines that run the gamut of the great railroad workhorses of the 19th century, their names freighted with strength and power, like Dragon, 10-Wheeler, Mogul, Camelback, Consolidation, Pacific and Hudson. Virtually all the pieces evoke images of movies about the Civil War, or the pioneers pushing across the West. Steps are built up to a few pieces of equipment so that visitors can get a closer look.

Outside are dozens of newer locomotives and rail cars, ranging from the steam-powered Freedom Train that was displayed around the country during the Bicentennial to streamlined cars from the 1940s and 1950s. Some of the equipment is retired from what probably was the B&O's best-known train in this century, the Capitol Limited.

Unfortunately, the museum has had a problem lately with vandals damaging the inside of the equipment, according to one of the curators. The rail cars and locomotives outside are locked up, with no public access. The museum does not have enough employees to guard against hooliganism, the curator said.

From June through October, every second weekend, the museum offers rides on some of its restored, working trains along 2.5 miles of track that starts at the station. The museum also has a very good shop, on the first floor of the station building, and there's a big collection of books, railroad souvenirs and some authentic pieces of memorabilia, including Centennial china, for sale.

The B&O Museum is at 901 W. Pratt St. at Poppelton Street, about 12 blocks west of the Inner Harbor, and about the same distance from Lexington Market. Open Wednesday through Sunday, 10 a.m. to 4 p.m. Admission, adults $2.50, children under age 12, $1.50; senior citizens over age 65, $1.50. Closed major holidays. 301-237-2387.

•

The Ellicott City B&O Railroad Station Museum has no less an authentic atmosphere. It sits at a bend where Main Street ducks under the Chessie System Railroad tracks. Main Street also is state Route 144, the road leading into town from Baltimore.

In the original stone station building, the first of two structures that are National Historic Landmarks, you enter through a small gift shop and then are guided through a series of sparsely furnished rooms that seem typical of an early rural train station.

Outside, you walk down the station platform, past the original stone foundation of the turntable where trains were turned for the return to Baltimore, to the old freight building. There volunteers have set up a wonderful HO-gauge display of the entire 13-mile original B&O line.

In case you didn't read all about it back in Baltimore, you'll learn here that the first trains on this line were horse-drawn, and it was several months after the line opened before a steam engine was added. Even then, on its first run back to Baltimore, the first engine, known as the Tom Thumb, suffered a mechanical breakdown and lost a race to a horse-drawn coach.

The whole show is remarkably well done, and the rail fans operating it will be happy to tell you more if you want to stay and chat.

Ellicott City, founded in 1772 by three Quaker brothers from Bucks County, has numerous other buildings that predate the 1830 train station. Some would argue, in fact, that there are plenty of reasons to come here to soak up some history other than the station museum. Main Street and a few alleys leading off it are lined with boutiques, antiques stores and restaurants, in case you want to linger.

The Ellicott City B&O Railroad Station Museum is open April 1 to Dec. 31, Monday and Wednesday through Saturday, 11 a.m. to 5 p.m.; Sunday, 12 to 5 p.m.; Jan. 1 to March 31, Saturday, 11 a.m. to 5 p.m.; Sunday, 12 to 5 p.m.; closed major holidays. Admission, adults $2; adults over 62 with ID, $1.50; children 5 to 12 $1; under 5, free. Information: 301-461-1944.

•

The other two railroad museums are farther from Baltimore, small and open only on a limited schedule. But they are fun, and interesting places to stop if you are passing through.

The Chesapeake Beach Railway Museum preserves the history of the Chesapeake Beach Railway Co. and Amusement Park, a turn-of-the-century resort on Chesapeake Bay

about 50 miles south of Baltimore and 30 miles east of Washington.

The museum, located in the only station still left on the old rail line, recently has hired its first full-time director and is trying hard to upgrade the collection. The town of Chesapeake Beach, which is undergoing a revival of its own, was a popular excursion spot from the early 1900s to the Great Depression for one principal reason — the railroad was built specifically to connect the resort to Washington.

The Chesapeake Beach Railroad Museum is on State Route 261 in Chesapeake Beach and is open Saturday and Sunday, 1 to 4 p.m., from the first weekend in April until Memorial Day, then every day throughout the summer. Special groups can be accommodated at other times. Admission is free. Information: 301-257-3892, or Calvert County Tourism information, 301-535-1600, ext. 357.

•

In Union Bridge, Md., about 30 miles northwest of Baltimore, you can see a collection of railroad memorabilia in Union Bridge Station, home of the Western Maryland Railroad Museum.

The station, built in the Victorian style in 1902 and now restored, housed the general offices of the Western Maryland Railroad. The place has a bountiful collection of plans, photographs and artifacts from both the Western Maryland and other railroads.

The Western Maryland Railroad Museum is on state Route 75 in Union Bridge. It is open Sundays from 1 p.m. to 4 p.m., May through October, and by appointment.

Admission is free. Additional information may be obtained from 301-868-5849, John Gruber; 301-775-2206, James McDermott.

•

For more information on Baltimore — hotels and restaurants, for instance — contact the city's Office of Promotion & Tourism at 301-752-8632.

Block Island, R.I.

A *haven of Victorian charms where it's all right to do nothing*

By Mary Jane Fine
Inquirer Staff Writer

The ferry chugged in at noon. Within the next hour, we had hastily surveyed the landscape and shared a sigh of relief: Nothing had changed.

There was still a swan family gliding prettily across the pond visible from our hotel window. The little art gallery at the foot of the hill was still open, as was the little gourmet market in town. Jazz still floated across the lawn each afternoon from the hotel across the open field. A flier promised a concert in the lobby of our Victorian hotel, just as in previous years. And the island newspaper, the Block Island Times, assured us that the folk singer we had liked so much last year was still performing "every sunny afternoon."

It has become a ritual for us. Because vacations on Block Island — off the coast of Rhode Island — are so idyllic, we have gotten very protective about the things that make it so. The peace, the quiet. The gently rolling, verdant hills. The vistas of ocean and pond, viewed from the wrap-around porch of the Spring House, circa 1854, to which we return as faithfully as swallows to Capistrano. The island architecture, Victorian and New England, unspoiled by anything taller than a tree.

Block Island was my husband's fa-vorite spot before we were married, and it has remained so since — and become one of mine, as well. Never one who wanted to visit the same destination over and over, I make an exception for this one.

The island's permanent population numbers about 800; its summer population balloons to around 15,000. It always surprises, and pleases, me to see how well the place absorbs people. The residents may moan about the vacationers and the vacationers may fuss about the day-trippers, but they all blend together as in any seaside resort.

Treated to a description of the island, people are wont to ask, "But what do you do there?" It is a question, apparently, that is asked of people often, because a resident wrote a mini-essay on the subject for the local paper, extolling the virtues of doing a lot of lovely nothing.

We read. We pack up the books we've been meaning to get around to, stagger under their weight in our luggage and then revel in the uninterrupted hours of reading on the porch, the ever-present breeze blowing over us.

We walk. Surrounded by the ocean, we never tire of the sight of it — or the bluffs down to the beaches, or the boats bobbing at anchor in Old and New Harbors, or the fields of clover and Queen Anne's Lace and black-eyed Susans.

We eat. A lot. The price of our accommodations at the Spring House — spartan decor, but we care little — includes a full breakfast for $108 per night. Lunch might be a lobster roll at Finn's by the harbor one day, a yuppie-ish hummus sandwich with sprouts at Tiffany's in town the next day, a picnic of fruit and cheese bought at the market and eaten oceanside the day after that.

We feed the swans and the ducks our leftover muffins and toast from breakfast. We sip drinks and listen to jazz on the veranda of the neighboring hotel. We visit the Historical Society and the library, reading up on island history or swan habits (aggressive hissing plus flapping of wings, usually countered by human flapping of arms). We go to the beach when the weather permits. And when it doesn't, we let other people complain about the rain or fog; we glory in it. Block Island fog turns the landscape gauzy, leaves droplets of moisture in my husband's beard and makes cats damp to the touch; the foghorn groans, like a ship's basso whistle, every 25 seconds.

Nightlife since our last visit had increased twofold, with a new cinema that showed foreign films and a new club that alternated between comedy nights and Irish singers. The cinema was small, crowded and friendly; during reel changes (remember reel changes?), they served coffee and brownies. The comedians, on the night we saw them (it was a different group each week) were young and quick and clever.

The island's tourist heyday was the turn of the century, and the ambiance lingers. At least two of the Victorian hotels — the Atlantic and Manisses — are recent restorations, furnished with antiques to retain their long-ago charm and boasting restaurants with excellent, if pricey, meals. Some hotels, like the Spring House, have only a summer season; others, such as the Atlantic and Manisses, stay open into the fall. A couple, and some guest houses, operate year-round.

Block Island is reachable by small plane or ferry. Our choice is the latter: The water route seems most appropriate for reaching an island. From New London, Conn., or Montauk on Long Island, the trip takes 2 to 2½ hours — a bit longer in soupy fog. From Point Judith, R.I., it's about an hour and quarter. You can drive to a departure point and bring your car along if you like, or you can try to mesh Amtrak's schedule with the ferry's. It takes some juggling, but it can be done.

During the fall and winter months, no ferries run from New London or Montauk to Block Island. Ferry service from Point Judith changes with the seasons and even the days of the week.

To avoid confusion, call the Block Island Ferry ahead and double-check: 401-783-4613.

There's no denying that Block Island has been "discovered," as evidenced by house prices that have climbed to ridiculous heights and hotel prices that are creeping up little by little.

When next we return, we will probably retrace our well-trodden steps again — in the hope that everything remains as remembered.

Chincoteague, Va.

An ideal spot for photographers, birders and pony-watchers

By Janet Ruth Falon
Special to The Inquirer

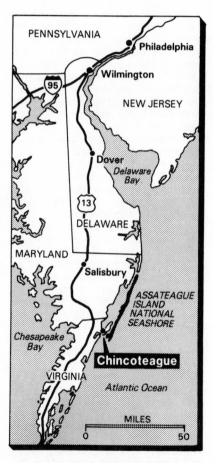

The annual wild-pony roundup and swim are so famous, so unusual and so popular that this unpretentious little fishing town is overrun with visitors, like an unguarded pie attracting ants at a summer picnic.

The roundup, which traditionally occurs on the last Wednesday and Thursday in July, has found its way into literature as the pivotal event in Marguerite Henry's delightful children's book, *Misty of Chincoteague.*

Early in the book, the grandfather explains to his grandchildren the raison d'etre for the event, which continues to benefit the Chincoteague Volunteer Firemen, who own the ponies:

" 'Twas this-a-way," he said. "In the yesterdays, when their corn was laid by, folks on Chincoteague got to yearnin' for a big hollerday. So they sails over to Assateague and rounds up all the wild ponies. 'Twas big sport."

"Like hunting buffalo or deer?" asked Paul.

" 'Zactly like that! Only they didn't kill the ponies; just rounded 'em up for the fun of the chase. Then they cut out a few of the younglings to gentle, tried some ropin' and rough ridin' of the wild ones, et a big dinner of outdoor pot pie, and comes on back home to Chincoteague. By-'n-by, they adds somethin' to the fun. They swum the ponies acrost the channel to Chincoteague and put on a big show. 'Twas so excitin', folks come from as far as New York to see it. And afore we knowed it, we was sellin' off some of the colts to the mainlanders."

"Why did they sell the wild things?" asked Maureen.

"Why!" echoed Grandpa. "Why, ponies was overrunnin' Assateague. They was gettin' thick as raisins in a pie!"

The pony roundup and swim encapsulate the contemporary tone of Chincoteague. What was once a bare-bones fishing village, existing mainly on catches of oysters, crab and flounder, now relies on tourism as its number-one year-round industry. T-shirt shops stand side by side with farm stands, and 24-hour convenience stores that sell croissants co-exist with dirty seafood stands that will never see the likes of sushi.

Visitors come to this area to commune with nature, to spot rare waterfowl at a wildlife refuge, to absorb the peacefulness of the pristine beach, but in order to meet their needs and bank on their presence, the town has responded with suburban-feel campsites and souvenir shops that sell seashells and with other "amenities" that entrepreneurs decide tourists must need.

Perhaps most telling of all, the ponies are no longer totally wild. Descendants of a band that swam ashore from a shipwrecked Spanish galleon in the late 16th century (or so the legend goes), they'll come right up to your car or campsite and nibble at your food and will snooze on the beach near your tent.

They almost seem to expect the roundup, which, in fact, serves to ensure the ecological balance by preventing overgrazing on the land. To keep the herd of perhaps 150 ponies in check, and to raise money for the volunteer fire department, some males are auctioned off each year. The average bid is $225.

There are two basic ways to "do" Chincoteague (pronounced SHINK-o-teague) and neighboring Assateague: You can camp right on the beach and have a no-frills seashore-and-nature

weekend, or you can stay at a cabin or motel in the town of Chincoteague for a somewhat less outdoorsy environment and go by car or bike to the sights and scenes that intrigue you.

Beware, however, if you choose the latter option, because car traffic from Chincoteague Island over the Assateague Channel through the National Wildlife Refuge and to the beach on Assateague can be brutal. And if you want to be a spectator at the pony swim, you have to arrive by 7 a.m.

The U.S. Fish and Wildlife Service operates the Chincoteague National Wildlife Refuge, heaven for birders, photographers and other devotees of the natural world. The refuge is open Nov. 1 to March 14, 6 a.m. to 6 p.m. and March 15 to October 31, 5 a.m. to 10 p.m.

The refuge is home to an enormous number of wildflowers, indigenous to either the field, forest or marsh habitats that compose it. Similarly, a trained eye can spot the birds, mammals, reptiles, marine mammals and amphibians that thrive in this protected environment.

Excellent illustrated brochures aid the uninitiated in spotting all this, but a bit of preparation with a field guide isn't a bad idea.

For the total novice, the refuge sponsors in the summer both a guided evening cruise of the Assateague Channel and a "wildlife safari" through the back roads of the refuge. A seven-hour family fishing day on Chincoteague Inlet or the Assateague Channel is also available, as are daily walks on different types of terrain. Call 804-336-6122 for information.

Wildlife that any visitor unquestionably will encounter includes the pesky mosquitoes and, sometimes, ticks. The sound of hands slapping flesh is common here, and it's a good idea to walk in the refuge with a can of repellent.

There are several trails in the refuge, the most dramatic being the 3.2-mile wildlife trail that is closed to cars until 3 p.m. A drive through it is like those drive-through safari theme parks. Birds seem to walk magically on water. Creaking trees sound like gentle snoring. The flat terrain with scrubby brush seems, at some spots, like the African plain.

One short trail leads to a red-and-white-striped lighthouse. Local artists show and sell their wares in a connecting shed on some weekends.

A 1.6-mile pony trail, open to walkers and bikers, offers a promise of spotting a pony, but there's no guarantee. A walk on this trail can be something of a search for a mirage, in which everything, including a haystack, appears from the distance to be a pony. Turn right when you enter the trail from the parking lot, and look for the boardwalk-type path that leads you to an overlook from which you can usually see ponies, if only far away. Deer, on the other hand, are plentiful.

You're certain to be ponied out if you stay in Chincoteague, however. Pony symbolism is everywhere: saltwater taffy called Ponytails, the Year of the Horse Inn.

For a real kick, visit the Pony Farm, which says it has, mounted, the real Misty from Henry's book. There are also a miniature pony farm, the Quarter Horse Video Arcade and miniature golf.

The town of Chincoteague also has the Refuge Waterfowl Museum, which houses a huge exhibit of waterfowl decoys. Hunting makes decoys a big business down here.

The town's Oyster Museum, open only between Memorial and Labor Days, is a low-key museum of the area's environmental history (the museum may be open during weekends in the spring and fall if volunteers are available: 804-336-6117). People who work at the museum can tell you all sorts of fish lore and will assure you that it is not true that you are supposed to eat oysters only in months with the letter R in their names.

Both museums are close to a waterslide ride on the road that leads to Assateague, opposite the Chamber of Commerce and the Maddox Family Campgrounds, next to the Dairy Queen, with its typically Chinco-teague parking lot of crushed oyster shells. You can't miss the waterslide: It's marked by a giant figure of a woman in a polka-dot bikini.

Even with these eclectic attractions, the town of Chincoteague isn't as tacky as it might sound. It's just that it seems to be at odds with itself, a fishing/beach village that doesn't quite know how to embrace commercialism. It never went through a "quaint" stage, during which rough edges smoothed out, but instead, jumped right from its pre-tourism identity to this uncertain mix.

Scholars of American quirkiness will find it intriguing; others will find its not-quite-this-or-that-ness irritating. The best way to take it in, perhaps, is on bike or foot or moped, on which you can poke around its side streets and back roads and see how people live. Houses have names. Most have screened-in porches, and some have back yards with free-roaming chickens. Roses abound, honeysuckle comes in early and a couple of homes use beat-up old buses for junk storage.

This is, after all, the South, and things are just plain different. Grits and hush puppies are easily found, as are Southern accents and postcards that read "Greetings from Dixie." Everything's at least a tad slower than we're used to, more laid back, and a rush-rush aura marks you immediately as an outsider. By the time you've been served breakfast at the Beachway restaurant, for example, it can be time for a soft-shell crab sandwich lunch at another restaurant.

Actually, it's not such a bad idea to have your meals later than you usually do because, in this town, which lacks such standard amusements as movies or clubs, a late dinner will probably be your evening's entertainment. Luckily, there are some eateries that fit the bill nicely, the most noteworthy being the excellent Oyster Catcher on Main Street, with sophisticated fish dishes and a nice sprinkling of New Orleans spicy side dishes. Children under 12 are not welcome. Although the Oyster Catcher takes credit cards, most Chincoteague and

Assateague restaurants and motels will accept only cash or traveler's checks.

Although McDonald's recently arrived in town, most of the fast-food places are seafood stands, such as McCready's, an indication that beef plays second fiddle here to fish.

The Oyster Catcher seems to be the exception to the rule. A more typical Chincoteague restaurant is Don's, also on Main Street (one of two main thoroughfares in Chincoteague). It's open for all three meals and, like a diner, the ambiance and service stay the same round the clock. You'd be crazy not to eat fish here, since it is magnificently fresh, brought in daily by the local fishermen, whose boats, at night, loom large against the soft pastel sunsets.

Chattie's Lounge, with real seashells serving as ashtrays, is one flight up from Don's and is famous for raspberry and peach daiquiris. You might catch a country-western band and some local stomping, and it's surely one of the places in Chincoteague to mingle with, or observe, the local residents. Without its touristy frills, Chincoteague is a down-home town. Souped-up American cars are much more common than imports, and their drivers don't go in for pretenses. There's something admirable in the town's honesty about what it is, even if what it is is not your cup of tea.

That's why a place such as the super-expensive Channel Bass Inn, even with its reputation for quality, sticks out as an impostor, an oddity. How can a place that charges $40 for "the Chef's Classic Dessert Souffles for Two" ever be truly part of a town whose commercial core on Main Street consists of the police and fire headquarters, a hardware store, a five-and-dime, a new convenience store and not a whole lot more?

If these dichotomies would turn you off, rather than intrigue you, maybe you'd better spend the bulk of your time at the beach, where the human influence is tightly controlled and the only real changes are made by the wind and the water. At the most unde-veloped spots, it's difficult to believe that the Assateague seashore is part of the same Maryland shore as Ocean City, with all the high-rises.

More than 22 miles of roadless barrier island beach and marsh lie between the visitor facilities at each end of Assateague Island. Be sure to bring a bathing suit, because the beach patrol, zipping around on Honda three-wheelers, makes sure that seaside frolickers are observing a decision to outlaw nude bathing.

An alternate sight to write home about might be the porpoises that play in the ocean, very close to the shore. They, too, are tame, and supposedly will permit humans to play with them.

Assateague's gently shelving beach is ideal for a variety of seaside activities, including swimming, surf-fishing and surfing. Sections of beach are designated for specific activities, so be sure to check first before diving in. And the dunes, planted with American beach grass and enclosed by fencing, are closed to people in an effort to preserve the island.

And for a different dimension to your visit here, you might stop at the National Aeronautics and Space Administration's Wallops Island Facility of the Goddard Space Center, right on the road to Chincoteague. There are models of rockets and satellites, a history of flight exhibits, spacesuits and presentations about America's spaceflight programs. The center, open Thursday to Monday 10 a.m. to 4 p.m., is free to visitors and can best be seen on a self-guided walking tour.

For more information, contact:

Chincoteague Chamber of Commerce, Box 258, Chincoteague, Va. 23336; 804-336-6161.

Assateague State Park, Maryland Park Service, Route 2, Box 293, Berlin, Md. 21811; 301-641-2120.

Chincoteague National Wildlife Refuge, U.S. Fish and Wildlife Service, Box 62, Chincoteague, Va. 23336; 804-336-6122.

Assateague Island National Seashore, National Park Service, Route 2, Box 294, Berlin, Md. 21811; 301-641-1441 or 804-336-6577.

Crisfield, Md.

Heading for the Eastern Shore to fill up at a blue crab festival

By Dan White
Special to The Inquirer

When I get that craving, usually on the third Wednesday morning in July, I jump into my car, take Interstate 95 south, and on the other side of Wilmington, pick up Route 13, the main highway into the Delmarva Peninsula.

As I move south of Dover, I lose WCAU on the car radio, but the craving is so overpowering it just pulls me on. I pass Perdue trucks packed with thousands of chickens panting in the heat. Corn and soybean farms stretch over the endless flatland. At Seaford, I cross the Nanticoke River, 31 miles from its Mississippi-size mouth in Tangier Sound. I enter Maryland at the town of Delmar, detour around Salisbury and finally, just when I think I'm not going to make it, I see the sign for Route 413.

Thirteen miles later, I reach Crisfield. Total time elapsed from Philadelphia to the annual J. Millard Tawes Crab and Clam Bake is three hours — not a bad drive at all, considering that the Tawes clambake is the biggest crab-eating blowout on the Eastern Shore and features the hard-nosed, hard-shell, delectable steamed blue crab, *Callinectes sapidus* (which translates as beautiful, savory swimmer), which I crave.

Crisfield itself is an interesting destination, although at first glance the town seems to offer nothing extraordinary to tourists. It lacks the boutiques and the studied cuteness of such towns as Annapolis. Its beaches are adjacent to marshland full of notorious insect "vermin." In the hottest months of the year, the waters fill with sea nettles, which inflict painful and sometimes dangerous stings.

Crisfield does have museums, some new restaurants, a few new gift shops, and, for those with boats, the marina at Somers Cove, which also has a swimming pool. Crisfield has an unusually intact array of homes representing late 19th-century Victorian and early 20th-century revival architecture and, surrounding the city cemetery, the largest collection of decorative iron fence in Somerset County.

What Crisfield also offers is verisimilitude. Those who aren't in a hurry can savor life in a working Chesapeake Bay port, can listen to the palaver of watermen as they unload their boats, can view unspoiled marshland and sunrises and sunsets that can be seen "all the way around" and can eat crabs and crab cakes bursting with meat.

But back to the clambake. By the time I arrive at Somers Cove on the edge of town, lines of people stand hundreds deep in a field of grass and crushed oyster shells, waiting. The sky and the water are the color of

61

limestone. The temperature is 92.

There will soon be about 4,000 people here, paying $20 each to come through the snow fence that surrounds the field. They have come from all over the state, and some, like me, from up north, across the Chesapeake and Delaware Canal from New Jersey, Pennsylvania and New York, the three states from which come most of the tourists on the lower Eastern Shore.

Two hundred and twenty-five bushels of *Callinectes sapidus* are being steamed in caldrons at one of the seafood plants down the road. When they turn reddish orange, they are loaded into baskets and hauled by truck to the crab booth and the lines.

Counter workers hoist them onto a serving table and spill them into piles. The hard-shells click against one another as they fall and slide. The servers stack the crabs on paper plates intended more for the shapes and weights of hot dogs and hamburgers than for crabs. A fine orange dust settles over their arms, and over the counter and table tops. Orange is the color of Old Bay Seasoning, which the workers scoop from bowls by the handful and fling over the crabs.

"Hey, more Old Bay Seasoning on there," I ask a counterman, returning my plate of crabs to him. I am used to crabs that are cooked and encrusted in the stuff.

"More Old Bay? You want it, you get it."

When I breathe the peppery aroma, I develop an Old Bay high. I experience something both deliciously salty and mind-clearing. The sensory gratification lasts just long enough to fuel that craving. Then suddenly it is gone, and in its place is a tickle, a gagging sensation, an immediate desire to cough, to find something wet and cool. Like beer.

"Let us know how you feel about our crabs. Come on, don't be scared." The people have been waiting to let the servers know how they feel.

They arrive at the front of the line with cardboard boxes the size of small suitcases, with parts of boxes,

with coolers, with pieces of board, anything on which they can carry away a load of crabs and other bounty of the bay area: corn, watermelons, clams, oysters and fried fish.

People stretch and contort to create new planes on their bodies on which they can balance their teeming plates as they weave their way to the large striped tents in which tables have been set up for eating. Some never reach the tents. They stop next to trucks and cars and eat off the fenders and hoods.

The patrons under the tents prepare to dine on tables covered with brown paper. They tuck in paper towels for bibs. They check their supply of soda or beer. Soda? "You go to hell if you drink soda with crabs in Crisfield," says a native. "Beer is the drink here."

For the price of admission, I can get all the beer I can drink. In this land of pleasant living, however, there is one caveat: Beer is served only in glass mugs, which are not included in the price of admission. They cost $1.50 at a separate booth. There are also wooden mallets for $1 to crack the crab shells, and paper aprons at 50 cents to protect matching shorts and tops, or Annapolis sun dresses, or blazers and cotton slacks, or whatever dress those who have never eaten crabs were advised by someone else who has never eaten crabs to wear for this extravaganza.

Some veterans advise you to "whip up" on the crabs, crushing right through the shell after the meat. I approach the task surgically, with quiet intensity, examining every nook and cranny for the tiniest morsel. I twist off the claws or pincers. Off come the remaining legs, and the broad, flat shell or carapace, that covers its organs. Out come the mustard, the gills, the extraneous essentials. All are flicked into a heap of discarded shell fragments and unattached limbs, bits and pieces of crab body and moist clumps of Old Bay Seasoning.

At some point, all that remains of the crab is its final defense: two cartilaginous chambers that protect what the most clinically dispassionate might think of as the muscles that propel the crab's legs and back fins. But, to those like me who endure the hardships and suffering wrought by the sharp edges of claws and shells, the lump of back fin that pops free from each cartilaginous chamber at the touch of the knife (that very same meat that retails at $10 a pound and is fancied by Philadelphians and New Yorkers and Arabs and West Germans) that is — the essence of seafood, the epitome of taste, the incarnation of what is godly about the Chesapeake Bay.

It is the sinful greed of both human and crab that has gotten the blue crab into this predicament. At $18 to $25 a bushel, a hard-working crabber on the water by 4:30 a.m. with 450 crab pots to tend can earn $400 or $500 a day, or as much as $3,000 in a six-day week. One waterman boasted of a $14,000 week. That's all based on early season prices, when the world is clamoring for crabs that have not yet returned in large enough numbers from their winter hibernation in deeper waters. By midsummer, crabs will be everywhere, and the price will drop.

The prospects of good money lure lots of part-time crabbers onto the water. Auto mechanics take their vacations crabbing. Schoolboys go crabbing in the morning before school opens or forget about school altogether. Tourists crowd the docks and piers to dangle strings with chicken pieces as bait. Watermen drop their baited wire-mesh pots in all the rivers and creeks and thoroughfares of nearby Tangier and Pocomoke Sounds. The faded floats of the pots are an essential feature in the watery terrain around Crisfield, as are the weathered faces of the watermen who place them.

With so much of the bay polluted with pots, it is a wonder any crabs remain. In fact, however, the blue crab has become the chief cash crop for Chesapeake fishermen.

More than 10,000 commercial crab licenses were issued in 1986 in Mary-

land, the largest producer of crabs in the country. Maryland and Virginia together harvested about 90 million pounds of crabs in 1986. That accounts for at least half of the entire country's catch of the blue crab, which in turn is half the annual harvest in this country of all crabs (Alaskan king, stone, rock, Jonah, Dungeness and snow crabs).

The two states supplied about four million pounds of soft-shell crabs in 1986, about 98 percent of the total national production. Those figures don't include sport crabbing, which is thought to equal anywhere from 10 to 25 percent of the commercial harvest.

It doesn't seem possible that a single species could be so fiercely hunted without disastrous effect on its ability to reproduce and survive. Yet the blue crab appears to be thriving, in part because it seems to have some natural advantages. It eats just about anything and goes just about anywhere, and it doesn't seem to accumulate in any quantity the toxic chemicals that are doing in the oyster and some fish, such as rockfish.

It was not the crab but the railroad and the oyster that made Crisfield. At the turn of the century, Crisfield had as many as 75 oyster-shucking houses. Oyster shells were piled as high as telephone poles. Trains ran down the middle of Main Street to dockside and left with their boxcars full of oysters and crabs and shad from the skipjacks that crowded the harbor. By 1910, Crisfield had become such an important port of entry that its custom house had the largest registry of sailing vessels of any American port.

Today, the railroad is gone and close behind it, in the opinion of many bay watchers, will be the glorious oyster, which has been imperiled by pollution and disease. In 1986, the harvest of oysters was the lowest since the Civil War. As a result, Crisfield is a fading seafood capital, its fortunes dependent now on the crab and on a tourist industry that is improving.

On that score, there is the Governor Tawes Museum in Somers Cove Marina, with Indian artifacts from the area, models of workboats, decoys by the famous Crisfield wildfowl carvers Lem and Steve Ward, and Millard Tawes memorabilia, especially from the period during which he was governor of Maryland, 1959-1967.

And the town has no shortage of restaurants that serve crab cakes bursting with meat. The Captain's Galley Restaurant and Bar, once an oyster-shucking house, now bills its crab cakes as the best in the world and throws in a panoramic, air-conditioned view of the harbor.

Just up Main Street, the Side Street Seafood Market has a second-story balcony eatery at which you can have crabs and steamed corn. The Circle Inn, as you enter town, serves terrific hamburgers.

There are three motels in town: the Pines (301-968-0900); Somers Cove (301-968-1900), and the Paddlewheel Motel (301-968-2220).

Downtown Crisfield, built over tons of oyster-shell landfill, resembles a coral atoll. Except for a few lonely saplings in the median strip on Main Street, where the railroad once ran, there are few trees in the downtown area.

On a typical July morning, the temperature on the electric clock above the Eastern Shore National Bank on Main Street, once the site of the Custom House, is likely to register 80 before 6:30. Tawes & Brothers Hardware, the third hardware store on the block, is open and selling ice to the Captain Genze, a party boat out of Stevensville, Md., packed with men and women going fishing for hardheads, trout, croakers or spot.

Halfway down Main Street, Gordon's Restaurant, a hangout for retired watermen, has been open since 4 a.m. The air is thick with cigarette smoke and the aroma of bacon and eggs frying. For $2, a visitor can get a bacon-and-egg or crab-cake sandwich, either of which comes as often as not with a thumbprint on the roll.

Main Street dead-ends at the Depot, where the railroad once loaded oysters. The Depot is now a public loading dock and terminal for passengers waiting for the mail boats that depart for Smith and Tangier Islands. The islands are popular with tourists fascinated by the lifestyle of the inhabitants, a way of living that harks back to the original settlement in the 1600s and that has yielded little to the passing centuries. There are tour boats as well as mail boats to the islands.

Although we have reflected on the life and times of Crisfield, the annual J. Millard Tawes Crab and Clam Bake has been winding down. A half-hour before closing time, at 4:30, the lines to the crab booth have disappeared.

The crab extravaganza is in its drinking phase. The sun has turned crab orange. In the distance, the marina shimmers, a beery mirage. The masts and sails of boats form dark, slowly expanding, geometric patterns on the water. A soft breeze has come up to clear the air. There are crab carcasses everywhere. They will be taken away by trucks.

As for me, I've done it again: overdosed on crabs. My lips are afire; I've gotten Old Bay on my eyebrows, under my fingernails, on my clothes. I smell like crab, feel hot and sweaty and want to plunge into something cold and refreshing, such as a huge watermelon.

I've also reached that point in my binge at which I can't stand the sight of another crab. But I know that by the time I reach Philadelphia, I will have already programmed my next craving.

It will coincide with the annual National Hard Crab Derby & Fair on Labor Day, a Crisfield festival that includes a boat-docking contest and, of course, piles of steamed, fat, succulent hard-shell crabs.

•

For more information about traveling in Maryland, contact the state's Office of Tourism Development, 45 Calvert St., Annapolis, Md. 21401. Phone 800-331-1750 and ask for operator 250 or call 301-269-3517.

Gettysburg, Pa.

The Civil War battlefield where war and oratory are remembered

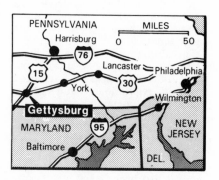

By Larry Fish
Inquirer Staff Writer

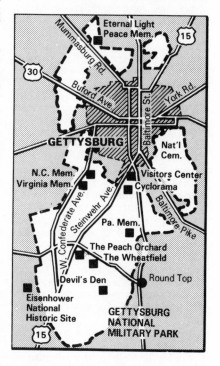

The late-afternoon sun seemed to be melting its way through a thick haze that hung over the battlefield like smoke.

"It looks so ethereal," said a woman from Virginia who, in spite of the suffocating heat, had climbed the 60-foot observation tower atop Culp's Hill. Her reward was not only a fine view of the green Pennsylvania hills gradually disappearing into shadows and steamy mist, but also a brush with what Lincoln called "the mystic chords of memory" that define America.

Gettysburg is a place twice sacred in the national memory — once for one of the decisive battles of history, and again for the short speech that made brilliantly clear what had been at stake.

Gettysburg is also a little county-seat town whose character was forever changed in three days of July 1863. Tourism is its only industry, and the Gettysburg National Military Park surrounds the village almost like a noose.

Happily, on a weekend expedition we found that the town, population

7,200, seems able to deal with the 1.5 million or so visitors who come each year without becoming jaded or callous.

Gettysburg undeniably harbors a certain amount of schlock — if wax-museum figures could vote, this could become the 51st state — but it never dominates. Prices seem reasonable, and the pace is relaxed.

Somehow, the town seemed typified by one of the first places we visited after the two-hour drive from Philadelphia: the Lincoln Diner, downtown, where we wanted a late lunch before hitting the battlefield.

The dining-room walls were decorated with two copies of the Gettysburg Address — apparently required by zoning regulations — and a photo-mural of the Canadian Rockies.

Our waitress was a high school girl, painfully shy, who brought us our grilled-cheese sandwiches with downcast eyes. The apple pie was good; when I mildly asked the cashier if it had been baked on the premises, she responded with a bit of surprised indignation. Where else would it be baked?

Nothing shrill about the Lincoln Diner. We left its Formica coolness and went back out into one of the hottest days of the year.

There were three of us. With me were two good friends: a certified Civil War expert and his wife, whose interests do not center on military studies.

I would like to be a Civil War expert, but, to tell the truth, I have a hard time keeping track of grand strategy. Fortunately, I had a handy guide with which to brush up: the National Park Service's 60-page historical handbook to Gettysburg National Military Park.

It's available at the Government Printing Office bookstore in Center City Philadelphia and at many Park Service sites in the East. It is generally a good, concise account of the battle.

In the first year and a half of the Civil War, the major battles were on Confederate soil, in part because of the Southern position that there would be no war if the Union army would go away and let Dixie secede in peace.

Many months of war made clear that the Union was not going to do any such thing, and Gen. Robert E. Lee began to realize the potential advantages of taking the war to the Union homeland. Besides creating havoc in the enemy's territory for a change, the move might be such a blow to Northern morale that a negotiated peace could follow.

Lee made his first attempt, in the border state of Maryland, in September 1862. The campaign ultimately saw his Army of Northern Virginia turned back at Antietam.

Early the next summer, Lee once again moved north out of Virginia, this time through the Shenandoah and Cumberland Valleys. His goal, he said, was to destroy the Pennsylvania Railroad's bridge over the Susquehanna River at Harrisburg, after which, he wrote, "I can turn my attention to Philadelphia, Baltimore or Washington as may seem best for our interest."

By late June, three corps of Confederate infantry had reached southern Pennsylvania. They were to converge on Harrisburg, but things went awry.

The Confederate cavalry — the eyes and ears for the infantry — had become separated from the rest of the army and was out of touch in eastern Maryland.

Lee, who was in Chambersburg, Pa., knew that the Union Army of the Potomac, newly under the command of Gen. George G. Meade, was closing in, from the direction of Frederick, Md.

Lee planned to take up a defensive position near Cashtown, eight miles northwest of Gettysburg.

A Confederate brigade was sent across fat, fertile Adams County toward Gettysburg for supplies, but it spotted Union cavalry about a mile west of town.

Lee was still on the other side of the mountains, so Lt. Gen. A.P. Hill took it upon himself to send two brigades along the Chambersburg Pike, northwest of Gettysburg, to test the Union strength there.

It was early on July 1, 1863. The two armies had more or less bumped into each other. Over the next three days, 165,000 Americans would fight, and more than 10,000 of them would die in the verdant countryside.

If the Union Army had been shattered at Gettysburg, there would have been no forces left between Lee and Philadelphia — which was convulsed with terror that summer — and only the defending garrison surrounding the capital at Washington.

The first day's fighting occurred on the ridge northwest of town around the Lutheran Theological Seminary, still very much a going concern. After that, the focus of battle shifted south of town, stretching from the high ground that contained the town's cemetery to a small, rocky hill called Little Round Top, 1½ miles away.

Most battlefield visitors, especially first-timers, start their tour at the Park Service Visitor Center at the southern edge of town. The Visitor Center has excellent, free maps of the battlefield roads, a hodgepodge of war relics and, for $2, a worthwhile, 30-minute "electric map" show that uses colored lights to explain what happened during the battle.

The only problem with beginning at the Visitor Center is that it is smack in the middle of the last day's battlefield. Each of us had been to Gettysburg before, so we decided to start our tour on Seminary Ridge, where the fighting started.

There is a clearly marked auto tour of the battlegrounds, a route of at least a dozen miles that completely encircles the town. It is the best way to see the field as a whole; even the most hurried tourist ought to allow three hours for the drive — most of it at about 10 m.p.h. with stops every hundred yards or so.

But as repeat visitors, we particularly enjoyed driving along the park roads that were not part of the circle tour. The fields were completely quiet in the hot afternoon sun, and there was a sense of fresh discovery when we came upon seemingly forgotten monuments.

Gettysburg is a vast encampment of monuments. There are granite Union infantrymen firmly withstanding their bronze foes across the fields. There is a monument with an Irish wolfhound, and another with a Tammany Indian outside a tepee.

There are stone knapsacks, drums and caps. There is a chaplain giving last rites, and there is a muse writing names on a scroll.

The biggest monument of all is the Pennsylvania Memorial, a massive, domed pavilion bearing the names of 35,000 Pennsylvanians who fought here. On top, a dark angel holds a terrible sword aloft.

Because we had started our tour in the heat of the afternoon up on Seminary Ridge, we found ourselves on what many consider the "main part" of the battlefield — between the Visitor Center and Little Round Top — in early evening.

This is where the monuments are clustered the thickest. This was the "high-water mark" of the Confederacy, where Gen. George D. Pickett's desperate charge failed. This is where it is easiest to see that the Blue was here, the Gray was there and this is where they met.

The crowds had now largely left for the day. The shadows behind the stone soldiers were getting longer. In the quiet, it was easy to think. Early morning and early evening are the best times to be out on Gettysburg's battlegrounds.

We drove over to Culp's Hill, east of the town in a part of the park where none of us had ever been. We drank from Spangler's Spring, as the soldiers from both sides had done, and we began to think about dinner. All armies travel on their stomachs.

We were definitely going to have to wash up first, so we went back to our rooms at the Gettystown Inn, a seven-room bed-and-breakfast arrangement connected with the Dobbin House Tavern, almost directly across Steinwehr Avenue (Business Route 15) from the Gettysburg National Cemetery and only a few yards from the Visitor Center.

Gettysburg seems well supplied with inexpensive motels for travelers with children — there was one directly opposite our inn. We had felt like treating ourselves to a B&B, and the Gettystown Inn got our business primarily because its advertising stressed that it had air conditioning.

Its fair-size rooms were furnished with antiques. My friends had a private bath; my bath seemed to be mine alone but was across the hall. I paid $54.45 for the night.

By the time we got ready for dinner, it was 7:30 on a Saturday night in the middle of tourist season. We had hoped to eat at the Farnsworth House on Baltimore Street, which offers period-style dining — peanut soup, game pie, spoonbread — in a house built in 1810. Without reservations, we discovered, we had no hope of dinner there.

Genuinely hungry now, we descended on the Sunny Ray Restaurant — "where friends and families meet to eat" — a family-style diner offering real mashed potatoes, apple fritters and a buffet for $6.95.

It was good, substantial food in a relaxed setting. Probably a bit too relaxed — the help was not at all bashful about vacuuming around the table as we finished. But the apple pie was better than that at the Lincoln Diner, so I switched my loyalty.

•

The first order of business the next morning was to visit the Eisenhower National Historic Site, the former President's retirement farm adjacent to the military park and behind former Confederate lines.

The only way to get to the Eisenhower farm is to go to the Visitor Center, buy a $2.25 ticket and board a shuttle bus for a 1½-mile ride to the estate. (Buses run from 9 a.m. to 4:15 p.m.)

Ike purchased the farm in the early 1950s, bewitched by the charm of the countryside and the opportunity to wander the battlefield at will.

During his presidency, he oversaw construction of the two-story, oddly suburban brick house, and he sometimes took world leaders there for a working weekend. After leaving the White House in 1961, Ike and his wife, Mamie, lived there until their deaths.

For baby-boomers, such as us, Ike was the national Granddad, beaming and chuckling and comforting. And this was Granddad's house. There was the sunporch where he ate dinner from a TV tray while watching *Gunsmoke*.

There were Mamie's manicure scissors and emery boards on the table next to the bed. Here was their kitchen, where we could almost see Mamie, wearing a dress and a strand of pearls, opening the Frigidaire while Ike pops in and says, "Hi, honey, I'm home!"

Most of the rest of the day was spent in or around Gettysburg's commercial attractions. If these are the sorts of things that particularly appeal to you, you will find a wonderland of them under the brow of Cemetery Hill — where Steinwehr Avenue and the Baltimore Pike form the top of a "Y."

We went to the National Civil War Wax Museum along Steinwehr, opposite the Visitor Center parking lot, for $3.75 apiece.

I don't have much good to say about wax museums, and that includes this one. But the place was packed with people who seemed otherwise normal, and they seemed to like it.

We went to the Farnsworth House for lunch. The luncheon menu does not include game pie or other exotica, but we did get excellent cups of the peanut soup and good sandwiches that cost about $2.50 each.

And just when I thought I had tasted the best in pies that Gettysburg had to offer, I tried their rum cream pie, a light, custardy filling on a graham-cracker crust. I wish I had ordered a second piece.

After lunch, we wandered back up to the area of the cemetery. Gun emplacements are still evident around the gate to the public cemetery, which is still in use but not open to tourists.

Immediately after the battle, the first of about 3,500 burials of Union casualties took place in a hastily purchased annex to the cemetery. (Most Confederate dead were taken home and reburied by patriotic societies after the war.)

The National Cemetery at Gettysburg has the dead, arranged by state, in a vast semicircle.

It was here, of course, that Lincoln (not the main speaker for the day — that honor went to famed orator Edward Everett) gave a two-minute address of dedication on Nov. 19, 1863, that ranks as one of the masterpieces of American writing.

The place where Lincoln stood is marked by a tall shaft called the Soldier's National Monument, erected shortly after the war. Not far away, there is also a monument to the address itself, where the text is reprinted in case you have somehow missed it elsewhere.

Hard by the cemetery is Old Gettysburg Village, a contrived collection of fudge shops and whatnot that we entered with no great expectations.

We were happily surprised to find the Horse Soldier here, a shop dealing in genuine war memorabilia — old photographs, Minie balls, newspapers, even an old saddle — and a collection of books, quality uniform reproductions and other goods.

The prices, if not cheap, seemed realistic — at least on those items about which I knew something. Anybody with a serious interest in the Civil War is likely to love the place.

I only wish I had also gotten to the Sword & Saber, south of town on a site where, the proprietors proudly note, Gen. Dan Sickles' leg was amputated. Sword & Saber's specialty is Confederate memorabilia.

As a final stop, we went to A. Lincoln's Place, almost next door. There, James A. Getty gives several 40-minute shows a day in the persona of The Great Emancipator.

The idea is that Abe — who seems to recognize on some level that he is dead — returns to Gettysburg to chat with the audience — $3.75 for adults — about his life and times.

Getty, whose name is simply a happy accident, has done his homework thoroughly and answers questions knowledgeably. It was almost spooky, the extent to which he persuaded the group we were with that he was indeed Lincoln.

Although Getty knows his stuff, whether he has the voice and mannerisms right depends on what you think Lincoln was like. I thought the accent sounded a bit more Down East Maine than central Illinois, but I enjoyed the show.

While the drive back to Philadelphia can be accomplished in about two hours, we managed to take almost twice that by stopping at antiques shops along U.S. Route 30 in New Oxford and other little towns. They are worth a trip in themselves.

•

For information on accommodations and attractions in and around Gettysburg, write to the Gettysburg Travel Council, 35 Carlisle St., Gettysburg, Pa. 17325, or call 717-334-6274.

Gettysburg National Military Park is open daily from 6 a.m. to 10 p.m., all year. The Visitor Center is open 8 a.m. to 6 p.m. during the summer but closes at 5 p.m. the rest of the year. For more information on the park, write to Gettysburg National Military Park, Gettysburg, Pa. 17325, or call 717-334-1124.

Hyde Park, N.Y.

Roosevelt and Vanderbilt mansions: Grand reminders of other eras

By Anthony R. Wood
Inquirer Staff Writer

The main road, Route 9, looks as out of place here as a McDonald's on a mountainside. The roadside motels, diners and fast-food outlets belie the fact that this is one of the nation's most historic neighborhoods. If it weren't for various signs associating the name "Roosevelt" with commercial enterprises, visitors might get the feeling they were lost.

But once on the driveway leading from Route 9 to the complex housing the Museum of the Franklin D. Roosevelt Library (it's not exactly a library) and the Roosevelt house (it wasn't exactly his house), there is nothing to fear but the eventual return to Route 9 itself.

One walk to the rear of the house, and its breathtaking view of the Hudson Valley, and it is clear why Sara and James Roosevelt settled here, and why their famous son, Franklin, spent considerable time here, at the house in which he was born.

How different this stretch of highway must have been in the Roosevelt years. FDR's son Elliott, who lives in California, recalled that when he was growing up in Hyde Park, the area along the highway, known as the Albany Post Road, was sparsely settled. The roadside buildup did not come until after the war that so heavily preoccupied his father.

Today, the Roosevelt era is a major attraction in the Hudson Valley. According to William R. Emerson, the Yale- and Oxford-educated historian in charge of the museum, during the spring and summer as many as 2,500 people visit the complex daily.

Technically, the complex rests on the Roosevelt-Vanderbilt National Historic Site, which also includes the Vanderbilt Mansion and the Val-Kill grounds. The latter is the site of the Eleanor Roosevelt house and the only National Historic Landmark dedicated to the wife of a president.

Many of the Hyde Park visitors have memories of the Roosevelt presidency. Emerson, 64, said he finds it especially interesting to watch older people go through the museum. In his words, "They're reliving their lives."

The Roosevelt presidency coincided with — and certainly contributed to — one of the most eventful periods in world history. If his greatness is in dispute, his importance is not.

The presidential years, from 1933 until FDR's death in 1945, dominate the museum exhibits. An exhibit on the New Deal years, 1933-41, commemorates the enormous body of social legislation enacted during the Roosevelt administration, much of which remains intact.

The so-called Reagan revolution

notwithstanding, interest in the New Deal has remained steady over the last decade, says Emerson. The Reagan administration may have applied some brakes to governmental growth, but it has hardly reversed it.

The museum's New Deal exhibition area offers a survey of the era when much of that government growth occurred. Included is the 1935 presidential statement announcing the institution of Social Security, "a law to flatten out the peaks and valleys of deflation and inflation."

Displayed is a picture of the first chairman of the Securities and Exchange Commission, Joseph P. Kennedy, and his son John, both sporting wide grins and a mighty show of the famous Kennedy teeth. In light of his activities as a Wall Street speculator, visitors are told, Kennedy's appointment was a controversial one and caused quite a stir in the financial community.

The most compelling photographs, however, are those that portray the despair and trauma of Dust Bowl victims in the 1930s. The photographs, of destitute farmers and their families, are part of a large collection taken at the behest of the Resettlement Administration in an effort to document human suffering.

It succeeded.

The museum's exhibits cover FDR's entire life. In one room are FDR's wicker, canopied bassinet in a glass case and photographs of his aristocratic parents, James and the legendary Sara. In another room is a headline announcing FDR's death.

Along the way is a draft of the speech that Roosevelt delivered after the Japanese attack on Pearl Harbor, seeking a declaration of war, with evidence of judicious editing. The opening sentence reads: "Yesterday, Dec. 7, 1941, a date which will live in ... Scratched out are the words "world history"; they are replaced by the single word "infamy."

Despite its imposing name — the Museum of the Franklin D. Roosevelt Library — visitors need not work up an intellectual sweat. There is an archive, used mostly by serious researchers, but the exhibition area is another matter.

It is the home of the frivolous as well as the historic. In the basement, for example, is FDR's 1936 Ford phaeton convertible. On the main floor is a campaign poster Roosevelt made while running for managing editor of the Harvard Crimson, in which he refers to himself as "Cousin Frank, the fairest of the Roosevelts."

The exhibit area, like the Roosevelts, has managed to affect the unaffected self-assuredness of the aristocracy, says Emerson. He describes it as "perhaps a little shabby around the edge. Shabby in the unselfconscious way...."

Just beyond the entrance is the cluttered but orderly desk, littered with knickknacks, that Roosevelt used during his 12 years in office. The visitor is told that it actually was the desk of FDR's predecessor, Herbert Hoover, and that in the blizzard of changes that followed Roosevelt's inauguration, he never got around to changing desks.

The human side of FDR is powerfully evident at the Roosevelt mansion, about 100 yards from the museum. Emerson strongly suggests that visitors begin at the mansion, which might well be called the Sara Roosevelt Museum, since the influence of FDR's mother is pervasive. "The leader of the free world was a tenant in his own house," says Emerson.

Elliott Roosevelt heartily agreed. During a recent interview, he recalled the power his grandmother exerted over the household. He noted with some irony that his mother, Eleanor, believed in the emancipation of women, whereas Sara Roosevelt accepted the tradition of male dominance. He added, however, that there was a twist to Sara Roosevelt's attitude toward dominance: "She knew women could establish some, without having any."

In the sumptuous mansion living room, bookended by Vermont-marble fireplaces, is a large oil portrait of FDR. During a recent animated house tour conducted by Park Service guide Haywood Smith, visitors were told that FDR didn't like the portrait. Nor did Eleanor. But Sara did. So in the living room it went. Near the living room is the lushly furnished Dresden Room, decorated by Sara. The furnishings are plainly too small for use. That was Sara Roosevelt's way of saying that this room was only for show.

A few miles away, but on an utterly different planet, is the Val-Kill complex, named for the nearby Val-Kill pond and dedicated to the memory of Anna Eleanor Roosevelt.

There has never been a first lady quite like Eleanor Roosevelt. She considered Val-Kill her home, out of sight and earshot of her domineering mother-in-law. While it may have been a refuge, it was hardly a retreat. The list of those she received at Val-Kill include Nikita Khrushchev, Tito, Jawaharlal Nehru and John F. Kennedy. That her marital life was less than romantically ideal is well-documented, but the vibrancy of her political life and the intensity of her social commitment also are well-documented.

Elliott Roosevelt said the cottage's furnishings are testimony to his mother's discomfort at the mansion, with its preponderance of heavy, light-absorbing furniture. "She built it [the cottage] to express her own personality," he said. The cottage's early American furnishings are lighter, more functional.

The cottage was once the site of a furniture factory operated by Eleanor Roosevelt and some of her closest friends. They envisioned the factory as a means of giving rural New Yorkers an alternative skill, should farming become unprofitable. The factory closed in 1936, and was converted into apartments for Eleanor and her secretary. Guest rooms were added to handle visitor overload at the Hyde Park mansion.

The main cottage at Val-Kill and another dating from 1925 can be reached by shuttle bus.

Only two miles from the Roosevelt manor is the Vanderbilt mansion. Although they are part of the same designated site, they have little in common but the fact that they are both in Hyde Park.

The Vanderbilt mansion, built in the Italian Renaissance style, is a palace rather than a mansion, a monument to the ostentatious wealth associated with the age of industrialism rather than to the aristocratic pedigree of the Roosevelt and Delano clans. The mansion was the home of Frederick Vanderbilt, the grandson of Cornelius Vanderbilt, who made a fortune in shipping and railroading.

The Vanderbilt estate has at least one advantage over the Roosevelt property: At the north end of the estate is a panoramic view of the Hudson superior to any offered on the Roosevelt grounds.

The Roosevelt mansion and museum are open daily from 9 a.m. to 5 p.m. except on Thanksgiving, Christmas and New Year's Day and Tuesdays and Wednesdays in November through March. Hours for the Vanderbilt Mansion are 10 a.m. to 6 p.m. Admission to the Roosevelt museum and mansion is $3.50, and to the Vanderbilt Mansion, $2. Those under 12 and over 62 are admitted free. The shuttle bus to Val-Kill, which operates daily from April through October, costs $2.50, or $1.65 for those 15 and under. The shuttle leaves from the parking lot of the FDR home. For information, call 914-229-9115, or write the National Park Service, 2499 Albany Post Rd., Hyde Park, N.Y. 12538.

If history is not enough of an enticement to visit this area, consider the Hudson Valley itself. It is worth the drive just for the privilege of crossing the Hudson bridges and taking in the magnificent views of the valley, with its mountain backdrop.

Hyde Park is about 80 miles north of New York City, on the east side of the Hudson. The probability of running into congestion and/or road construction is near 100 percent, but the drive is no longer than four hours. To circumvent some of the worst of New York traffic, take the New Jersey Turnpike to the Garden State Parkway to the New York Thruway. The simplest route to Hyde Park is Route 84 east from the Thruway to Route 9 north.

An alternative, slightly longer route, which avoids the New Jersey-New York traffic, is to travel through the Poconos via the Pennsylvania Turnpike's Northeast Extension. You can link up with Route 84 east in a variety of ways (consult a map), and then follow that to Route 9 north.

Once there, lodgings should be plentiful, except during the foliage season, when rooms are booked well in advance.

Although they are in no danger of winning any architectural design awards, inexpensive but clean motels dot the roadside. A short distance from the Roosevelt museum are the Dutch Patroon, 914-229-7141; the Golden Manor, 914-229-2157, and the Hyde Park Motel, 914-229-9161.

Ten miles up the road in Rhinebeck is the more expensive but far more charming Beekman Arms, 914-876-7077, an 18th-century, 49-room hotel.

The Beekman Arms has a restaurant offering elegant dining. To the south on Route 9 is the Culinary Institute of America, 914-471-6608. The institute has three restaurants: the Escoffier Room and the American Bounty, which require jackets, and the less formal St. Andrew's Cafe, which does not. For those on a tighter budget, there are a number of diners in the area.

Then there are always the Big Macs and the Whoppers, and all their competitors.

The Roosevelts and Vanderbilts wouldn't believe it.

•

For more information on this Hudson Valley area, contact the Dutchess County Tourism Promotion Agency, Box 2025, Hyde Park, N.Y. 12538; phone 914-229-0033. Also see the Tarrytown, N.Y., story in this book.

Jennerstown, Pa.

Forsaking the Pa. Turnpike to roam the Laurel Highlands

By William H. Stroud
Inquirer Staff Writer

The regulars at the counter at Babe's Corral, a rustic cafe on Route 30 here, were ragging a fellow who had come in wearing Bermuda shorts.

"Aw," said their victim, edging toward the door, "you guys are just jealous 'cause you ain't got legs like these."

One of his tormentors shouted after him, "If I had legs like those, I'd cut them suckers off at the knees."

Babe's Corral, with its plank-paneled walls and ceilings and its wagon-wheel light fixtures, is not Le Bec-Fin. But then Le Bec-Fin doesn't offer a good New York strip steak, baked potato, green beans, home-baked bread and a salad for $5.75, or a two-pork-chop dinner for the same price, or a fried-fish special with coleslaw and french fries for $3.

Babe's, which was recommended by a local resident as good and cheap, lived up to its billing. It was one of a number of happy surprises our family discovered when we left the turnpike and followed the two-lane blacktop into the heart of Pennsylvania's Laurel Highlands.

The Pennsylvania Turnpike is an antiseptic highway. West of Carlisle, its deep cuts, long tunnels and gentle grades make crossing the Allegheny Mountains probably less challenging than driving the Schuylkill Expressway from City Avenue to King of Prussia. There is little to suggest that these rugged hills were once a formidable barrier to armies, merchants and pioneers.

Recently, taking a daughter to summer camp near Ligonier, Pa., about five hours west of Philadelphia, we had to leave the turnpike and drive awhile along its predecessor, Route 30, the Lincoln Highway.

We were so impressed with the scenery, the charm of the small towns and the style and comfort of an inn where we spent the night that we decided to turn our return trip, two weeks later, into a weekend vacation.

We would experience a part of Pennsylvania that we had driven through countless times on the turnpike but had never really seen.

We discovered a region of considerable natural beauty, fascinating history, down-home warmth and quirky commercialism. We nibbled hearth-baked bread and homemade jam, watched flax being spun into linen thread and bought maple syrup by the jug and berries by the quart.

Our daughter played in a mountain brook, sliding 40 feet or so down a slippery rock into a pool of clear, cold water. We hiked through a dark forest of mixed hardwoods and evergreens, where huge wild rhododendron (mountain laurel) formed a flowery canopy just above our heads, and we slaked our thirst at a mountain spring.

For our headquarters we chose the Ligonier Country Inn at Laughlintown, on Route 30 just east of Ligonier. The inn has been recently renovated and for $65 we had a huge, cheery, air-conditioned room with a king-size brass bed.

The inn has a bar and an excellent dining room.

For a guide, we used the *Laurel Highlands Annual Guidebook,* an expanded edition of a local tourist magazine called the Laurel Highlands Scene. The Scene, published by the Laurel Group Press in Scottdale, Pa., is available free at some tourist-information centers and for $1 at hotels and gift shops.

The annual guidebook, which lists and describes parks, historic sites, museums, sports facilities, campgrounds, theaters, restaurants, hotels, motels and inns, costs $1.75. Each book contains a regional calendar of events.

The tiny town of Ligonier centers on the Diamond, an immaculately groomed village square with a Victorian gazebo as its centerpiece. Shops near the Diamond specialize in gifts, craft items and expensive clothing. The overall style is touristy in a subdued New England style.

There is no mistaking the Laurel Highlands for an unspoiled, undiscovered mountain region. This is a highly developed vacation area less than two hours' driving time southeast of Pittsburgh, with an abundance of commercial tourist attractions. On the other hand, we found the pace unhurried and the places we visited relatively uncrowded.

One of our first stops was Fort Ligonier, a reconstruction of the British fort that was established here in 1758 during the French and Indian War and became the staging point for the successful British assault on the French Fort Duquesne (now Pittsburgh).

The reconstruction of Fort Ligon-

ier began in 1946 with an excavation of the fort site. Artifacts recovered in the excavation are displayed in the fort museum. The fort itself consists of a stockade of sharpened poles surrounding a number of log buildings: officers' quarters, soldiers' barracks, the commissary, the infirmary, the quartermaster supply room, the armory and powder magazine.

The buildings are furnished with reproductions of frontier military equipment. In each, the push of a button brings a tape-recorded explanation of a display. Admission to the fort and museum is $3 for adults, $1.50 for children ages 6 to 12, free for those under 5.

After our visit to the fort, we drove east from Ligonier on Route 30, then turned south on Route 381 to Linn Run State Park. The tree-shaded seven-mile drive to the park winds through beautiful horse farms and private estates.

In the park, we stopped at the Adam Falls picnic area and hiked Flat Rock Trail, winding our way through the rhododendron and along a clear, stony creek. After less than a mile of walking, we came upon a place where the creek bottom was a huge piece of smoothly sculpted rock. For about 40 feet the rock angled gently downward with a thin current flowing over it to form a natural water slide. At the bottom was a wide pool about three feet deep.

Two families were frolicking in the water. Children and adults were experimenting with sliding down the rock, sometimes standing up and sometimes lying on their backs, sides or stomachs. A squealing toddler took the ride on her father's ample belly.

Our daughter Mary, 12, ran back to the car to get her swimsuit so she could join in the fun. She locked the keys inside, so she had an hour to play on the water slide while Mom, Dad and a friendly park ranger figured how to break into a car with electric locks.

Linn Run State Park has cabins

available for rent, and the ranger informed us that they recently had been renovated and insulated for year-round use.

Linn Run is at the northwest corner of the Forbes State Forest. Linn Run Road leads out of the park and southeast across the forest to Laurel Ridge State Park, where it joins a road that turns northward toward Laurel Mountain State Park. The three state parks, which are connected by hiking trails as well as good roads, mark the points of a triangle with sides roughly two miles long. The state forest fills the area between the parks.

Throughout the parks and state forest, there is an almost continuous undergrowth of mountain laurel, the state flower. Branches as thick as a man's arm arch high over the heads of hikers on the forest trails.

After driving through the parks and state forest, we headed back to Route 30, Jennerstown and our late dinner at Babe's Corral.

The next morning we followed the advice of the loquacious proprietor of Big Paps, a sandwich shop in Ligonier, and dropped in at the Ligonier Country Market, an every-Saturday summer event at the Ligonier Valley High School.

There, among the baked goods, produce and bric-a-brac, we found some exceptional handcrafted furniture. For $35, we bought a marble-top pedestal table made of weathered oak from an old barn, and for $5 we got two quarts of plump fresh blueberries.

From the market, we returned to Laughlintown, where on the third Saturday of every summer month, pioneer crafts are demonstrated at the Compass Inn, on Route 30 next door to the Ligonier Country Inn.

The Compass Inn is a log tavern built in 1799 as a stop for drovers and traders on the old road from Philadelphia to Pittsburgh. The tavern, restored by the Ligonier Valley Historical Society, has a common room, kitchen and ladies' parlor on the first floor and sleeping rooms upstairs. Volunteers in costumes of the early 1800s explained how the tavern was run, how food was prepared and how weary travelers shared the rope-strung beds upstairs if there was room and slept on buffalo skins on the floor if there was none.

In a reconstructed cookhouse, a volunteer baked bread on the hearth in an iron pot and cooked soup and made jam over the fireplace fire. In the yard, women were spinning and weaving with flax and wool. A barn and blacksmith shop also are part of the tour.

When we finished the Compass Inn tour, it was time to head back to Philadelphia. We decided to shun the turnpike and drive back on Route 30, taking our time, enjoying the mountain scenery and reflecting on the time when it was Pennsylvania's main road west.

●

For more information, write or call Laurel Highlands Inc., Ligonier Town Hall, 120 E. Main St., Ligonier, Pa. 15658, phone 412-238-5661. Laurel Highlands Inc. is a tourist-promotion agency with members in Westmoreland, Somerset and Fayette Counties and the Johnstown area.

Mystic, Conn.

The Mystic Maritime Museum: Reliving an old port's glory days

By Neill Borowski
Inquirer Staff Writer

Leaning over the counter of the 19th-century drugstore, Jan Bell held that popular remedy for headaches and other symptoms of bad blood humors: the leech.

Just let the critter set awhile attached to the forehead and the troublesome pounding deep within the skull will disappear, advised Bell, a "historical interpreter" at the Mystic Seaport Museum.

The museum was the chief lure for me, my wife and our two young children, but there was more than enough to see and do in the area to fill the weekend.

The museum itself, in this village of federal blues and slate grays, is worth the 230-mile journey from Philadelphia. And although the area can be packed with visitors in the summer, in typical New England understatement it is low on the glitter and clutter that often rise around such tourist attractions.

At the museum, with its more than 60 buildings on 40 acres and ships sitting in the Mystic River, well-trained interpreters and "role-players" (who dress in period costume and assume identities of Mystic characters) outline the maritime history associated with their specialties — carpentry, blacksmithing, sailmaking. They are trained by the museum

staff and must do their own research in the museum library for several months before they are allowed to host any of the exhibits, said museum spokeswoman Lisa Brownell.

In the pharmacy, Bell, who is both an interpreter and a role-player, held out the bottled leech for inspection.

Maybe the leech worked for those who sought out the local druggist for relief in 1870. It might have been psychological — simply a repulsive placebo in the pre-Tylenol era. Or, as Bell suggested, the leech-prompted bleeding might have reduced blood pressure or had another such effect.

Leeches were a basic necessity in the inventory of a good seaport druggist a century ago, when ships pulled in and their medicine chests had to be stocked. And, beginning in the 1600s, plenty of ships dropped anchor in this harbor just off Long Island Sound on the Mystic River.

The seaport also was a thriving shipbuilding center. Between 1838 and 1878, about 100 vessels were launched here. Mystic also had become a major whaling port by 1840 and, although the village had fewer than 1,500 residents, its merchants owned 18 whalers, according to a history of the seaport.

"Mystic, in its time, contributed to the nation's maritime stature in a manner out of all proportion to its size," according to one brochure.

The 59-year-old Mystic Seaport Museum effectively achieves its stated objective of "preservation of our maritime heritage."

The museum is laid out on the shore of the Mystic River and on a peninsula that reaches out into the river. In the preservation shipyard, the visitor can study how early wooden ships were built.

Ships open to browsing include the Charles W. Morgan, an 1841 whaling bark, and the Joseph Conrad, an 1882 training ship.

Important shops and suppliers to the 19th-century maritime trade line the streets of the Seaport Museum.

A cooperage, lobster shack, nautical-instrument repair shop and rigging loft are among the exhibits in the replica of the early village.

Other exhibits and galleries include a ship's cabin from an 1883 vessel, figureheads, scrimshaw, ship models and changing art shows.

Visitors can walk away from each of the exhibits with tidbits of historical knowledge. These facts won't arm you to win at Trivial Pursuit, but they will be a packed lesson in the nation's early maritime history.

Here, for example, you can learn how the various grades of coal and charcoal were blended in the shipsmith's shop to manufacture iron rigging and other hardware. As they explain how it was done, smiths work the giant bellows and pound out replacement hardware for the museum's ships and other exhibits.

A walk through the oystering exhibit will brief the visitor on the history of oystering, with photographs, oyster-output charts and an oyster dugout and a sharpie.

A warning: Expect to walk and walk. And walk. Comfortable shoes are essential.

You will walk miles through the museum village. You easily can spend a day or two browsing. A note on the museum map outlines a quick tour "if you have a short time to visit us." That tour alone takes two hours.

Although many families can be seen touring the museum, a weekend visit could be ideal for someone traveling alone because it is not the kind of experience that necessarily is enhanced by companionship. Visitors traveling alone can browse at their own pace and take time to read the documentation with each exhibit.

Our children's interest was held by the exhibits, but the youngsters didn't permit us to linger long at any one exhibit to read about it.

The Mystic Seaport Museum is open daily 9 a.m. to 5 p.m., May 1 to Oct. 31. During the rest of the year, it closes at 4 p.m. Admission is $7.50 for adults and $3.75 for children.

While a day can be spent at the museum learning about what went on above the sea, you can also learn what goes on below it at the Mystic Marinelife Aquarium, not far from the museum. The aquarium, operated by the nonprofit Sea Research Foundation Inc., was the high point of the weekend for our children (followed closely by the indoor swimming pool at the Ramada Inn).

The aquarium is well-maintained and stocked with a diversity of sea life. Scarred, mean-looking sharks glide round and round through a giant tank, with their razor-sharp teeth bared. Seals dive and surface in open pools. And every hour on the hour, trainers stage demonstrations of operant conditioning with whales, dolphins and sea lions in the aquarium's large Marine Theater.

Ironically, in a village that owes its early existence and growth to the butchering of countless whales, the aquarium plans to build a $4.3 million Whale Study Center to rescue sick marine mammals.

From the beginning of July through Labor Day, you can enter the aquarium 9 a.m. to 5:30 p.m., but you don't have to leave until 7 p.m. Throughout the rest of the year, admission hours are 9 a.m. to 4 p.m., with the aquarium closing at 6 p.m. Admission is $6.25 for adults, $5.25 for senior citizens and $3.25 for children ages 5 to 17.

A history of other undersea creatures — submariners — can be explored in nearby Groton at the Nautilus Memorial Submarine Force Library & Museum.

Browsing through the free museum and taking a self-guided tour of the USS Nautilus, the nation's first nuclear-powered submarine, launched in 1954 and decommissioned in 1980, will consume about 1½ hours.

In 1982, the Nautilus was designated a national landmark, and in 1985, it was towed to Groton. Before its decommissioning, the submarine had journeyed nearly a half-million miles in its career.

The museum, maintained by the Navy's Atlantic Submarine Forces, teaches visitors about the submarine service through memorabilia and exhibits of submarine equipment.

The museum is open 9 a.m. to 5 p.m. from mid-April to mid-October and 9 a.m. to 3:30 p.m. the rest of the year. It is closed Tuesdays and every three months for one week, so it is advisable to call ahead.

The Mystic area has an ample supply of fast-food, "ye olde" and trendy restaurants. We chose to avoid desk-clerk recommendations and cracked open the Yellow Pages to find places for dinner Friday night and for Sunday brunch. Worn out, we ate an unremarkable dinner in the hotel restaurant Saturday evening.

Our relatively random restaurant-selection process produced winners on both tries.

On Friday night, we found a homey ad for Sailor Ed's, which is one mile east of Mystic in Stonington. It's a casual, cozy seafood restaurant with fish mounted on knotty-pine walls. With tired, soda-spilling and sloppy children in tow after a long drive, we found this to be just the kind of restaurant we were looking for.

We later discovered that this restaurant is a favorite among the locals. It should have come as no surprise — we knew that we would return to our hotel room the victims of overeating after the appetizer.

It was an innocent-enough order: a $1.95 "small mountain" of onion rings. Clearly, there is a difference between the Philadelphia version of "mountain" and the Connecticut version. This order was on a foot-long platter piled at least six inches high.

The fried clams were real, fat and juicy, and not the ubiquitous chopped and sized pieces of clam. The fried scallops were plump and plentiful. And my lobster was tasty, what I got of it — my 4-year-old son saw this as a chance to begin developing an appreciation for the sweet and expensive meat.

For Sunday brunch, we selected the Capt. Daniel Packer Inne in West Mystic based on the inn's Old-English-lettered ad.

Brunch was $9.95 for adults and $7.95 for children. It included prime rib, beef brisket, baked ham, stuffed chicken breasts, beef tips, fish and the usual choice of eggs, waffles and pancakes.

The inn is run by Richard Kiley, who rescued the 18th-century building three days before the town was going to tear it down because it was a safety hazard. The former owner had started to restore the inn by gutting it, but then gave up. After he took it over in 1980, Kiley spent 3½ years renovating the place.

The inn was owned in its early history by the Packer family, which included one or two sea captains and the owner of a soap-manufacturing plant. Now in the National Register of Historic Places, the inn has random-width pine flooring (some planks are 30 inches wide) and six working fireplaces. During the winter, fires are kept alive in all the fireplaces, Kiley said.

One of the inn's businesses was operating a ferry on the Mystic River for stagecoaches and travelers from the seaport side of Mystic to the other side. When Kiley renovated the building, he found the tackle for the ferry's pulley system. Rods that anchored the ferry's rope guide still are embedded in the inn's foundation, he said.

Clearly, in this part of the world, history is everywhere around you.

Onchiota, N.Y.

From lake to lake, a canoe outing in the wilds of the Adirondacks

By Mike Shoup
Inquirer Travel Editor

It was the edge of fear in my 17-year-old son's voice that had me awake in seconds, sitting bolt upright, in fact, under the pitch-black tent canopy.

"Listen," he said in a whisper. "There's some nut out there throwing rocks into the lake. Who'd be doing that at 2 in the morning?"

I had no answer, but I felt the adrenalin surge in my own body as a loud "kerplash" echoed in the absolute stillness outside. This was the first night of a four-day canoe trip in the northern Adirondacks, and we hadn't seen a soul since choosing the remote campsite on Clear Pond in late afternoon.

"Kerplash." I grabbed the flashlight, unzipped the tent flap and emerged into the lacy moonlight that filtered down through the pine and spruce boughs high overhead. "Kerplash." The sound — like a flat, heavy rock being dropped from overhead — seemed to come from the edge of a nearby inlet that was horseshoed by trees and thick scrub growth.

"I don't know who you are or what you're trying to do, but knock it off," I boomed in my most authoritative voice as I stood there in the cold, feeling more than a little vulnerable in my boxer shorts. The splashing stopped for perhaps two minutes, then resumed for five or six smacks, in a slow but almost rhythmic pattern.

Tim said it first. "Beaver. Could that be a beaver?" As the logic of the noise that huge, flat tail could make on water sank in, we began to relax and chuckle at our needless trepidation. Soon, we were back in the tent and laughing so hard tears rolled down our cheeks.

We pictured Papa Beaver, now happily esconced in his nearby home of branches, mud and twigs, regaling the family with hilarious accounts of how he had once again scared the humans, especially the lunkhead with the hairy legs and knobby knees.

This Night of the Beaver, as we came to call it in the ensuing days, occurred in the northern reaches of the so-called Adirondack Park, about six million acres bounded very roughly by the St. Lawrence River and the Mohawk River Valley on the north and south, and Lake Champlain and the Black River on the east and west. It's an area about the size of Vermont, but with a population of only about 125,000, and, while heavily used by tourists and outdoors-lovers, still boasts some of the East's most pristine and untrampled terrain.

Forty percent of the park was legislated "forever wild" in 1894, but the rest is privately owned. Since the ownerships are piecemeal, the park presents a crazy-quilt of private and public use that permits ski centers, lakeside summer cottages, cheap motels, resorts and places with names like Santa's Workshop and Frontier Town to exist practically cheek-by-jowl with designated wilderness lands that have changed little since the Algonquins and Iroquois roamed the forests.

In the late 19th and early 20th century, the rich and super rich — Morgans, Vanderbilts, Rockefellers and many other well-heeled families of the industrial robber-baron era — built palatial estates on remote lakes in the mountains.

Guide-boating between and among the hundreds of lakes and ponds gradually became a cottage industry as hotels and summer homes sprang up along the lake shores and in the mountains. The railroads made this vast area more accessible to the millions — just a few hours away in New York City — but it was left for the automobile to completely open the Adirondacks to the masses. This occurred with construction of the New York Thruway to Albany in the late 1940s, and with completion of Interstate 87 from Albany north to Canada in the 1960s.

Today, it is the lake system that makes the Adirondacks stand out from other wilderness areas of the United States. There are about 2,300 major lakes and ponds, many of them to remain forever undeveloped. Many are also connected, either naturally or by canals and waterways dug when guide-boating first became popular a century ago, or by well-tracked portages — all of which makes for an unusual and varied canoe-and-camping experience.

There are a variety of outfitters throughout the Adirondacks that are willing, for a price, to put you out on a chain of lakes. We chose St. Regis Canoe Outfitters, a small company run by two brothers and their wives and situated a few miles northeast of Saranac Lake in a little settlement called Lake Clear. Unlike most Adirondack outfitters, St. Regis handles the complete package, right down to the food.

The cost seemed reasonable: $39 a day per person for a four-day, fully outfitted excursion with lightweight equipment, or $49 for ultra-light, the main distinguishing feature being a 13-pound difference in the canoe.

Not much of a weight variation, but no small consideration when contemplating several portages. Price was a bigger consideration for us, so we opted for the cheaper package.

But that included everything: canoe and paddles and tarp and rope, rain gear, tent and sleeping bag and foam-rubber pads, stove and cookware and eating utensils. The food, some freeze-dried and some (like bacon, eggs, butter and lunch meats) stored in a neat little plastic cooler, was much better fare than we'd have packed for ourselves.

All of this was placed in two large waterproof packs, and we'd brought a third backpack for our own personal needs — mainly clothes and small items. And our fishing rods; we'd obtained three-day licenses the day before.

On the morning of departure, Dave Cilley provided an hour's canoe instruction on a nearby pond, mainly for Tim, who'd had little canoe experience, before Cilley's sister-in-law, Sue, drove us northeast about 15 miles to our put-in on Lake Kushaqua. Cilley had done the packing and provided maps — half done by a cartographer and half his own hand-drawn version — and we had talked about the route, but I was later to learn three discomforting things: (1) He was hardly a professional cartographer; (2) we hadn't discussed the route thoroughly enough, and (3) he — and we — forgot the rain gear.

Although it was the end of August, the day had an autumn feel to it, the air crisp and the sky that deep, clear blue one associates with fall weather in the Northeast. The tone for the day was set when we drove through the little settlement of Onchiota and past a sign that read: "Leaving 67 of the nicest people in the Adirondacks (Plus a couple soreheads)."

After unloading the canoe and gear from the Cilleys' Jeep, we put in at the head of Lake Kushaqua, balancing the three packs in the middle and settling the fishing rods beside them.

The wind was up, tossing some mild whitecaps, which gently slapped the sides of the green Mad River canoe as we paddled to the center of the lake.

Tim turned back to me. "What do you think?," he asked.

"Great," I answered. "You?"

"Outstanding."

And it was. If there was a civilization out there somewhere, we saw none of it on Kushaqua. Within 15 minutes, though, we saw a great blue heron winging overhead, and paused to watch a kingfisher dive for some unsuspecting fish that had lingered a moment too long near the surface.

We fished, with less success than the kingfisher, as we lazed our way across Kushaqua, under a culvert, and through some narrows into Rainbow Lake. In late afternoon, we passed through a gap in Rainbow and into Clear Pond, still heading in a general southwesterly direction toward our campsite. From out of nowhere, it seemed, a speedboat pounded into Clear Pond from Rainbow, then roared south, throttling down and disappearing in the foliage through some unseen channel. So much for wilderness.

Actually, the remaining daylight passed much as the day had — in total isolation. We paddled the canoe up a backwater called the Flow, and spent a lazy, pleasant time casting unsuccessfully for bass as the sun inched its way toward the horizon.

Dinner was at dusk: boiled and buttered potatoes, freeze-dried peas and two small but excellent steaks done over the campfire and its coals on a folding wire grill. While I washed the dishes in the woods with warm water and nondetergent soap, Tim landed two smallmouth bass. Good for breakfast, we decided.

Then came the infamous Night of the Beaver, and dawn found Tim snoring away. I got the little Coleman stove going and heated water for coffee. Casting from the bank with worms, I landed two more smallmouth bass. All were a little too small to get much from fileting, so I gutted the four and pan-fried them in butter for breakfast. They were a pain to eat — bony and not very meaty — but tasty nonetheless.

The going got tougher this day. Rainbow Lake narrowed down to a developed shoreline of summer homes; there was even one with a float plane docked out front. Marsh grass and other vegetation choked the way in spots, and finally the lake just ended. Portage time.

First, we had lunch — cheese-and-lunch-meat sandwiches and cookies for dessert. We'd brought along our own water — 2½ gallons in one container and another half-gallon in a canteen — and fixed that up with some powdered fruit punch the outfitter had provided. When the water ran out, we had purification tablets; the water may be clean for the fish, but it's hardly potable.

We took it slow on the portaging, carrying the canoe on opposite sides with two of the backpacks inside. When we reached Jones Pond, Tim went back for the third pack. I was happy that he'd volunteered earlier; he wasn't. It all took close to two hours.

In the interim, Sue Cilley had driven by on the country road beside the pond, returning to the base camp at Lake Clear after running another canoe party up to Kushaqua. Dave forgot the rain gear, we said, but it's OK; the weather looks clear. No, she said, it's going to rain tomorrow. She promised to meet us that night with the gear at a lean-to on Osgood Pond where Cilley had suggested we camp the second night.

But now things began to unravel. The long channel between Jones and Osgood Ponds was immediately blocked by a beaver dam, a totally unexpected and rather obtrusive impediment. The pesky devils had it in for us and were passing the word along, we figured. I skirted the adjacent marshes on foot and reconnoitered, determining that the channel was traversable. But the brush and marsh grass were practically impenetrable to portage.

We decided to go over the beaver dam, and so we both got out on the springy dam breast of branches and pulled the canoe forward past the center balance point.

Then Tim got in the rear and I pushed it into the channel below. He backed up to take me aboard. We would repeat the process twice more, which proved to be exhausting, before emerging into Osgood Pond in late afternoon, with rain threatening.

Now, because I could not read the hand-drawn map, we were uncertain about where our campsite was. We found several lean-tos; they were already occupied. The only others, campers told us, were back out on Osgood Pond. So we reloaded the canoe and set out for 10 minutes' more paddling that took us to a vacant lean-to on the pond, one of several not located on the map. We doubted Sue Cilley would find us in this lean-to, but it seemed much preferable to sleeping under the canoe.

Dinner was freeze-dried beef in a sherry sauce, with noodles, and freeze-dried green beans. The beef wasn't bad at all; the beans were like the peas the night before: a little tough to handle.

When darkness had arrived on the Night of the Beaver, it had brought stillness, save for the quavering hoot of an owl and an occasional fish breaking water nearby. But on this night, somebody in a lean-to farther down the shoreline had a radio, and hard rock echoed across the pond.

"What an idiot," said Tim, a sometime fan of these cacophonous creations.

Then it started to rain. And it rained all night and it was still raining and gray when I again fired up the little Coleman for coffee the next morning. We decided to linger and see what turn the weather would take.

If it cleared, we'd push on for the final day; if it remained cloudy and cold, I'd hike to a phone and call the outfitter to pick us up.

Intermittent rain was the order of the day, so we joked around and chatted in the lean-to and enjoyed each other's company while we watched the raindrops spatter an infinity of tiny ringlets on the lake surface. When it wasn't raining, we did a little fishing and strolled the nearby trails. Mushrooms and toadstools had poked up everywhere from the forest floor; I'd never seen such a proliferation of them. There was a lot of fungus among us, we agreed.

In late morning, I hiked out to the campus of Paul Smith's College, found a pickup spot nearby, then called the Cilleys and asked them to come by in late afternoon. They'd tried to find us with the rain gear last night, said Sue Cilley.

Well, the lack of rainwear gave us an easy excuse. Truth to tell, our urbanized bones already yearned for a sit-down meal and a warm bed. As we nosed northward toward the St. Lawrence River in the car later, we passed a sign that said, "At the End of the Road, You'll Find God."

"And hopefully a Holiday Inn," added Tim.

We had to settle for a roadside motel that night and a local restaurant, both little noted nor long remembered, but we were still laughing about the Night of the Beaver. And we probably will be for years to come.

•

Those contemplating canoe trips might contact St. Regis Canoe Outfitters, Box 318, Lake Clear, N.Y. 12945. Phone: 518-891-1838. This is one of the few outfitters in the Adirondacks that does complete outfitting, including all food.

Names of other outfitters and canoe and boat liveries in other areas of the Adirondacks may be obtained from the Adirondack Regional Tourism Office of the New York State Department of Commerce, 90 Main St., Lake Placid, N.Y. 12946. Phone: 518-523-2412.

Tangier Island, Va.

Savoring a spot where there is nothing to do

By Fawn Vrazo
Inquirer Staff Writer

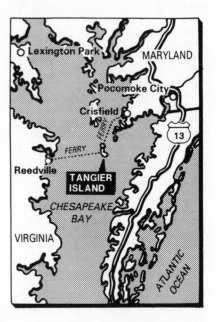

M y ahn-kul's house is on the sow-weed."

The what?

"The SOW-WEED."

Wha?

They talk differently on Tangier Island, a less-than-five-mile-long speck in Chesapeake Bay that in some ways seems as though it has become stuck in a time warp that holds it forever in the 18th century.

The island's unusual dialect, which perhaps half of its 750 or so residents speak, is a throwback to the English spoken by the island's first settler, John Crockett of Cornwall, England, who came here with his family in the late 1600s. Some of the islanders call it Elizabethan English; to mainland ears it may sound Cockney, with a heaping of Gaelic, smoothed out with an overlay of Southern.

Head tilted, you have to listen very hard at times to figure out what a Tangier Island resident is saying to you. "Oh — side !" I said like a suddenly enlightened student when I realized what the dark-haired, friendly tyke beside me meant by the word sow-weed. His uncle's house was on the side of the house where we had taken a room for the night.

Tangier Island is a strangely wonderful place.

Charming, odd and completely unexpected, it's a sweet diversion in a country generally as homogenized as milk. You'll find it by looking at the fattest part of the Chesapeake Bay, just under the Virginia state line, where it floats, like a small pork chop, out of reach save by water or air. For years, my husband and I have stared at its shape on our map and wondered about it, only to be held off by reports that once you arrive on Tangier, there is nothing, nothing at all to do.

And so we weren't prepared for the unusualness of this island, where the men rise at 3:30 a.m. to go crabbing and oystering just as they have for hundreds of years; where the dead residents — their above-ground crypts are often located in families' front yards — seem to outnumber the living; where roaming cats outnumber everything else.

On Tangier, all roads, including the main one, are no wider than a sidewalk. The island is essentially carless, yet the population is highly mobile — grandmothers, fathers, mothers, babies, teens are constantly whizzing up behind you on motorbikes, motorcycles, scooters, bicycles and golf carts. One traffic sign was a bent piece of plywood reading "15 m.p.h."

On Tangier, you can walk through the marsh to a pleasant yellow bayside beach and stare at the spot, now under water, where thousands of British soldiers camped in 1814 before embarking on their doomed attack on Fort McHenry near Baltimore — the attack that inspired Francis Scott Key to write the words of "The Star-Spangled Banner." (On your way back, the young turks of the island may roar past on motorcycles with boom-box radios held to their heads and girlfriends riding on back seats.)

On Tangier, you get the feeling the residents like you, really like you. And it's not just because tourists provide needed jobs for the mostly homebound island wives, but also because Tangierians just seem to enjoy people.

Walk past a strange man on one of the little roads, and he will invariably say, "Hey!"

Land is precious here. Houses are clustered on the island's "ridges," which rise a mere five feet or less above sea level. The bay takes nibbles off the island's edges each year — it's only a mile and a half wide — and islanders are beseeching government officials for a seawall. Large storms have occasionally flooded the entire island.

With hardly enough land left to bury the dead, it's not surprising that there is not much space for live guests. Two private homes and one guest house (the Hilda Crockett Chesapeake House) offer a total of just 15 rentable rooms for the summertime tourists who chug in daily to Tangier on mail boat, cruise boat and small plane.

We came on the 90-foot cruise ship Steven Thomas, which makes the 14-mile trip from Crisfield, Md., each day at 12:30 p.m. It's impossible to get lost on the way to the boat; just follow Maryland Route 413 toward the bay until you are about to land in the water. The cruise-ship office will be at your left, and you leave your car at a parking lot there. A mail boat also departs daily for Tangier at 12:30 p.m. from the Crisfield city dock. The cost is $14 round trip on either vessel. Children pay $7; those under 6 are free.

As we docked after an hour-and-15-minute cruise, our first sights on Tangier were some large Exxon tanks, a turquoise water tank and a tall church spire. On the shore, a passel of Methodist youth choir members in souvenir sea captain's caps was sitting at picnic tables waiting for the cruise back. This is a churchgoing island, and dry.

We lugged our bags down a grassy walkway and up to what seemed to be a sidewalk — actually Tangier's main drag. We stood there forlornly for a while, and then a large golf cart pulled up. We said that we needed a ride and the driver invited us on. The island's golf-cart rides are $1.50 a person, and apparently the way to arrange one is simply by flagging one down.

The usual tourist here doesn't get even this far. Most pile off the cruise ship and rest for a while at the picnic tables of the very reasonably priced Waterfront Restaurant (actually a small takeout place featuring such seafood as soft-shell crabs). The visitors take short walks down the island's small streets, stop at the handful of gift shops, then sit down to dinner at Hilda Crockett's before catching the 4 p.m. cruise ship back.

We thought it would be a shame to spend just a few hours here. And so we golf-carted to a private residence with room to rent, stretched out in a room cooled by bay breeze and window fan, and then faced the imponderable Tangier Island tourist question: What do we do now?

Tourist Alert: Tangier Island will seem like a very dull place if you like action and bright lights. But if you are looking for a place to slow down without isolating yourself from humanity, it will seem just about right. In our own 24 hours on Tangier, we found more than enough to do.

We took a long walk down little roads and over humped wooden bridges to the Hilda Crockett Chesapeake House, where dinner is served daily from 11 a.m. to 5 p.m. We were seated at a long table with three high-spirited couples who fly small planes all over the country. They had landed on Tangier that afternoon just to have dinner and check out the place. Our table's blue vinyl cover was heaped with enough food to get the islanders through the winter: large plates of crab cakes, ham, glazed bread, clam fritters, corn pudding, coleslaw, applesauce, potato salad, peas and pound cake.

The next morning, my son and I stopped by the house of Frank Dize, a longtime resident and Tangierian historian. Islanders take their history extremely seriously; we found several pamphlets about Tangier's beginnings for sale at every gift shop.

Dize told us about his stay on Tangier during the island's terrible storm of 1933, known since as the August Storm. The wind blew 107 m.p.h., he said. "I was as tall then as I am now," he said, "and water was up to my chest."

After lunch at the popular Fisherman's Corner restaurant, where they'll serve you a crunchy softshell crab on white bread for $3, we rented sturdy old bikes, then bumped along the narrow roads past the island's numerous cemeteries. We bicyled as far as we could on a path leading to the beach, then took a footpath through the marsh to the bay's edge.

If you walk far enough along a gritty little beach covered with dried seaweed, you will reach a wide yellow beach that drops sharply into the warm — and sometimes jellyfish-infested — waters of the bay. A local man showed us an arrowhead he had plucked from the sand. I found weathered pieces of pottery. I want to believe that they were remnants of the large British encampment and an Indian settlement long before that.

Many days after we left Tangier, I called the island's mayor, Bobby Crockett. I wanted him to help me understand Tangier's most appealing quality — its ability to keep up with modern times and yet stay unchanged in many ways.

I told him that the island's residents seem to have something that most of us would like to find: the peace that comes with knowing your place in life, without forever wishing you were someplace else.

The mayor said this was true for some of the islanders, but not all. He could recall when there were 1,100, maybe 1,200, residents on the island; because of young people leaving for the mainland, that number has dipped to about 750.

But there is hope here, too. One of the mayor's sons is having a house built on the island, a costly proposition because he must bring in the materials by boat. The house is on Tangier's west side, where the island is most threatened by the waters of the bay. "When you write your story," the mayor said, "you want to say how desperately we need a seawall. We don't have a big future if we don't have something or other."

"It's unique — our way of life is unique," said Crockett, a descendant of John Crockett, who settled here in 1686 or thereabouts. "But it's just a matter of time before we lose it."

West Glover, Vt.

Heading for Canada by bike without a care or much of a plan

By Rick Nichols
Inquirer Staff Writer

Suffice it to say, we're not heavy planners. My wife and I strap the bike rack on the car, select a quadrant — in this case, the summer-green quilt of dairy farms, steepled hamlets and lake country that is northeastern Vermont — and wing it somewhat on the route.

It's a "method" that has provided a few disappointments but far more surprises and unexpected joys.

There is, of course, the more organized way to go: In Vermont, especially, bike-touring outfits have it down to a pleasant science, setting up no-fuss reservations at rustic country inns and offering luggage-toting services that take the strain out of all but the most strenuous of expeditions.

But biking, the cheapest way to cover a lot of territory and still feel as if you really savored it, needn't be left to professionals. Our latest venture strengthened my feeling that bike-touring was well within the capabilities of complete amateurs and that even killer hills could be conquered by the simple, humble act of walking.

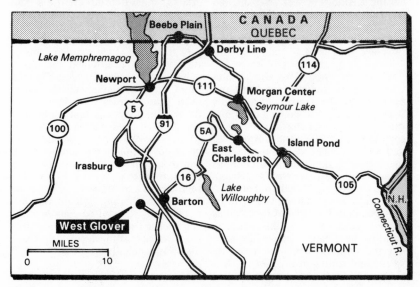

Base camp for this summer excursion was a cool, breeze-riffled cottage on the shore of Parker Lake, a dot on the map beside the village of West Glover just up the road from Barton, Vt. Over a pre-July 4 picnic, our friends Chris and Ellen Braithwaite helped us chart a two-day trip.

Later we picked up a fine, detailed road map from the Greater Newport (Vt.) Area Chamber of Commerce. Newport, by the way, also has a fully stocked bicycle shop.

Before leaving Vermont, we spent a lazy fireside afternoon with a dairy farmer and his artist wife, who tap sugar maples and make sweet pecan brittle from the syrup. We chowed down on corncob-smoked ham and delighted in an uproarious stay with Dan and Gayle Phillabaum, the unreserved proprietors of the Seymour Lake Lodge in Morgan.

My teenage son, Coan, was along for this journey, and for some reason we felt compelled to add an objective to the trip. The Canadian border, about 35 miles away, fit the bill, though we were assured that Derby Line, the destination, was not particularly scenic, except for an opera house that straddled the U.S.-Canadian line, providing the site for intrigue, international trials and meetings of rock stars banned from one country or the other.

It was Dominion Day, Canada's national holiday, when we got there, and the place was closed.

•

Setting out from West Glover provides one of the most encouraging cycling-trip beginnings on God's Earth. We crunched down a hard dirt road, passed gentle morning meadows sprinkled with black-and-white cows, and at the crossroad began a sweeping, streaking descent for three miles or so, rolling all the way to Barton. That's where Coan's chain fell off.

Seconds later, Ellen Braithwaite, our friend, pulled up and inquired as to our readiness for the venture, handing us a can of spray lubricant out the window. Soon we were repaired and rolling again, past the C & C Grocery (home of corncob-smoked bacon and ham, not to mention wonderful Cabot Cheddar), up Route 16, through farmlands to Lake Willoughby, a sparkling, narrow, glacier-carved lake cupped by low mountains.

Down a driveway bounced a car with a carpenter spread-eagled on top, hanging on to a load of lumber (and for dear life). "Take it easy," he was hollering at the driver, joining our laughter, as we cut northwesterly and stopped at a hilltop snack stand that was just opening for the afternoon.

A few miles up Route 5A, we hailed a tractor emerging from a dirt road and got directions for a short cut through the country to East Charleston. The short cut was on hard dirt and gravel roads that, at least at this time of year, were in fine condition for biking and provided a great way to tour, with virtually no traffic. The entire area is laced with such roads, some of them on maps, some of them known only to local tractor drivers.

East Charleston, like many Vermont villages, is a post office, a general store, a church and a used-furniture/antiques shop. Bikes, of course, aren't the best vehicles for toting home country furniture. But we spent a half-hour rummaging through two floors packed with stripped pine chairs, glass-doored cabinets and crockery, and compiled a list of finds that one day may end up in a rental van for a journey to Philadelphia.

At Island Pond we wandered into a time warp: a health-food restaurant run by a Northeast Kingdom Community Church commune (the women in faded granny dresses and long scarfs, the men in ponytails) that a few years ago figured into national news accounts of overly strict disciplining of children. The place was dim and a bit weird for our tastes, so we ended up down the street, eating hot turkey sandwiches and browsing at the Buck & Doe Restaurant, which was announced by the stuffed countenances of a buck and doe. The place was across from a once-bustling depot of the Canadian National Railway.

•

The only sure thing when we set out

was a reservation at the Seymour Lake Lodge (802-895-2752). "If you're looking for excitement every minute," the brochure had said, "this is NOT the place for you. If you want a relaxing vacation spot, a sandy beach with super swimming, a lovely lawn, quiet Vermont countryside and a chance to sit on a porch-swing and enjoy the every-changing view of lakes and mountains, this IS the spot for you."

Sounds sedate, right? Well . . .

"The owners are out for a few minutes," boomed a fisherman, whom we came to know as J. Barton, reposing on the porch swing. He herded us into the kitchen, which was undergoing reconstruction, thrust an ice-cold Old Milwaukee Light into our hands and gave us a rundown on the family, the fish, the purity of the lake water (you can drink it) and the evening's schedule, which involved a Little League game for young Tod Phillabaum, son of owners Dan and Gayle.

It was a warm and comforting welcome, particularly after having passed through the foreboding gateway to Morgan Center, where the village name is burned into a sign hanging from fence-style ranch gates leading straight into the cemetery.

Seymour Lake, it turned out, was anything but dead. Bass and salmon abound, and at the grocery opposite the lodge, boats and wind-surfers are available for rent. In the winter, ice fishermen and cross-country skiers find it a more off-the-beaten-track spot than the more popular and often oversubscribed New England resort areas.

The lodge, eight miles from Canada, is a homey, dark-green wooden affair, stripped across the front with a creaking porch and cluttered inside with long dining tables, a piano and a dusty, mounted moose head. It claims the distinction of having the first indoor plumbing in Morgan, Vt.

Soon the Phillabaums burst in: Gayle chucking a frozen Dreamcicle across the porch to my son; Dan and J. Barton regaling him with a box of risque fishing lures (and inviting him to join them on a dawn expedition on the lake), and Tod, finding an extra baseball glove for a game of catch.

Supper, usually a home-cooked, family-style occasion, would be pizza that night served with a six-pack ("Your genuine Vermont country inn experience," Dan announced. "Pizza and beer at eight!"). Soon we were sharing jokes (inn jokes?), watching the night fall on the lovely rolling lawn and climbing the stairs, exhausted, to a rustic room papered with pine sprigs: the Pine Room. Capacity is 15. Baths are at the end of the hall.

For breakfast, Dan fried eggs and bacon and insisted on a second course of buckwheat cakes with maple syrup served in a corner of the torn-up kitchen. As we finished, the carpenters invaded, stuffed boards through the window and hammered on the counter, all the while being harassed and cajoled by Barton and the Phillabaums, who simultaneously were plotting the leg of our trip between Seymour Lake and the Canadian border.

The cycling to Derby Line was once again through hilly, uninterrupted farmland, much of it on dirt roads until the checkpoints at Canada with its sudden switch to French signs. We biked along the border to Beebe Plain, munched fruit from a stand that sold "fruits et legumes" and coasted back into the United States a few miles later on a roll, up and down a few steep hills, toward Newport, where we ate at an old-fashioned, polished-wood diner, and on to Lake Memphremagog.

About 35 miles later, after ice cream on the village green in Irasburg and a stop at one of the largest rummage barns in the East (everything from hard hats to theater seats), we were back in West Glover, wading out into Parker Lake to wash the road off.

All told, we had covered 80 miles at most. But in two bright Vermont days, our bike-it-alone confidence was renewed and our faces were sun-tanned. As for facing the meanness of July in the city, we crossed that bridge when we came to it.

•

At Seymour Lake Lodge, the dinner, bed and breakfast package is $34 for one and $62 for two.

West Orange, N.J.

The lab where Edison's ideas were transformed into reality

By Janet Ruth Falon
Special to The Inquirer

Part of what used to be Thomas Alva Edison's 40-acre laboratory complex is now an A&P supermarket. Only five of the original buildings — in which creativity begat invention and invention sometimes became reality — still stand.

But 100 years after Edison created his "invention factory," an inspiring spirit of enterprise still hovers over the well-preserved brick remnants of the laboratory complex, now run as an eight-acre museum by the National Park Service. And a visit can still charge up the creative juices of would-be inventors and fill with awe any student of the process of invention.

Edison, a 40-year-old success, came to West Orange in 1887 after having operated for 10 years what amounted to a research and development center in then-rural Menlo Park, farther south in New Jersey. It was at Menlo Park that he invented the phonograph and the first practical incandescent light bulb.

Before Menlo Park, Edison did his thinking and creating in Newark, where he made his early fortune by inventing an improved stock ticker and selling a patent for it, at age 21, for $40,000.

Although Edison was a millionaire by the time he was 36, it was in West Orange that his empire really mushroomed. From the library, Edison ran 30 companies and employed as many as 5,000 factory workers. It was a multidimensional plant — with its own fire department, glass blowers and other skilled-trade operations — in which the creation of new ideas coexisted with the manufacture of already-devised inventions and supporting parts.

Edison's library, a magnificent multilevel oak "think tank" that opens into a central atrium, is the most beautiful of the spaces in the complex. It was here, on his bed in a small alcove, that Edison took some of his fabled catnaps. Periodic naps were all that the inventor needed to fuel his creativity. Before his wife sent over a cot from their home, Edison would nap on the floor, at a table or at his desk.

But, more important, it was from the library, amid the 10,000 books and signed photographs of American presidents, that he ran his quintessentially American empire.

The library features some delightful oddities, such as Edison's 1929 honorary Academy Award, the first such award to be presented; a statue called Triumph of Light that holds an early Edison light bulb, perfected when the inventor used bamboo as the filament; an enormous movie screen, and a copy of Edison's favorite motto — "There is no expedient to which a man will not resort to avoid the real labor of thinking" — attributed to Sir Joshua Reynolds.

A 20-minute videotape, *The Invention Factory*, provides visitors with a useful overview of the Edison plant. The forthright tone of the tape is perhaps epitomized by an Edison quote, "I never quit till I get what I'm after."

Thanks to the tape, by the time your guide takes you to the tool crib, or stockroom, you'll already have a sense of what was produced by the tools contained within — the drills, planes, lathes, gears and grinders that are testament to the nitty-gritty underbelly of the creative process.

The tool crib fed the adjacent machine shop, which contains many 100-year-old machines, most of which still work. Two 40-horsepower motors run all the machines and the freight elevator by way of leather belts and drive shafts.

The plant's massive time clock is also located here. Edison had card No. 1 and punched in and out every day. His original time cards are now in storage, and they show a range of 80 to 115 hours of work a week.

It's all very impressive when you think that some very important creations passed through these rooms: the dynamo, an electricity generator; the cement that Edison used in his concrete structures, including the Traymore Hotel in Atlantic City (a cement house could be poured in six hours); the nickel-iron-alkaline storage battery; talking dolls, and the carbonized cotton-thread filament that burned for more than 40 hours in Edison's light bulb.

The chemistry lab, which at one time employed 12 chemists, looks as if the workers have simply gone home for the night. (Edison's own lab coat hangs in a corner.) It was here that scientists created the chemicals that made the Edison-invented battery work, as well as the waxes and other materials used to create phonograph records. Seeing how many of Edison's ideas were converted into reality by his employees — some of whom worked for him for many decades — makes one realize how much the credit for invention should be shared.

In addition, you learn that Edison's ideas were often the result of solving a technological problem presented to him by some other entrepreneur. Many of his inventions were clever, business-savvy solutions to specific problems. Edison had 1,100 patented inventions during his career.

One room in the plant shows the development of the phonograph, including Edison's initial-idea sketch, early tinfoil records, a spring-driven cylinder phonograph and a 1909 Amberola, marketed in competition with the Victrola. Although Edison first envisioned the phonograph as a business tool that would dramatically improve dictation, he eventually realized that it would be most successful as an entertainment device. To capture his share of the market, the Edison diamond-disc phonographs played 80 r.p.m. records, which, of course, were only produced by his company. You can even hear a recording of Edison's voice, speaking the first words ever heard on a phonograph: The "Mary Had a Little Lamb" nursery rhyme.

Also on display is a 1928 Edison phonograph/radio, which, at a time when a Model T Ford cost $700, sold for a hefty $1,100. The radio still works, and it's somewhat disconcerting to hear it playing Janet Jackson or the Beastie Boys.

Visitors get to rest their weary feet in the movie-viewing area of the West Orange plant. You'll get to watch several short silent moves originally shown on Edison's Strip Kinetoscope — great stuff if you're tickled by sight gags — as well as the 1903 classic *The Great Train Robbery*. Filmed in West Orange, it was the first western ever made and, with a running time of 11 minutes, was then the longest movie ever filmed. There is also a newsreel-type film about Edison's life and work.

Just outside is a replica of the

Black Maria, the world's first motion-picture studio. It is about the size of a house. The original, a tar-paper contraption, was built in 1893, and was called Black Maria because of its resemblance to the police paddy wagons of the day that bore the same slang nickname. Not only could the entire structure pivot on its axis to keep sunlight on the stage, but the hinged roof of the Black Maria could open to let in light, a necessity for working with the slow-speed cameras and film of that era.

The original Black Maria was torn down in 1903 and replaced by a large studio in New York. Edison left the movie industry in 1917 because a fire at the lab had destroyed much of his motion-picture equipment.

The reopening of Glenmont, Edison's 23-room Queen Anne-style home, located one-half mile away from the West Orange laboratory, is scheduled for 1988. Although the grounds of Glenmont were open to visitors during a two-year renovation, the home was closed so the sagging roof could be stabilized.

Glenmont is in Llewellyn Park, a private residential community of more than 400 acres within the town of West Orange. When Llewellyn Park was built in the late 1850s, it was the first planned suburban residential community in the nation. It catered to wealthy merchants, businessmen and bankers working in Newark and New York City. It's still a private community, and visitors to Glenmont are required to check in with a guard at the gate.

Edison purchased the 13-acre estate in 1886, six years after Glenmont was designed and landscaped for a New York executive whose property was seized when he was discovered to be embezzling from his company. Edison added his own touches to the estate, such as the poured-cement garage, erected in 1907, complete with gas pump, battery charger and turntable for parking.

The home includes a dining room which, at holidays, could accommodate 30 people; the den, converted from a ballroom to a more informal space for the family; a conservatory, and Edison's library, or "thought bench," in which he came up with the ideas that he would try to bring to reality at his "workbench" — the laboratory in the valley below.

The inventor moved into brick-and-wood Glenmont with his second wife, Mina, and his three children from his first marriage, and lived here from 1886 until his death at age 84 in 1931. The couple's own three children were all born at Glenmont.

The graves of Edison and Mina — both of whom were originally buried in Rosedale Cemetary in nearby Montclair — are now located in the rear yard of Glenmont.

•

Although the Visitors Center is open every day, guided tours of Edison's West Orange laboratory are only offered Wednesdays through Sundays on the half-hour, starting at 9:30 a.m., with the last tour beginning at 3:30 p.m.

For information about the laboratory or Glenmont, write to the Edison National Historic Site, Main Street and Lakeside Avenue, West Orange, N.J. 07052, or call 201-736-0550.

The other place to visit while you're on Edison's New Jersey turf is the Edison Tower in Menlo Park, a 131-foot concrete tower on the site of the inventor's workshop between 1876 and 1886. (The workshop buildings are now in the Henry Ford Museum-Greenfield Village in Dearborn, Mich. Edison's Menlo Park home has been destroyed.) An adjacent museum houses a few of Edison's inventions.

The Edison Tower is open, between Memorial Day and Labor Day, Tuesdays through Fridays from 12:30 to 4 p.m. and Saturdays and Sundays from 12:30 to 4:30 p.m. The tower is closed on Mondays. During the winter, the Tower is also closed on Tuesdays. For more information, write to the Edison Memorial Tower, Christie Street, Menlo Park, Edison, N.J. 08820, or call 201-549-3299.

Williamstown, Mass.

A college town where the focus is on the arts

By Michael Kimmelman
Special to The Inquirer

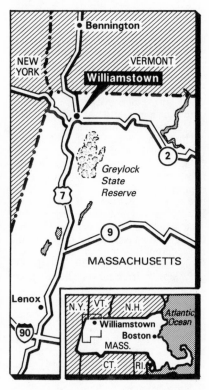

"I'll check again; it can't be right," I said, getting up from the table to find the maitre d'. We had been supplied with a rather wonderful menu and told that, as part of our weekend package here at the Orchards Hotel, we could choose anything we'd like for dinner.

"Anything — and as much as you wish," I was told again, and so we gleefully set out to chart a gluttonous culinary course.

The feeling, all in all, about our stay at the Orchards was of a weekend spent in cheerful satisfaction. This new hotel, set along the town's main street, is, nonetheless, a little outside the center of things and admittedly not in the prettiest of spots. But it is a pleasantly quiet, civilized retreat.

The place feels more like a spacious inn than a full-fledged hotel. It offers the sort of amenities found in larger establishments, including a fine restaurant; large, gracefully appointed accommodations; cable TV; a sauna, and a pool. But it's relatively small (49 rooms, some with working fireplaces), and it has adopted the air of a New England inn, offering afternoon tea, Sunday afternoon concerts and generally discreet, friendly service.

We went there on a two-night-three-day excursion: For roughly $350, we were offered not only our elaborate dinner but also two breakfasts, which were no less impressive. It was costly but seemed worth the price.

We traveled there during August, having spent a few days at nearby Saratoga Springs, N.Y., roughly an hour and a half to the west. Williamstown is surrounded by interesting places, among them Bennington, Vt., to the north and Lenox, Mass., and envi-

93

rons to the south, home during the summer to the Tanglewood Music Festival, the Berkshire Playhouse and Jacob's Pillow Dance Festival.

Williamstown is one of those places that looks good year-round. While we were there, the winding, tree-lined streets and apple orchards were wonderful places to take walks. During the fall, the town becomes packed with leaf-watchers; during the winter, it's a cozy, snowy getaway, not far from various ski slopes, and during the spring, it's full of flowers.

Williamstown's worth the trip, wherever one stays. Even getting to the quintessentially New England town, tucked in the northwest corner of Massachusetts, can be a pleasure. Surrounded by several mountains, it is filled with clapboard houses, elegant churches and grand old college buildings all resting gently in a valley.

The town was settled in 1765 near a line of forts protecting the colonies from the French to the north. It took its name from Ephraim Williams Jr., a commander of the region who died in battle and in whose will money was left for the town to start a free school. That school, by 1793, became Williams College, and pretty quickly the farming community took on an increasingly academic tone. The population grew slowly, from 1,000 in 1800 to 5,000 a century later.

The town fell in population after a railroad line through the area ceased operations in 1950, but now it's home to 8,700 residents, some of them still farmers, many of them teaching or attending college or one of the nearby prep schools.

Aside from its college, the place is probably now known best for its art museum and its summer theater festival, each of which is worth a special trip. We spent a good part of one day wandering through the Sterling & Francine Clark Art Institute, one of the country's best small museums, with a broad collection and fine group of French Beaux-Arts, impressionist and post-impressionist paintings. There are an extensive art library in the museum and changing special exhibitions. The institute is open year-round, Tuesday through Sunday 10 a.m. to 5 p.m.; there is no admission charge.

The rest of our days were spent peacefully wandering through town, up Spring and Water Streets, through small shops and good bookstores and into a few coffee shops. There's still a '60s feel to the town, and a couple of the places to eat display works of local artists on their walls. A trip to a food store along Spring Street supplied us with cheese, fruit, meat and bread, and off we went to picnic on the Williams campus, where we found a small hill overlooking a duck-filled pond. A short drive out of town took us through lovely farm country and to several picture-postcard views of Williamstown and the surrounding hills.

The town itself is also filled with historical spots to see, such as the 1753 House along Hemlock Brook and the 1765 Red Saltbox House on Main Street. And Williams College, one of the nation's prettiest campuses, is well worth a look around.

After our elaborate meal during our first night at the Orchards, we were in no condition to venture out, but the next evening we got seats for a performance of Sheridan's *The School for Scandal* at the Williamstown Theater Festival, justifiably one of the pre-eminent summer playhouses. There are always a good number of big-name actors who take the stage there (during a recent season, for example, Christopher Reeve, Mary Tyler Moore, Richard Thomas and Stephanie Zimbalist), and the productions, our evening's included, have always been of reliably high quality. Local theater groups play year-round, and the college offers regular performing-arts events and films.

After breakfast the final morning, we headed off toward Boston, along Route 2, the old Mohawk Trail. Even if you're not planning to go in that direction, the trip, through beautiful rocky terrain, up a mountain or two and along a winding river, is worth a drive anyway, as part of a day trip.

It, like Williamstown itself, is New England at its most graceful and ingratiating.

94

FALL

Fallingwater is no ordinary house. Designed
by Frank Lloyd Wright in the 1930s, it is built
over a waterfall in Mill Run, Pa.

Boston, Mass.

Revolution with a mixture of history and urban freshness

By Janet Ruth Falon
Special to The Inquirer

I'll tell you why I love this town, and why I always have: Year-round, even in the dead of a New England winter, everyone eats ice cream. An enormous Bailey's hot fudge sundae, a sophisticated gelati from Quincy Market, a plebeian Brigham's cone, a dip from the original Steve's.

My kind of town.

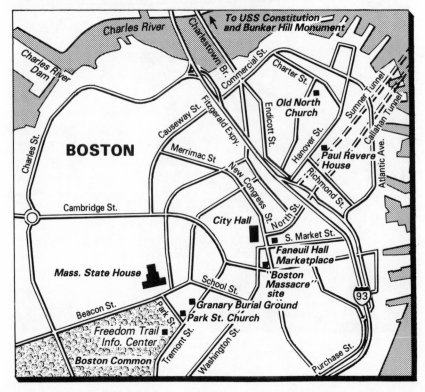

Its residents also speak with that crazy accent, at times not realizing how odd it is to pretend the letter "r" doesn't exist, and, at other times, suddenly feeling the need to append it to the most "r"-less of words.

I also love the city's public transportation system, the color-coded MBTA, with those ever-present student musicians underground, churning out Vivaldi, and that sensational view of the Boston skyline you get crossing the Charles River on the Red Line. The system may get awfully crowded, and it's not as antiseptically efficient as Washington's subways, but in the long run, it's reliable, and it's easy ... sort of like Boston itself.

The city is an absolutely great place to spend a weekend, and here is a subjective but nonetheless utilitarian guide to the best of it. Boston today is in great shape, much better than when I left it almost a decade ago. It's safer, less divided over school-busing controversies and, best of all, the downtown area is thriving and growing like mad. There's a real feeling of optimism in the air.

The best example of the downtown's comeback, perhaps, is the rejuvenation of the financial district, which has developed as Boston has become the mutual-funds capital of the world. High-tech companies are also coming downtown, while the "Silicon Valley" of suburban Route 128 is reaching the bursting point. The addition of French and Japanese banks to the scene, making this an international city more than ever, has also contributed to the financial district's health.

There are immense new skyscrapers, such as Exchange Place and One Post Office Square, in the financial district. There are wonderful renovations, such as the transformation of the city's former Federal Reserve Bank building — a Renaissance-revival structure modeled after a palace in Rome — into the classy Hotel Meridien. The area bustles, even at night. And although Boston is very

much a college town, you don't feel that youthful, academic presence downtown; cosmopolitan is more like it.

This is a city to walk in, but not to drive in. (Parking is a headache.) It's a place where lobster pots co-exist with neon, where glass has been integrated with brick, where the city's waterfront has been restored for the '80s. (Many executives take a commuter boat from the suburbs, and there is a new water shuttle connecting the airport to downtown that runs every 15 minutes from 6 a.m. to 8 p.m.)

Now, a look at the city's top attractions.

Freedom Trail.
This walking tour of Boston's most significant historical spots takes about two to three hours and continues to be the most popular attraction in town.

Sixteen sites, spanning 2½ centuries of important American events, are connected by a red brick or painted stripe that runs through town. Beware, though. Although you need to follow your feet for this self-guided tour, you should look up a lot to keep yourself aware of any shenanigans by Boston's notoriously impetuous drivers.

It's not just the Freedom Trail's historic sites that are appealing, but the trail itself, which takes you through the modern city into which the sites have been integrated. An example of this then-and-now interweaving is the ring of cobblestones marking the site of the 1770 Boston Massacre, where nine British soldiers shot into an unruly mob and killed five colonists. This marker is set in the pavement at Washington and State Streets, a very busy downtown intersection. The Boston Massacre site, therefore, is not the best place to have your children stand to say "cheese" as you snap their photographs.

You'll also pass through some of Boston's famous neighborhoods when you do the Freedom Trail: the Italian North End, Irish Charlestown and the old-money Boston Brahmin neighborhood of Beacon Hill.

Other highlights of the Freedom Trail include the Paul Revere House, built in 1676, which is the oldest surviving structure in Boston. While he lived here, the silversmith took part in the Boston Tea Party and departed on his famous ride to warn the residents of Lexington and Concord of the approach of the Redcoats. Revere moved from here after his brood — 12 children from two marriages — outgrew these quarters.

You'll also pass the Old North Church (officially, Christ Church) on your walking tour. A sexton hung two lanterns from its steeple as a warning that the British were crossing Boston Harbor on their way to Concord.

The Freedom Trail includes the site of the first public school in America (attended by Benjamin Franklin, Cotton Mather and Samuel Adams); the Old Corner Bookstore, where Emerson, Longfellow, Hawthorne and Thoreau used to hang out and chat; the USS Constitution ("Old Ironsides"), the undefeated battleship of the War of 1812, and the Bunker Hill monument (resembling a smaller version of the Washington Monument obelisk), which commemorates a Revolutionary War battle that was fought on adjacent Breed's Hill. The tour starts on Boston Common on Tremont Street. The tour is self-guided, with a map available for $1. Some of the sites are free and others cost 50 to 75 cents.

Quincy Market. The original Rouse Co. shops-and-eats development, a smashing success more than a decade after its opening, has become the second most popular attraction in Boston. This is the place to check out the "natives," day or night, seven days a week. (To initiate closer contact with these Bostonians, the bar at Lily's restaurant, with the piano accompaniment, is the recommended hot spot.)

This is where Boston comes to unwind, to blow frivolous bucks, or to play — and the crowds would make you think it opened last week.

The market is a den of potential culinary sins — and you can sin in any number of ways by combining nationalities and any kind of gustatory predeliction: Ice cream and gelati (of course!), sausage on a stick, huge fries, clams on the half shell, brownies, tacos, barbecue, pizza, Chinese delights, Mediterranean goodies, exotic coffees, giant bagels — the list goes on, sometimes literally ad nauseam. The Market is open 10 a.m. to 9 p.m. Monday through Saturday and noon to 6 p.m. on Sunday.

You can also spend more money quicker than you might imagine at Quincy Market, either at the fancy shops or the trendy boutiques or at the vendors who peddle exotic gadgets such as tools for lefties, or anything purple. And unlike most of these shop-till-you-drop complexes, even window-shopping is fun here.

The North End/Haymarket.

The North End, now Boston's Italian enclave, feels like Europe, what with its 17th-century street patterns, old folks arguing the day's events on the corners and the strong sense of neighborhood. If you're lucky, your visit here might coincide with one of the lavish festivals on Hanover Street.

The Union Oyster House is here; it is considered Boston's oldest restaurant. Be sure to indulge in a cannoli from one of the many area bakeries.

Haymarket in the North End is an open-air farmers' market, operating Friday 5 to 10 p.m. and all day Saturday until 6 p.m. It's terrific for photography and finding that perfect apple for your snack. But don't squeeze the lettuce, or the vendors will scream at you. The best bargains can be obtained at the end of the day.

JFK Library Museum. Boston's native son (who was actually born in nearby Brookline) is revered in this more-than-a-just-a-library memorial, in the Columbia Point section of the city.

The museum opened in 1979. The dramatic structure, designed by I.M. Pei, pays tribute to John F. Kennedy's life and career and, by extension, the nature of the presidency. The career of the late Sen. Robert Kennedy also is traced here.

A biographical film, *John F. Kennedy, 1917-1963*, is a good start to a visit here. There are also excerpts from Kennedy's televised press conferences, the Nixon-Kennedy debates and Rose Kennedy's recollections of her son's early life.

The view of downtown Boston's skyline from the Kennedy Library is stunning. The library is open 9 a.m. to 5 p.m. daily; admission is $2.50 for adults, $1.50 for senior citizens and free for those under 16.

Museum Wharf. Three new or recently relocated museums make for a wonderful and diverse cluster of fun-and-learning experiences. A sign shaped like a milk bottle leads you here, in honor of the enormous milk bottle ('50s roadside kitsch) dairy stand on the wharf.

Children love the Boston Tea Party Ship and Museum, especially because they get to throw overboard a tea chest (which is then hoisted back on board to indulge the next tyke) from the Brig Beaver II, a full-size, permanently moored replica of one of the original Tea Party ships. The museum is open 9 a.m. to 8 p.m. daily; admission is $3.25 for adults, $2.60 for senior citizens, $2.25 for children 5 to 12 and free for those under 5.

The Computer Museum, said to be the only one of its kind in the world, is a terrific place, even for those who've only recently traded Bics and typewriters for an Apple. In an easily understood fashion, the exhibits trace the history of this technological phenomenon, and along the way show major innovations, ranging from an Air Force computer of the 1950s to the first Speak-and-Spell. There are hands-on exhibits, a computer that talks, and a museum shop that sells microchip jewelry, fancy diskette holders, books and other

gifts to please any hacker. From Memorial Day to Labor Day, the museum is open 10 a.m. to 5 p.m. daily, except Friday when it stays open until 9 p.m. (It is closed on Monday the rest of the year). Admission is $4.50 for adults, $3.50 for college students and senior citizens, free for children under 5.

The Boston's Children's Museum almost makes one want to be, or have, or hire a little child for a couple of hours. It has particularly appealing "exhibits" (really, too formal a word) that can be explored internally and externally. The Museum is open 10 a.m. to 5 p.m daily. On Friday, the museum stays open until 9 p.m., and admission is free after 5 p.m. Regular admission is $4.50 for adults, $3.50 for children and senior citizens, and free for children under 2. The museum is closed on Monday during the school year.

Museum of Fine Arts. This is a repository of beauty that's a speedy trolley ride from downtown. It's a pleasant place to visit — especially because of its recent expansion. The museum is closed Mondays. It is open Tuesday to Saturday 10 a.m. to 5 p.m. On Thursday and Friday, the West Wing is open until 10 p.m.; the entire museum stays open until 10 p.m. on Wednesday. Admission is $5 for adults, $4 for senior citizens, free for children under 16. No admission is charged on Saturday mornings.

Gardner Museum. Just a quick walk away is the Isabella Stewart Gardner Museum. The palatial museum was the home of the very rich, very eccentric patron-of-the-arts Isabella Stewart Gardner. The art inside is as diverse as were its owner's interests, and lovingly tended flowers bloom year-round in a courtyard.

The museum is open Tuesday to Friday noon to 5 p.m., and Saturday and Sunday 10 a.m. to 5 p.m. A $3 donation is requested.

Downtown Crossing. Here, on Washington Street, is the original Filene's, with its progressive-discount-basement shopping, as well as other stores.

Lafayette Place, an urban mall attached to Jordan Marsh, the other flagship department store downtown, has the requisite mix of trendy shops and a fast-food "court."

Beacon Hill. Long regarded as the most desirable residential location in Boston, Beacon Hill has cobblestone streets, gas lights, brick and brownstone townhouses, all set on hills that give walkers a workout. This is a haven for lovers of architecture and urban planning.

Louisburg Square, a residential square with a park in the middle, is considered quintessential Beacon Hill. Louisa May Alcott is only one of several notable Bostonians who have lived on the square.

Shopping on Beacon Hill's Charles Street can be a pleasant interlude, especially if you're hunting for antiques.

Back Bay/Copley Square. You'll probably spend a lot of time in this part of town.

It may even be the place to start your tour of Boston. The 60th-story view from the John Hancock Observatory, right at Copley Square, offers a panorama of the city's skyline of angles and odd juxtapositions. There are also several multimedia exhibits here. Without doubt, my favorite sight in the city is of the Romanesque-style Trinity Church reflected in the Hancock Tower: the epitome of new and old, and how they can enhance each other. (Another "anchor" of Copley Square is the Boston Public Library.)

The newest attraction in Copley Square is Copley Place, with an enormous upscale mall (Neiman-Marcus, Charles Jourdan, Bally of Switzerland, Williams-Sonoma), hotels (Westin and Marriott), offices and residences. The mall also has a collection of boutiques selling items from several Boston museums.

There's a Durgin Park restaurant in Copley Place, a toned-down version of the original, still-operating institution near Faneuil Hall, known for its crowds and nasty waitresses . You go there for great Boston dishes — corn bread, fish cakes, baked beans — and a side order of abuse. ("I don't think you should have any dessert," a waitress once told a plump friend of mine).

Back Bay's Newbury Street is lined with elegant shops, European boutiques, art galleries, restaurants and sidewalk cafes. The street is sometimes closed for art festivals.

Also in Back Bay is the Prudential Center, with shops, offices and the Skywalk, an observation deck on its 50th floor, and the Christian Science Center, with its mother church and tours of the Christian Science Monitor newspaper.

Boston Common. The adjacent Boston Common is a 48-acre tract set aside in 1634 as a cow pasture and training field; by law, it is still available for these purposes, although the most common use today for both the Common and Public Garden is as a walkway connecting Back Bay and downtown. Roller-skaters, street musicians, flower vendors and tenacious pigeons are "regulars" here.

At the head of the Boston Common is the golden-domed Massachusetts State House, designed by Charles Bulfinch. Free tours are available during the week.

Et cetera. Also worth taking in are Boston's Museum of Science, of the touch-and-feel school of "museumology"; a ferry ride to George's Island or any of the other Harbor Islands; a Red Sox game at Fenway Park; the Bull and Finch Pub, across from the Public Garden, the bar on which the TV show *Cheers* was based; a Boston Symphony Orchestra concert; and of course, all the options of the fun-and-funky city of Cambridge, just across the river.

For more information, contact the Greater Boston Convention & Visitors Bureau, Prudential Plaza, Box 490, Boston, Mass. 02199, 617-536-4100.

Cornish, N.H.

A 19th-century artists' colony set in a world of natural beauty

By Ann Keefe
Special to The Inquirer

Sequestered in rural Cornish, N.H., on a high bank of the Connecticut River, are the house, studio and gardens that belonged to Augustus Saint-Gaudens, whose monumental works grace parks and public buildings from Maine to California.

More than 100 years ago, the property's inspiring view of Mount Ascutney first captivated the man that many critics regard as this nation's greatest sculptor in the classical tradition. Soon he, his fellow artists and their students had transformed Cornish into a flourishing summer colony numbering more than 60 artists and writers. It is now a National Historic Site.

Here, an *allee* of white birches leads to the working plaster casts for the Shaw Memorial, a bronze relief that stands on the Boston Common opposite the State House, showing a mounted Col. Robert Shaw leading his Civil War regiment of black volunteers.

In a formal garden, shadowed by hedges of white pine and hemlock, is a copy of the haunting Adams Memorial that broods over the Rock Creek Church Cemetery in Washington, D.C. It shows a seated, shrouded woman, sometimes known as *Grief,* which Henry Adams commissioned after his young wife took her own life.

Other statues — some original, others reductions of immense equestrian generals, presidents, goddesses and angels of victory — are found in the Little Studio, a high-beamed, converted horse barn where much of Saint-Gaudens' remarkably prolific work was accomplished.

Saint-Gaudens' idyllic estate is much more than a museum. Maintained for hiking by rangers of the National Park Service are almost three miles of woodland trails that plunge down a ravine where the athlete-artist used to toboggan, traverse old wagon roads where he skied, skirt a beaver pond where he and his friends played ice hockey, pass a grist mill, cross a stone bridge and wend through a grove of sycamores.

Music is another pleasure often included in the 50-cent admission on summer afternoons. On Sundays, before the 2 p.m. concerts, young families in blue jeans picnic on the sweeping lawns where elaborately costumed members of the Cornish colony used to amuse themselves by staging pageants, *tableaux vivants,* masques and Renaissance theatricals.

Before the musicians strike up, there is time for a tour of the house. Built as a tavern in 1805, the austere brick structure was painted white and given an open, Mediterranean flavor by Saint-Gaudens. He added a spiral staircase and a wide porch with Ionic columns to frame the broad view of Mount Ascutney, rising across a river laced with five covered bridges.

He and his wife, the American painting copyist Augusta Homer, whom he had met in Rome, managed to make the rooms both homey and distinguished. Three of them are furnished as they were 90 years ago, with antiques and art objects acquired during the couple's years abroad.

The bearded, lean-faced sculptor named his new home Aspet after the Pyrenees village where his father, a shoemaker, had been born. His mother was Irish and he had been born in Dublin shortly before the potato famine caused the family to immigrate to New York. There, apprenticed to a cameo cutter, he attended Cooper Union night school and, eventually, Ecole des Beaux Arts in Paris.

A cheerful, gregarious young man of great personal charm, he acquired as friends influential patrons, who recognized his enormous talent, and youthful architects, like Stamford White and Charles McKim, who were soon in a position to aid his career. The great breakthrough was a commission to execute a bronze statue of Admiral Farragut for New York's Madison Square. After critics praised its vigor and original composition, the commissions began to pour in.

Among them was one for a likeness of the Great Emancipator, to be installed in Chicago's Lincoln Park. A friend of Saint-Gaudens', an extremely wealthy New York lawyer named Charles Beaman, assured him that "Lincoln-shaped men" abounded in a New Hampshire farming village called Cornish. Beaman had bought more than 1,000 acres in the region, which included 23 houses that he would rent for the summer to artists and writers, hoping that they would eventually settle in Cornish and afford Beaman the double pleasure of civilized company in a region of extraordinary scenic beauty.

Saint-Gaudens actually found the lanky model for his *Standing Lincoln* across the river, in Windsor, Vt. But Cornish, and the estate called Aspet, became his summer home, then eventually his year-round residence and, in 1907, after a long bout with cancer, his final resting place.

Behind the latticed walls in back of his house, a carriage barn now functions as a small museum for antique phaetons, rockaways, cutters, buggies and other conveyances of a type used when Saint-Gaudens lived here.

If you go to the Saint-Gaudens home, here are some practical tips:

Coming from the south, take Route 95 to New Haven to Route 91 to Exit 8, marked Ascutney. Remain on the Vermont side of the river, taking Route 5 five miles north to Windsor so as to be able to cross over into Cornish through the nation's longest covered bridge. Then, take Route 12A north a mile or two, watching on the right for the entrance sign. Coming from the north, take Exit 9 from Route 91 and proceed south on Route 5 to Windsor.

The site is open from the last weekend in May until October 31. The grounds are open from 8 a.m. until dark; the buildings, from 8:30 a.m. until 4:30 p.m. Admission is 50 cents for those 13 or over.

For information, write Saint-Gaudens National Historic Site, R.R. 2, Cornish, N.H. 03745, John H. Dryfhout, superintendent. Phone: 603-675-2175.

When you're looking for a place to stay, Hanover, one of the prettiest college towns in the nation, is 20 miles north of Cornish. It makes a good base camp for a visit to Cornish. Here, the elegant and venerable Hanover Inn overlooks the Dartmouth College common. Rooms begin at $88 single, $93 double. Phone 603-643-4300.

The charming old Occum Inn at 35 N. Main St. has rates that range from $32 for a single without bath to $41 for a single with a private bath. Phone 603-643-2313.

Hanover abounds in restaurants. At the Hanover Inn, New England clam chowder and a curried chicken salad go for $6.50.

Peter Christian's Tavern at 29 S. Main St. has a cozy rathskeller atmosphere. Open daily. Phone 603-643-2345.

Delaware Canal, Pa.

A leisurely trip without a real destination

By Janet Ruth Falon
Special to The Inquirer

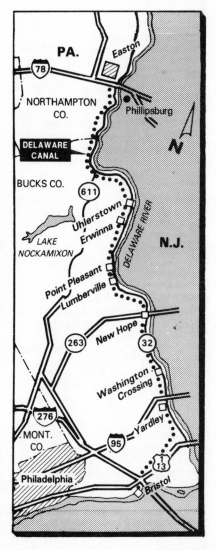

Plunging temperatures and crisp breezes mean that it's too far along for serious leaf-peeping, but it's a perfect time to explore one of eastern Pennsylvania's oldest and prettiest manmade waterways.

The 60-mile Delaware Canal is one of the best places to immerse yourself in the special pleasures of this time of year — barring a long haul into New England. You can hike for a day or a weekend along the towpath, perhaps staying overnight at one of the famous inns along River Road, Route 32, Bucks County, or across the river on Route 29 in Hunterdon County, N.J.

It's the kind of getaway where the getting-to is an integral part of your pleasure. There's no real ultimate destination, except, maybe, Easton, the head of the canal, with its informative Canal Museum and Hugh Moore Park.

The canal, which runs from Easton to Bristol and is formally known as the Delaware Division of the Pennsylvania Canal — or Roosevelt State Park — is a wonderfully askew landmark around which to plan a weekend. Never too far from the Delaware River, the canal plays with the road, sometimes appearing to your left, sometimes to your right, forcing you to guess its next move.

You can stroll along the towpath, or bike it, or ride horseback on it, or pound it at an eight-minutes-a-mile clip. You can picnic or watch for the deer, pheasant, rabbits and other wildlife that live along it (not at the more industrialized Bristol end, mind you).

You can also canoe or fish in the canal — when it holds water, that is. In August 1987, there was water only from Center Bridge to New Hope and that was scheduled to be drained for repairs to the canal.

The canal, a National Historic Landmark 153 years old, is a sliver of a now-defunct way of life that was crucial to this country's industrial development. And with its 23 locks, 10 aqueducts, 125 bridges and 165-foot drop between Easton and Bristol, the canal is undoubtedly the most interestingly shaped of the Pennsylvania state parks, no more than 60 feet across in many places.

In its heyday, in the mid-1800s, the canal was a main link in the transportation of Northeast Pennsylvania's anthracite coal, used not only in iron production but also as home heating fuel. Canal boats also brought produce to market from upstate farms.

The engineering know-how that went into the construction of the dams and aqueducts, as well as the financial savvy, were put to good use by the fledgling railroad industry, which ultimately did in the American canal network. Railroads could carry more goods a lot faster. Even so, the canal was used until 1932.

The canal era also gave rise to a cast of rough-and-tumble characters. Descriptions of many can be found at the Easton Canal Museum, as well as in the exhaustive Delaware Canal Journal by C.P. "Bill" Yoder. The journal, with its photos, charts and enough legends for a century of stories, is available at the museum.

All canals had locktenders, who lived rent-free in company-owned houses in exchange for maintaining a section of the canal and operating a lock. The locks were used to lift or lower boats between different elevations along the canal. It took five to 12 minutes to "lock through" a boat. Some locktenders were women; the wives of male locktenders often took in laundry or operated stores for extra income.

The mule tender, who often walked as far as 30 miles a day, led the mules down the towpath. Sometimes children as young as 6 years old had this job, needed year-round (as long as the canal didn't ice up).

The most prestigious job was boat captain — the man who steered the boat and was responsible for the crew, mules and cargo. His family sometimes lived aboard. Young children were fastened to the deck for safety.

You can follow the canal route by car through Bucks County and into Northampton County, near Riegelsville. A purist's route might start in Bristol and head north through Morrisville. But on this stretch in lower Bucks County, according to park maintenance manager Sandy Miller, the canal doesn't get much respect: It's common to see the banks littered with old tires and trash.

Most canal buffs start in Yardley and head up through Washington Crossing and New Hope, which gets large weekend crowds of tourists, as does its sister town, Lambertville, N.J. After New Hope, the area becomes more rural, with stretches of fields punctuated by charming hamlets.

There are plenty of points on River Road to visit: The David Library of the American Revolution, just above Washington Crossing; the Bowman's Hill Tower, with a great view of the famous section of the Delaware that "General George" crossed; the Bowman's Hill Wildflower Preserve, and in New Hope, lunch or dinner and the one-hour mule barge rides.

The River Road route goes through Lumberville, with its all-needs-answered general store that rents bikes, sells books, food and gas, and has an art gallery. There's also the Lumberville foot bridge, which crosses the Delaware into pleasant Bulls Island State Park.

Lumberville is the home of two of Bucks County's most popular inns, the 1740 House (215-297-5661) and the Black Bass Hotel (215-297-5815), either of which could be home base for this easy-puttering getaway. The Cuttalossa (215-297-5082) and Centre Bridge Inns (215-862-2048) are also nearby. The famous Golden Pheasant Inn (215-294-9595) in Erwinna, farther north, is also a classy option.

You'll pass through Point Pleasant, the site of the controversial pumping station, and drive near Ringing Rocks, the Ralph Stover Park and the Boy Scout Camp at Treasure Island. There are plenty of antiques shops and farm stands on this route, as well as the Stover Mill art gallery. The terrain turns hillier and rockier — there's even a stretch next to what are called the Palisades, sometimes frequented by eagles. Grafitti like "Barry loves Cheryl 4 Ever" appear on cliffs.

Also, be sure to turn left (if you're going north) by the bridge to Frenchtown, near Erwinna, and look at the covered bridge at Uhlertown, the only one of its type to span the canal. It is also the only covered bridge in Bucks County with windows on each side. Uhlertown was known as Mexico but was renamed for Michael Uhler, a boat builder and operator of a line of canal boats.

There were two types of boats on the canals: barges, and packet boats, the pleasure-ride passenger vessels. "It was like a hayride," explains Miller, the park maintenance manager. "In those days you couldn't jump on a bus to go somewhere, so you'd get on a packet boat."

Your canal meandering can end in Easton — where the Delaware, Lehigh and Morris (in New Jersey) Canals meet — with a visit to the Canal Museum and Hugh Moore Park. The museum tells the canal story through photographs, audio-visual exhibits (such as a replica of a coal boat cabin) and relics (including the "night hawker" lamp, for guiding canal boats in the night). In addition, on-staff canal experts will answer any canal questions.

This is not a museum that jumps out and wins over uninterested visitors. It's small, and you have to have some interest in the topic. It is especially interesting if you are familiar with the role that other towns played in the canal world, such as Mauch Chunk, now Jim Thorpe, which was the "funnel" for anthracite coal.

The museum also runs one-hour and 2½-hour mule-drawn excursion boat rides during the summer (including a lock raising and lowering) and operates a restored locktender's house during the prime tourist season. The museum is one mile south of Easton on Route 611, and is open year-round Mondays through Saturdays from 10 a.m. to 4 p.m. and Sundays from 1 to 5 p.m. Admission is $1 for adults, 50 cents for children ages 5 to 12; the boat ride is extra.

If you've taken River Road and then Route 611 up to Easton, you might coinsider crossing the river at Riegelsville and taking the back roads down to Frenchtown, where you can pick up Route 29 and go south through Stockton and Lambertville, eventually picking up Interstate 95 at the Scudder Falls Bridge north of Trenton. Or you can cross back to Pennsylvania at bridges in Frenchtown, Center Bridge, New Hope or Washington Crossing, N.J.

Hartford, Conn.

Mark Twain's house reflects the eccentricities of its owner

By Tom Infield
Inquirer Staff Writer

It seems fitting that America's most celebrated writer of the 19th century — an eccentric figure who at various times was a riverboat pilot, a Confederate army deserter, silver prospector and humorist — should have built one of the century's oddest houses.

His name was Samuel L. Clemens, a.k.a. Mark Twain, and he made his home here at 351 Farmington Ave. during the years when he produced his greatest works, including *The Adventures of Huckleberry Finn.*

Twain came to Hartford in 1871 from Buffalo, N.Y., where he had bought the Buffalo Courier with a loan from his rich father-in-law. He was beginning to achieve wealth in his own right from his first book, *The Innocents Abroad,* and he told his architect, Edward Tuckerman Potter, "I want a house that will be noticed."

He certainly got it.

The queer and gaudy mansion that Tuckerman designed still stands on a leafy slope at the western edge of the city, not far from the insurance companies that helped make it wealthy in the late 1800s. The house alone is worth a weekend journey to Hartford.

The biographer Justin Kaplan described the Victorian Gothic mansion in a marvelous passage in his Pulitzer Prize-winning book, *Mr. Clemens and Mark Twain.* It goes like this:

"Outside and inside, it defied all categories. It presented to the dazzled eye three turrets, the tallest of which was octagonal and about 50 feet high, five balconies, innumerable embrasures, a huge shaded veranda that turned a corner, an elaborate porte-cochere, a forest of chimneys. Its dark brick walls were trimmed with brown stone and decorated with inlaid designs in scarlet-painted brick and black; the roof was patterned in colored tile.

"The house was permanent polychrome and gingerbread gothic; it was part steamboat, part medieval stronghold, and part cuckoo clock."

Restored to its original appearance, the house is now called the Mark Twain Memorial. Many of the furnishings are originals that were dispersed at auction in the 1890s and have been collected one by one during the last 20 years.

Twain's neighbors in Hartford included Harriet Beecher Stowe, the author of *Uncle Tom's Cabin,* whose house next door also is open to the public, and Charles Dudley Warner, the co-editor of the Hartford Courant, who was a literary giant of his time but is now mostly forgotten.

Together they formed a small literary community known as Nook Farm. Their guests included many of the great men of the day, among them steel magnate Andrew Carnegie, novelist William Dean Howells and Civil War Gen. William T. Sherman. Also invited to dinner was the explorer Henry Morgan Stanley, the man who asked, "Dr. Livingstone, I presume?"

Twain and Warner collaborated on *The Gilded Age*, the book that gave a name to the period of material excess following the Civil War. Twain captured the essence of the era when he said of the financier Jay Gould: "The people had desired money before this day, but he taught them to fall down and worship it."

Twain moved into the house with his wife, Olivia, in 1874, and refurbished it in 1881 with all the amenities that money could buy, one of which was the first residential telephone in Hartford. The expense of running the house, and wining and dining the constant stream of visitors, eventually would help bankrupt him.

For most of the time in Hartford, he partied and lived the life of a literary gentleman. He did his real writing while summering at Quarry Farm in Elmira, N.Y., his wife's home town. Still, the house in Hartford was the only real home he ever knew, and the 17 years he spent there were the happiest and most productive of his life.

Twain liked to spend money. He also was prone to poor investments. "You are one of the talented men of the age," he was told by the famed preacher, the Rev. Henry Ward Beecher, brother of Harriet Stowe, "but in matters of business I don't suppose you know enough to come in from the rain."

The worst of his investments was in a mechanical typesetter built by James W. Paige. At 17, Twain had worked at The Inquirer setting type by hand. The machine seemed to him a "mechanical marvel" that made "all the other wonderful inventions of the human brain sink pretty clearly into the commonplace."

The Paige typesetter might have rivaled the Linotype, which was developed about the same time and still is in use in some places more than 100 years later. But Paige's machine was horribly complicated, containing 18,000 parts, and could never be made to work. Twain poured $300,000 — virtually his entire fortune — into the venture. He lost it all.

The only model of the typesetter ever built now rests heavily in the basement of the Twain house, a monument to futility.

The typesetter is the last stop on a leisurely tour that begins, logically enough, in the grand entrance hall, where Twain kept his telephone in a closet. It is said that he found the device confusing and a bother. More likely, he didn't like it because, having once been given an opportunity to invest in the telephone, he passed it by.

The house is filled with the heavy, ornate furnishings of the period. Most striking of these is Twain's mammoth black walnut bed, which already was 200 years old when he bought it in Venice. There are photos of him sitting backward in the bed, his pillows resting against the footboard, so that he could look at the fancy carvings on the headboard and the chubby little cherubs on the posts. He died in that bed.

Twain's billiard room — his favorite — occupies a wing on the top floor that is said to resemble a pilot house from the steamboats Twain remembered from his boyhood on the Mississippi River. Here was his study, where he wrote when he could.

Oddball touches abound in the house, which when seen in light as dim as that cast by the gas lamps of the 19th century, appears dark and foreboding. Twain ordered a window to be cut above the fireplace in the dining room. This required workmen to reroute the flue. He said he liked to watch flames and snow at the same time.

Over one section of the house he

installed tin roofing. He said he liked the sound when it rained.

Kaplan concluded in his biography that Twain's house was a symbol of his mixed-up feelings about himself. He was the rough-hewn Westerner, poorly educated, who had mined for silver and bounced around on newspapers in California. He even had gone AWOL from the Confederate army and never returned. Kaplan wrote that he wanted to poke fun at the genteel society of Hartford. But he wanted to be part of it, too.

Twain's lifestyle and business failures eventually drove him to Europe, where he could live for less. He closed up the house in 1891 and sailed for France. He remained away from America for eight of the next nine years, destined never to return to the house.

His favorite daughter, Susy, who attended Bryn Mawr College, died of meningitis in the house in 1896. Twain received the cable in England. He and Olivia could not bring themselves to set foot in the house again.

When the family finally did return to Hartford in 1900, Twain rented a smaller house on West 10th Street. The Farmington Avenue house was sold at a loss in 1903 to a vice president of the Hartford Fire Insurance Co., and, thereafter, passed through a variety of uses and owners. Twain himself, by then a widower, spent his last years in Redding, Conn. He died in 1910 at the age of 75.

For a time, the grand old house served as a dormitory for the Kingswood Boys School. Then it was the property of a coal company, which used it for storage and later divided it into 10 apartments. Finally, in 1929, the Friends of Hartford bought the mansion as a memorial to Mark Twain. Restoration began in 1955.

"No restoration is ever finished," said Wynn Lee, director of the Mark Twain Memorial. But the work was declared substantially done in 1974, in time for the house's centennial.

The work the restorers have done is hard to overpraise. Old photographs show the house was in awful condition. Once it was even stripped bare and filled with bookshelves to serve as a public library.

Now, though, it looks as if Mark Twain really did live there. If you use your imagination, you can hear his voice rumbling in the dining room, and the squeals and laughter of little girls on the stairway. Is that a lingering smell of cigar smoke in the air?

There can be no doubt: This is the house that Mark Twain built.

Hartford is a pleasant city of 130,000, with one of America's most attractive state capitols. It is a four-hour drive from Philadelphia via interstate highways.

Next door to the Twain house, across a green, is the large but more austere house where Harriet Beecher Stowe lived.

Harriet Stowe was 62 when she moved into the house in 1873, two decades after publication of *Uncle Tom's Cabin*, the book that made her rich and world-famous. Her husband, retired Bible scholar Calvin Ellis Stowe, was 71.

The Stowe house is airier and more modestly decorated than the Twain house; less interesting, also. Still, it's worth a look.

The Mark Twain Memorial and the adjoining Stowe house are open from 10 a.m. to 4:30 p.m. daily from May 1 until September 1. The rest of the year they are open from 9:30 a.m. to 4 p.m. Tuesday through Saturday and 1 to 4 p.m. Sunday. Admission for a tour of both houses is $6.50 for adults, $5.50 for senior citizens and $2.75 for children ages 6 to 16; children under 6 are admitted free.

Lowell, Mass.

Remembering when this mill town was the 'Venice of America'

By Robert J. Pessek
Special to The Inquirer

I t has been many decades since this old river town rang out with the constant clackety-clack of machinery from its dusty 19th-century textile mills. This birthplace of American industry has long since ceased to be a major player in the nation's manufacturing economy.

But, fortunately for visitors, much of what made Lowell important in its heyday is still here today. This unique mixture of red brick mills, canals and ethnic diversity owes its recent emergence as a major tourist

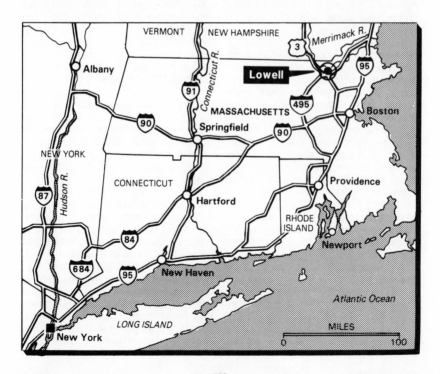

attraction in part to its earlier economic decline.

Unlike some other urban centers that experienced growth and change — with the attendant destruction of historic structures, whole neighborhoods and other irreplaceable elements of life from an earlier era — Lowell, Mass., simply moldered for much of this century.

Thus, when ambitious federal, state and city efforts began converting this first battleground of the American Industrial Revolution into parks, public waterways, museums and working displays a few years ago, much of Lowell's past survived as raw materials with which to work.

The result is a compelling account of not only what was endured in earlier generations but also an insight into a socio-economic upheaval that forever changed what America would be and even how we live today. More than Williamsburg, Va.; Plimouth Plantation in Massachusetts and other living history displays, or the monuments of Washington, Lowell is truly a "roots" tour in microcosm for many of the nation's citizens.

A 7½-hour drive from Philadelphia can bring you to Lowell's doorstep, affording the opportunity for a unique and offbeat two- or three-day weekend journey. Or you can make Lowell part of a side trip on your next sojourn to Boston.

Lowell's past began in 1821 with a visit to a farming village on the banks of the Merrimack River by a group of Boston entrepreneurs. They sought sufficient water power to run textile mills that would not only provide cloth for a growing country but also usher in a model community of contented workers cared for under corporate paternalism. They found what they wanted along Pawtucket Falls, where the Merrimack's flow drops 30 feet.

This combination of astute business vision and utopian social concepts started with great success and served as a model for the many New England mills that followed. As one brochure notes: "After Lowell, life in the United States would never be the same. From then on, men and women would leave their farms and families in ever-increasing numbers to work in cities; to submit their lives to the tyranny of timetables and factory bells; to become essential but interchangeable parts in the mighty new machines of industrial progress."

Today, many aspects of that distant, often painful period have been brought back to life in exhibits that offer unvarnished accounts of the manufacturing organization, social systems and daily lives of the workers who tended the whirling, clattering machines.

The key to this revival is a downtown core of 137 acres with 19th-century buildings and a 5.6-mile canal system. It has been designated a National Historic Park with federal efforts supplemented by state and local governments as well as the private sector.

Not long ago, the Lowell Manufacturing Co. mills, built in 1882 and 1902, were fire-damaged structures abandoned by owners who refused to pay property taxes on them. But in 1982 the once-crumbling eyesores were reopened as Market Mills, a gateway to the national and state parks and the downtown.

Within Market Mills — with adjacent visitor parking — are a visitor's center for information and tour reservations; a multi-image slide show; a bookstore and exhibits organized around the themes of labor, capital, power, machines and the industrial city.

There is a 2½-hour mill and canal tour (operating from Memorial Day to Columbus Day) that includes guided walks, trolley rides and canal boat rides to the canal gates, locks and dams. Another tour visits mills with cotton textile production demonstrations along with a depiction of working conditions. In the works is a major addition, dealing with labor and immigration to further dramatize the first planned American industrial city; called the Boot Mills Complex, it will be located in a restored 1836 boardinghouse. All tours and admissions are free, but tour reservations are required. (For park information and tour reservations, call 617-459-1000.)

A water-power exhibit is housed in the former Mack Building near the visitor's center. Outside is displayed a massive 17½-ton bull wheel taken from a mill. Inside, life-size sculptures dressed in authentic garb "talk" about the canal system that once earned Lowell the name "Venice of America." Its canals not only channeled swift river across turbines that in turn drove the looms and other textile machines, but also divided the downtown into five islands.

There are operating models and demonstrations of the special qualities of water power. The final display is a videotaped interview with one of the few remaining water turbine operators. In homespun unrehearsed language, he explains his duties and extols the engineering and mechanical prowess originally needed to harness the Merrimack.

Other restorations and renovations include hiking and bicycling paths along the river and the use of period light fixtures, park benches and materials to maintain an authentic air — even the trolley is an exact replica of a car made in 1901 by the J.C. Brill Works of Philadelphia. With tuck-pointed masonry, pristine brickwork and generous open spaces and plantings, there is a restful and gentrified air about the plazas and serene mill buildings.

Adding to the refined atmosphere is the Melting Pot, a food court of seven ethnic restaurants with common seating and A Brush With History, a gallery with studios of local artists and craftsmen.

But the knowledgeable tour leaders and excellent exhibits make it quite clear: Lowell may have been the mighty and oft-praised textile center of the nation, but life for its mill workers was much less than refined.

Even before the first millions of locally kilned bricks were laid for the mill walls, the few local residents were learning about the new business methods that would come with big money and big industry. To induce area farmers to give up prime lands along the Merrimack, they were told that the mill companies wanted to develop the world's finest orchards. The unsuspecting tillers — who believed a man's word could be trusted — agreed.

But nary a promised apple was to come from the fields. Instead, giant buildings and machines took over the land and only 15 years later — in 1836 — Lowell was incorporated as a city of 20,000 people.

The then-radical "Lowell System" of manufacture first recruited a hitherto untapped souce of labor — farmers' daughters. These "mill girls" were awakened at 5 a.m. and worked until 7 p.m., six days a week with only a half-hour break each day. Sunday was their day off, but on that day Irish laborers — who had dug the canals by hand — were sent into the waterways to scour and clean them. The Irish were then still considered unfit for more sophisticated labors.

The mills were hot, humid and noisy with the windows kept closed so that swiftly moving threads would not dry and snap — conditions that also produced foul, dust-filled air.

The women lived in company dormitories with an evening curfew, mandatory church attendance and rules against "improper conduct." Many of them used their meager earnings to send male siblings to school, to aid their poor rural families or for their own dowries. One visitor, seeing their plain bonnets and sober demeanor, called them the "nuns of Lowell."

During the mill girls era, life was not entirely grim. Limited amounts of leisure time could be spent reading, visiting or attending evening classes and lectures at which such luminaries as Ralph Waldo Emerson and John Greenleaf Whittier spoke.

Hundreds of American and European visitors, including Charles Dickens, Davy Crockett, and many economists and social reformers, journeyed to this seemingly ideal mill town that apparently was industrializing society without the brutalizing squalor and degradations accompanying similar ventures in Europe. If foreign dignitaries and academics were impressed with glimpses of conditions they did not actually experience, however, the mill girls were increasingly disenchanted.

As early as the 1830s, "turn outs" — strikes — pitted disgruntled workers against companies determined to dictate the terms of their employees' lives. As mill owners — one is described as having a "colorful personality, indomitable energy and arrogant self-confidence" — demanded wage cuts and more production, labor unrest increased.

In what was to become a standard employer tactic, management eventually ended the dissension by replacing the mill girls with a more vulnerable and thus docile labor pool: recently arrived immigrants.

In successive waves, starting with the Irish Potato Famine at the close of the 1840s, Lowell's mills absorbed Irish, French-Canadians (Canadian-born beat writer Jack Kerouac spent his boyhood in blue-collar Lowell and is buried in Westlawn Cemetery), Portuguese, Italians, Polish, Jewish and other immigrants.

Each ethnic group would establish its own community, erect a church and build social clubs, coffeehouses, language schools and other institutions particular to its heritage. Lowell often was referred to as a "City of Nations."

But this cultural diversity sometimes resulted in suspicions and hostility between the new, newer and newest Americans. These rivalries, stemming mostly from competition for jobs, tended to divide the workers and curb employee solidarity. Mill bosses were adept at swiftly replacing disgruntled employees with the most recent — and most needy — immigrants. Also with the departure of the mill girls, workers were responsible for providing their own housing, giving rise to rows of tenements circling the mills.

Today this multihued background is celebrated in a series of ethnic festivals.

After World War I, a permanent decline of the Lowell mills set in as companies closed down or moved south to be closer to cotton and cheaper labor. By 1940 only three of the original mills were left and the last of them disappeared forever when it was razed in 1966.

But many of the structures, where industrial history had been made, and the Victorian commercial buildings that served the once thriving community survived. Fortuitously, some were not only abandoned to the city for back taxes but many were so well constructed that they were left standing because it would have been too costly to destroy them.

Ultimately, this unplanned preservation resulted in today's revitalization that draws 800,000 people annually and includes the recycling of other mill buildings for high-tech industries, offices, housing, restaurants and other functions.

The final product is a fascinating and human story of early America: an energetic and tumultuous time that is depicted with unsparing objectivity but within an atmosphere that has transformed those once onerous work setting into placid plazas and restful parks.

One only wonders what the mill girls and immigrant laborers would make of it.

The mill complex is open year-round, 8:30 a.m. to 5 p.m.

Where to stay: The downtown Lowell Hilton is located at 50 Warren St., Lowell, at the lower locks of the Pawtucket Canal. Telephone: 617-452-1200. Other options include: Town House Inn and Restaurant, 850 Chelmsford St., Lowell, 617-454-5606; HeritageInn/Quality Inn, 10 Independence Drive, Chelmsford, 617-256-0800, or 800-228-5151 toll-free outside Massachusetts; Howard Johnson's, Route 110 at I-495, Exit 31, Chelmsford, 617-256-7511.

Mill Run, Pa.

Frank Lloyd Wright's Fallingwater: A house like no other on earth

By Mack Reed
Special to The Inquirer

Fifty years ago, Frank Lloyd Wright finished building his epic Fallingwater — over a serene waterfall in the deep woods along Bear Run — as an ultramodern vacation retreat for the wealthy Pittsburgh department store magnate Edgar J. Kaufmann Sr.

Twenty-four years ago, the owner's son, Edgar Jr., donated the house to the Western Pennsylvania Conservancy, which buffed it to a high polish and opened it to tours.

Six days a week, six hours a day, for the paltry price of $5, one can walk with learned guides through the cool rooms and stone halls over the falls, and experience Fallingwater for what it is — an engineering marvel and a testament to inventive home-building.

Fallingwater sits in a rural area of southwest Pennsylvania, surrounded by natural and historic attractions that make it an ideal weekend destination. The 275-mile cruise out the Pennsylvania Turnpike from Philadelphia probably necessitates a three-day weekend to make the trip comfortable. But the journey is rewarded the minute you turn the corner on the gravel path and spot the gentle, horizontal ocher lines of Fallingwater breaking through the soft, green verticals of the forest around it.

The house is a miracle of visual symbiosis.

The round-edged rectangular planes of its balconies and roof lines jut over the waterfall like the facets of some fantastic crystal growing from the rocks that support it. Horizontal lines are repeated in visual rhythm throughout the house, from the flat sandstone blocks that make up its walls to the horizontal wood grain running through the walnut wardrobes in the master bedroom.

The very materials that make up Fallingwater work in harmony with its surroundings — smooth, steel-reinforced concrete made by man, assembled with sandstone quarried just 500 yards from the site, and built upon solid rock formed 230 million years ago by the slow folding and erosion of the Earth's crust.

Wright once wrote of stone: "There is suggestion in the strata and character in the formations. I like to sit and feel it, as it is. ... In the stony bone-work of the Earth, the principles that shaped stone as it lies, or as it rises and remains to be sculpted by winds and tide — there sleep forms and styles enough for all the ages for all of Man."

By a modern homeowner's standards, Fallingwater is alternately brilliant and impractical.

The master bedroom appears no larger than 20 by 20 feet. Low ceilings throughout the house were meant to squeeze the eye of the beholder toward the woods outside, but one can feel almost claustrophobic in the smaller rooms.

Some doorways, such as the ones connecting Edgar Kaufmann Jr.'s third-floor study via a passageway to his bedroom, are elbow-scrapingly narrow.

The flagstone-paved, glass-walled living room is so wide that it would be difficult to have an "intimate" gathering of any fewer than 20 people without feeling like a bunch of mice huddled on the broad floor of some futuristic gymnasium.

But there is nothing else like Fallingwater on Earth, and to this day, it seems to have been designed not for the 21st century but the 22d.

The history of Fallingwater is even more fascinating than its structure, and the guides intertwine architecture and anecdotes for the visitor.

True to Wright's notorious reputation, the house came in behind schedule and over budget. It was also full of flaws.

Modeled after some of Wright's desert homes and built without downspouts, the house's flat roofs leaked. Insulation in the floors had been sealed in wet, and the redwood substructure rotted and had to be replaced.

The cantilevered, reinforced-concrete balconies were improperly built and drooped in a way "that worried [the elder] Kaufmann for the rest of his life," says one history.

In *Frank Lloyd Wright's Fallingwater*, author Donald Hoffman writes that Kaufmann was receiving Fallingwater damage reports from engineers until the final weeks of his life. One was, according to the book, "politely ominous":

"We believe that for some years this structure has been quietly asking for help (by bending stair hangers, twisting frames, and breaking glass) and that in the near future it will demand assistance in a more forceful manner," the engineers wrote.

You wouldn't know it to look at it.

Whatever Fallingwater's demands then, they seem since to have been lulled to whispers.

Walk down the laurel-lined path and enter Wright's vision — a rich hybrid of rock and steel made whole by calculating design.

• Wright had the broad sandstone of the living-room floor glazed with a high-gloss wax, to give the illusion of stream-washed rocks.

• A glass hatch, much like a ship's hatch, was installed in the living room. It opens to allow cool air to rise from the stream and to let people descend steps hanging from beneath the first floor and dip their toes in the currents of Bear Run. The steps are closed now, but one can look down through the hatch to the water rushing past and imagine the luxury that the Kaufmanns must have felt.

• One corner of the house, made of red-framed glass windows, rises through three stories, unbroken from foundation to roof line. The frames meet when closed, to form a shaft of light in each room on that corner, or open to show an unobstructed view of Bear Run. The glass edges are socketed into grooves in the stone walls, making more seamless the marriage of nature and artifice.

• Nine-inch-diameter industrial shower heads hang ready in cork-lined bathrooms to rain down on bathers, giving the feel of standing beneath the falls. Both the guest house and main house have small pools for bathing — separate from the stream's current, but one with its substance.

Wright built Fallingwater for two men, and there lies the most important symbiosis at work in the house: the meeting of architect and client, of artist and patron.

The elder Kaufmann first built a prefab cabin about 1,500 feet southeast of the site in 1921, on land set aside for Kaufmann's Summer Club, a vacation camp for female employees of his store, Hoffman wrote. The store employees' association bought the land in 1926 but later boycotted the site because of labor troubles, and the site lay dormant when the Depression hit the country. Kaufmann remained fond of it, though, and took title to the grounds with his wife in 1933.

Intrigued by Wright's autobiography, Edgar Kaufmann Jr. asked Wright for an apprenticeship, and six days later, Wright's secretary mailed the elder Kaufmann a copy of a book of Wright's work. When Edgar and Liliane Kaufmann visited their son and met Wright at the architect's home/workshop, Taliesin, near Spring Green, Wis., the artist and the businessman swiftly forged a friendship that would last for decades.

In December 1934, Wright began surveying the site. Neither he nor Kaufmann dreamed of the ordeal ahead — the cost overruns, the artistic spats, the engineering mistakes — or of the fame that the house would bring its maker and its owners.

Wright spent much of 1935 working up sketches and surprised Kaufmann — who envisioned a country home across Bear Run from the falls — with sketches of a house on the falls.

A Wright assistant remembered the 67-year-old master explaining to his client, "E.J., I want you to live with the waterfall, not just to look at it, but for it to become an integral part of your lives."

Wright had heard that Kaufmann used to enjoy sunning himself on a large boulder, and contrived to put it at the heart of the house, in fact making it part of the fireplace hearth.

There was a little business done at first, such as Kaufmann's specifying that the house should cost between $20,000 and $30,000, and that it must have a living and dining space, a master bedroom, a separate dressing room, a bedroom for Edgar Jr., a guest bedroom and a wing for servants' quarters and more guest space.

But for now, they were artist and patron, bringing flesh and bones of stone and steel to the spirit of an architectural vision.

In February 1936, though, when Wright sent blueprints to Kaufmann, the two quickly reverted to architect and client.

Kaufmann's engineers assailed the plans as incomplete, unsound and downright inadvisable — especially the notion of centering the whole structure atop a boulder constantly washed by a waterfall, which could kick the props out from under it with sudden blows from flood-borne driftwood or erode the foundation with the sure, slow force of running water.

"Mr. Kaufmann sent the report to Mr. Wright," recalled Abrom Dombar, assistant display architect at Kaufmann's Store and once a Wright apprentice at Taliesin, according to Hoffman's book.

"Mr. Wright told Mr. K to send the drawings back to Taliesin ... whereupon Mr. K apologized and said to go ahead with the working-drawings."

By May, work had begun on the stone piers and tapered concrete bolsters that would function, with the natural boulders, as the revolutionary cantilever system that gives Fallingwater its structural support and rakish shape. The flat, reinforced-concrete slabs of the floors were meant to balance on the boulders like levers on fulcrums, with the 30-foot-tall stone chimney mass at the house's core balanced on the largest boulder of all.

Construction progressed. The second-floor slab was poured on Sept. 16, and throughout the autumn and winter of 1936-37, the end product began to outshine the faulty parts and the off-schedule construction.

Then came the fine details that now are so much a highlight of the tour: Craftsmen built in horizontal-grained walnut wardrobes fitted with sliding wicker shelves to keep clothes from mildewing. They installed fluorescent tubes behind Japanese-inspired wood-and-rice-paper screens to light the living-room and guest-house ceilings. Wright was the first to use fluorescents to light homes, and he is also credited with creating the king-size bed, one of which takes up a considerable part of the small master bedroom.

In 1937, Kaufmann and his wife and

son began using the house, but it was not until 1939 that all the details were added and the guest wing was built.

And the raves came down.

The entire January 1938 issue of Architectural Forum was devoted to Wright's work, including 12 pages on Fallingwater, with text by Wright himself.

Time hailed it as Wright's "most beautiful" work.

In 1976, the house was designated a National Historic Landmark.

By the time all was said and done, the last window installed in the last corner of the guest wing, Kaufmann had spent $155,000 — quite a bit more than the $20,000 to $30,000 originally envisioned.

Then in the twilight of his career, Wright went on to design some of his most famous buildings, including the Johnson Wax Co. in Racine, Wis.; the TWA terminal at John F. Kennedy International Airport on Long Island and the Guggenheim Museum in New York City.

The pact between Kaufmann and Wright had been richly fulfilled.

In Hoffman's book, Architectural Forum staffer George Nelson remembers: "There is no doubt in my mind that for Wright the Kaufmann house was one of his great favorites. . . . For Wright, Edgar Kaufmann was one of his truly great and favorite clients, and as far as I am concerned, this high regard was well placed. Kaufmann was a true merchant prince, a man of great personal power, full of what we have come to call charisma and possessed of a vision that is anything but common. In retrospect, I would say that they did very well by each other."

•

Fallingwater is easy to reach, inexpensive to tour and surrounded by natural and historic attractions.

Take the Pennsylvania Turnpike west to Exit 9, for Donegal. Turn left off the exit onto Route 31 east. Go about two miles, and turn right onto Route 381 south. The road will take you through rolling farmland and forests, for about 19 miles, to the entrance of Fallingwater, which is at a slight rise on the right.

Follow the driveway to the guard shack, pay the $5 admission (there's a 50-cent discount on weekdays for senior citizens) and proceed to the hospitality pavilion, which has a restaurant and a day-care center for children younger than 10. The Western Pennsylvania Conservancy recommends leaving children in the care of its staff for $1 per child per hour, but special tours for them may be arranged.

At the pavilion, you will be assigned to a tour. When your number is called, go down the laurel-lined woodland path to the entrance to meet your guide.

Afterward, you will be allowed to walk down any of several paths to the base of the falls. But caution: Those unsure of their footing might take a free ride down the cliff face if they venture too close to the water-slicked edge, and parents will want to keep close control of their children. There are no guardrails at the cliff tops.

The lush woods around Fallingwater are seamed with nature trails, most notably those preserved and maintained by the conservancy itself and open free of charge, and no fewer than four rafting companies offer whitewater trips nearby.

Golfing and skiing are available in season at the nearby Seven Springs Resort in Champion, and just off Route 40, Fort Necessity National Park offers a tour of a reconstruction of a fort used by George Washington during the French and Indian War. Most hotel and motel accommodations are more than 30 minutes away from the house, so plan accordingly.

For more information, call the Fayette County Tourism Office at 412-439-5610.

Fallingwater is open 10 a.m. to 4 p.m. every day but Monday, and is also open on Mondays designated as national holidays — such as Memorial Day, Labor Day and Columbus Day. For more information on the house, write Fallingwater, Box R, Mill Run, Pa. 15464 or call 412-329-8501.

Natick, Mass.

New Englanders hoard their secrets and that includes candlepin bowling

By Douglas A. Campbell
Inquirer Staff Writer

Suppose you're in the kitchen with a grapefruit — a very hard grapefruit — in your hand and you suddenly have the urge to bowl the little sphere across the Congoleum.

Hurry to Massachusetts! You'll have company.

Thousands of New Englanders seem to get just such an impulse every Saturday at lunchtime, and they are not being weird. They are watching *Candlepin Bowling*, the highest-rated regular sports television program in the Boston market, a staple along with hot dogs and beans in many a New Englander's Saturday.

During a given week, thousands of viewers regularly jam into the 89 vintage-1950s candlepin bowling establishments remaining in Massachusetts and southern New Hampshire and, individually and in leagues, attempt once again the seemingly impossible — knocking down 10 slender pins, shaped like slightly pregnant candles, with a ball that is the size of a grapefruit and not much heavier.

Clearly, the local fascination with candlepin bowling suggests that there must be something to this century-old game. And there is. This is a sport in the truest sense, and it is truly egalitarian, offering the same opportunities to the athletically inept as to the gifted.

New Englanders hoard their secrets, though. Like their bitter soft drink, Moxie, bottled since 1888 but still sold only in a few dusty rural general stores, candlepin bowling is known in the United States only in a narrow swath that spreads from Massachusetts north to New Hampshire and Vermont. (Canada has lively groups of candlepin devotees, too.)

To experience the lure of candlepins, then, one must travel north from the Philadelphia area. Frustrated athletes — those of us chosen last in the sandlot ball games of our youth — are well-advised to make a weekend pilgrimage to the endangered habitat of a game in which the advantages of sex and age disappear and one's ability to excel may have more to do with a familiarity with grapefruit than with conventional athletic prowess.

One need never have bowled to enjoy candlepins. The ball weighs two pounds and a few ounces, not 15 or 16 pounds like the conventional bowling ball used in tenpins. The immediate benefit is that your shoulder never becomes dislocated.

There are other advantages. The ball is smooth. There are no finger holes to give you blisters. And if you drop a candlepin ball on your toe, nothing will be broken, so even the hopelessly clumsy are welcome.

As in other forms of bowling, the object is to roll the ball down a wooden lane toward 10 pins and to knock down as many of the pins as possible. Though the game of tenpins allows you only two tries, candlepin rules give a player three balls per frame with which to knock down 10 candlepins on a lane the same size as a tenpin lane.

Be forewarned. You will need all three. The average bowler exhausts his or her supply of ebonite balls and relinquishes the lane to the next player with a few pins still upright. (As in tenpins, 10 frames constitute a game, or string. But, unlike tenpins, where a perfect score of 300 is not uncommon, no one has ever scored a perfect game of candlepins, according to the Massachusetts Bowling Association, the candlepin trade group. In fact, the record is a score of 240, bowled in December 1984.)

If indeed you knock down some pins with one of your first two balls, the fallen pins are left in place, adding to the geometry by which the next ball may be deflected. The fallen pins are called "wood" or "deadwood" and can be used by the bowler to knock down the standing pins.

A second warning: A ball striking deadwood is just as likely to rocket into oblivion, leaving the standing pins untouched.

These are about all the things you need to know about candlepins except this: The most legendary figure in candlepin history is a grandmother from Webster, Mass., named Stacia Czernicki, 65, who has won more state and national championships than anyone else in history. She is an active professional bowler and has no thoughts of retiring.

Bolstered by this knowledge, drive north toward Hartford, Conn., where you will have to make the first decision.

Interstate 91 North will take you to Springfield, Mass., the westernmost outpost of candlepins, where three establishments offer from 16 to 34 lanes each.

Interstate 84 East will direct you into Massachusetts toward Sturbridge, Worcester (the birthplace of candlepin bowling) and Boston, in the suburbs of which are the majority of candlepin establishments.

The largest collection of candlepin lanes in Springfield — which is closest to Philadelphia — is at State Bowl, 1431 State St. Rates are $1.25 per string and 60 cents rental for a pair of shoes.

("We can fit any kid that's walking and any size adult.")

Travelers can stay at the Springfield Howard Johnson's, a half-mile from State Bowl in downtown Springfield, or at the Best Western motel in Chicopee, about four miles from the lanes.

More adventurous travelers willing to add an hour or so to their journey can find in suburban Boston: the smallest bowling establishment (Sawyers Bowladrome Inc.) in the bedroom community of Northboro, where six lanes are located in the basement of an old frame building that also is home to a store selling dancing attire; the largest bowladrome (Wal-Lex Recreation Center with 60 lanes) in Waltham, just off Route 128, the electronics-industry corridor around Boston, and the lanes that are used by Channel 5 in Boston to tape *Candlepin Bowling* (Fairway Sports World with 32 lanes) in Natick.

Being in a candlepin establishment is not a whole lot different from being inside a salmon and white '58 Ford Fairlane 500 hardtop. You will find that some lanes are in about the same shape as most of the few remaining '58 Ford Fairlanes — nicked, faded, maybe a little bit musty, with grooves worn in the yellow hardwood lanes that once glowed with new coats of varnish.

Wal-Lex and Sawyers are among these.

Ernest Sawyer, 59 and laconic, has owned his Northboro lanes for 35 years. He closes down from June to September but is open from 9 a.m. to

11 p.m. seven days a week the rest of the year.

When you've found 13 Blake St. in Northboro, look for a set of stairs descending on the southern side of the building. Walk down, open the door and hear the rumble of balls and the resonant whack of colliding pins.

To your right will be the humble counter, to your left, the salmon-colored plastic benches, the white Formica scoring tables on aqua metal pedestals. Lane 1 appears to be thoroughly grooved and might be a good choice. The grooves may just keep the balls from expending themselves in the gutter.

If you bowl during the day, Sawyer charges you $1 a string. At night, the rate rises to $1.40.

About 20 miles to the east, on Lexington Street in Waltham, the Wal-Lex is made up of three facilities. One building has 20 lanes upstairs and 20 lanes on the ground floor. And an annex in the back parking lot houses the third set of 20 lanes.

The walls of the lanes are decorated with carpeting in brick red, gray and gold, cut and fit together to spell out Wal-Lex and to depict bowling balls and pins falling. The benches are varnished hardwood, but the salmon-colored plastic seats are not far behind them, just in front of the bank of video arcade games.

Wal-Lex charges $1.25 a string, though there is a $1-per-string special Monday through 9 a.m. to 5 p.m. Shoe rental is 50 cents a pair.

A decent meal in a room with the same ambiance experienced at the Wal-Lex can be had at the Lani Island restaurant at 147 Winter St., about two miles from the Wal-Lex. A meal for seven there cost $78, including tip, and incorporated spontaneous entertainment when a flaming dish ignited the table cloth. The area around Waltham offers a variety of accommodations, and the Wal-Lex people are willing to make suggestions.

One of the gems of candlepin bowling — maintained much the way all the lanes looked when they were built in a bowling boom in the 1950s — is the Fairway Sports World at 721 Worcester St. in Natick. Decorated like the Wal-Lex, the Fairway has little of the grit and chipping that mark the former.

That is important because a big chunk of the New England television audience sees the heart of the Fairway on Saturday mornings.

"Our show started in October 1958 on Channel 5, and it's been on every week, every year since then," said Phillip S. Rubin, director and producer of *Candlepin Bowling* on WCVB-TV.

"I'm pretty sure why it's so popular is because anyone can do it," Rubin said.

Even you with the grapefruit in your hand. Think of it — the nearest candlepin lane is only a five-hour drive away.

•

For more suggestions on places to stay and things to do when you've finished bowling, see the stories on Boston, Concord, Lowell, Sturbridge and Williamstown in this book.

The Poconos, Pa.

A magnificent view is par for the course on these greens

By Tom Belden
Inquirer Staff Writer

At this time of year, when the fertile green hills of the Poconos turn gold and rust and red and brown, there are few places prettier than the 17th tee at the Glen Brook Country Club near Stroudsburg.

Glen Brook is not a particularly fancy place. Just an 18-hole public golf course with a well-stocked pro shop, a friendly bar and restaurant, several modern cabins for rent, fairly modest prices and an efficient operation that gets you through a round of golf in a reasonable time. It's one of the more interesting course layouts in the Poconos, providing great variety in its holes and a solid challenge, no matter what one's handicap.

But the real appeal of Glen Brook and a lot of other golf courses scattered across the lush Poconos is enjoying the added benefits of a visit, such as the pastoral mountain scene you can see from the elevated tee of the tough little par-3 17th hole. You can't see a long way but you gaze across a verdant valley cradling the course to the surrounding hills. Unless you've got an enormous bet hanging on the next shot, just being up on this knoll is relaxing enough to tell you why you came up to the hills in the first place.

Glen Brook is only the beginning, too. The Poconos can provide days, weeks, even months of variety in its golf courses. Although a number of courses can pose a serious challenge to even a very good golfer, there are others where beginners are welcome and will not feel out of place. A few Poconos courses are of such minimal standards that only children and rank duffers probably would enjoy them.

But we want to concentrate here on details of the better courses in the Poconos region that are open to the public, with a semblance of order given to the quality, amount of challenge and interest factor each one generated. A lot of personal preference obviously has gone into the evaluations, aided by other golfers who have played most of the courses in the region.

Not included are some golfers' highly regarded favorites, Skytop near Canadensis and Tanglwood Lakes near Lake Wallenpaupack. This is a guide to courses that anyone can play, without knowing a member of the club or staying at a certain resort, and those two courses didn't meet that test.

The courses featured all have pro shops with golf equipment for sale and clubs for rent, and some kind of snack bar, restaurant or bar, unless otherwise noted. Powered golf carts are a requisite at some of the resort courses, at least on weekends. Just as in urban areas, reserved starting times are necessary on weekend mornings at most courses. Later in the day and on weekdays, they are recommended but not always needed. The yardages listed after the greens fees are from the white or middle tees.

Another thing to remember is that many courses at resorts or lodges offer golf packages that include room and greens fees for one price, and many courses also offer reduced greens fees after 3 or 4 p.m. The Pocono Mountains Vacation Bureau also offers a free "Golf a Round" booklet that has coupons good for discounts at many courses on weekdays. The bureau's phone is 717-421-5791.

•

Hershey Pocono Resort. This is one of the Poconos' more dignified and elegant resorts, situated near White Haven, just off the junction of I-80 and the Northeast Extension of the Pennsylvania Turnpike. The golf course is several miles away from the hotel itself, off Route 534 (exit 41 of I-80), and has the fine conditioning, appearance and amenities of a small but well-to-do private country club.

The greens are some of the best around. There are a number of long, challenging holes that are a delight to attack, such as the 9th, a 535-yard par 5 that requires a tee shot threaded between two big ponds and then a march uphill to a big green. The short, 310-yard 10th hole comes back down the same hill but requires a precise second shot between more ponds to the green.

The flagsticks on this course also have a feature that all courses should. Big plastic balls are placed on the sticks to indicate how far back on the green the hole is placed — high for the back of the green, middle for the center, low for the front. That's a very helpful feature at a resort, where most of the customers

don't know the layout well.

Greens fees: $15 weekdays, $17 weekends. Powered carts: $9 per person. 6,122 yards.

Glen Brook Country Club. Located on Dreher Avenue, this course is just south of the middle of Stroudsburg, surrounded by one of the town's nicest residential areas. In addition to its other attributes mentioned earlier, this layout has pleasant changes from one hole to the next throughout most of its layout and pretty mountain vistas in numerous spots. There is only one sort of dull stretch in the course, the 12th through the 14th holes, with flat, parallel fairways. Glen Brook also has a good golf teacher in the friendly and loquacious pro, Mike Wells.

If there is a single drawback to Glen Brook, it is its popularity. It gets a lot of play from its loyal members, tourists and nearby residents. That means that while it is usually in very good condition, parts of it sometimes show wear, and play occasionally moves slowly.

Greens fees: $11 weekdays, $14 weekends. Powered carts: $21.20 for 18 holes, $10.60 for nine holes. 6,445 yards.

Mount Airy Lodge. This big resort complex, off Route 611 near Mount Pocono, bills its links as America's most challenging golf course, with each hole copied from a famous one on another course. It is, indeed, a very tough, finely conditioned test. It is one of the few courses in the Poconos that sell a yardage guide to the course, giving distances from many places on each hole to the green, and the purchase of one is a necessary step to survival.

The 1st hole here, for example, is a monstrous, winding, uphill 541-yard par-5 capped with a big pond in front of the green. There are many similarly terrifying experiences, with narrow fairways squeezed by yawning fairway bunkers and greens protected by water and more sand. You also have to go up and down a lot of hills.

In short, at Mount Airy there is almost no letup from beginning to end, and that is one of its problems. It may be such a challenge for the high handicapper, or even the middle handicapper, that you may wonder just how much fun you really had. In addition, you are allowed to drive the mandatory golf carts on paved paths on only one side of each hole, so it can easily take five hours to play a round. There are tales told locally of seven-hour rounds.

The hotel itself ought to be checked out, too, before deciding to stay here. It may be too big and commercial, and too close to the golf course, for your taste. On one recent visit, for instance, a radio playing through a loud speaker, apparently for the amusement of people around the hotel, was blaring disco music loud enough to be heard many places on the golf course.

Greens fees: $15 for hotel guests, $25 for others at all times. Powered carts: $10.60 per person. 7,123 yards.

Pocono Manor Inn and Golf Club.

This fine old resort, dating to the early 1900s, sits atop its own mountain just south of Mount Pocono. "The Manor" attracts a lot of people who come just to play golf. There are two 18-hole courses, the East and the West, both in very good condition.

The first few holes of the East course are near the clubhouse, but then the course plunges down into a deep ravine, with wide fairways on several par-4 holes and precipitous par-3s, where you shoot blind off elevated tees. There are lots of deep woods guarding all the fairways. A few of the holes in the middle of the 18 are rather similar on top of a plateau that affords views of the Delaware Water Gap. The course then closes with a pretty set of holes requiring a variety of good shots.

The West course is longer and flatter than the East but includes the same kind of fierce wooded roughs.

The greens on both courses are fairly small, too, especially on the older East. The very peculiar — and rather boring — aspect of the West course is that there are no sand traps and no water hazards. Most of the holes bear an amazing resemblance to one another.

Greens fees: $14 weekdays, $18 weekends. Powered carts: $10 per person for 18 holes, $6 for nine holes. East: 6,295 yards. West: 6,675 yards.

Pocono Farms Country Club.

Off Route 196 between Mount Pocono and Tobyhanna, this is one of a number of Poconos courses surrounded by a big second-home development, complete with tennis courts, swimming club and community center. To many people, this is one of the region's most difficult and interesting courses.

Pocono Farms was hacked out of a fairly flat but rocky and heavily wooded piece of ground. Most of the roughs that line the narrow fairways are loaded with boulders that will cause stray shots to careen off into the forest. And like many challenging, well-designed courses, this one gets longer and tougher as you go along. The three closing holes, with doglegs at 16 and 18 and a long par-5 17th, make sure you don't let your guard down. The front nine is a little shorter than the back nine, but still has the same tight fairways.

Greens fees: $14 weekdays, $16 weekends. Powered carts: $12.75 for 18 holes, $7 for nine holes. 6,219 yards.

Wilkes-Barre Golf Club.

This municipal course, owned and run by the city of Wilkes-Barre, is on Laurel Run Road, off Route 115 in Bear Creek Township, and is not usually thought of as a Poconos resort course. But numerous golfers familiar with the area suggested it be included. After only one round, it is easy to see why, for it's as well-kept, interesting and challenging a public layout as most people will ever play.

A number of the holes on the

course run parallel to one another, but you don't get a feeling of real interference from other players. The 8th and 9th holes are especially tough pieces of work, and there is ample variety and difficulty to keep up one's interest. To top it off, there is a very pleasant, handsomely designed contemporary bar-restaurant over the pro shop. Overall, this place wins the sleeper-of-the-year award.

Greens fees: $7.50 weekdays, $9 weekends. Powered carts: $15 for 18 holes, $9.50 for nine holes. 6,690 yards.

Wayne Newton's Tamiment Resort.

This course, off Route 209 north of Bushkill, probably has the best pedigree in the area. It is the only one designed by the premier architect of the past 40 years, Robert Trent Jones, and has been ranked among the top 200 U.S. golf courses by Golf Digest magazine.

The course starts out by dipping into a ravine and then spends most of both its front and back nines going back and forth on a plateau. The second nine is the more interesting and challenging, getting progressively longer and harder as you proceed back to the clubhouse.

The Tamiment course has been kept in good shape, but the same cannot always be said for the rest of the sprawling resort and vacation home development around it. Take a walk around here, both inside and out, before deciding this is where you want to check in.

Greens fees and mandatory cart rental: $25.60. 6,858 yards.

Buck Hill Golf Club.

This venerable old resort off Route 191 had the first golf course in the Poconos, built early in this century. Like Pocono Manor, it gets many repeat visitors who like to come back year after year. There are a total of 27 holes, on the Oak, Spruce and Maple courses, and a country club atmosphere in the pro shop and around the starter's station.

Although it has some interesting and testing holes, much of the Spruce and Maple nines (the only two tested personally) are cut out of a hilly piece of ground where goats would be at home. The layout can make golf a tiring chore, going up one hill and down another. The tough 541-yard par-5 4th hole on the Spruce, and a sharp dogleg, the 6th hole, also a par 5, on the Maple, are among the best.

Greens fees and mandatory cart rental: $24 weekdays, $26 weekends. Oak, 3,127 yards; Spruce, 2,955; Maple, 2,800.

Mountain Manor Inn and Golf Club.

You can see a couple of holes of this course from Route 209 at Marshall's Creek, but that may be the only way you would ever know about it. The place is practically a golfing factory, with a very busy 27 regulation holes and another 18 in a par-3 configuration, all surrounded by a handsome hotel, cabins and townhouses. But this spot is already so popular, with both guests and members of the club, that ads for it are virtually unknown, nor does it promote itself through the vacation bureau. The three regulation courses are of average length and in good condition, but the Yellow and the Blue courses are not particularly varied, with many holes fairly flat and similar to one another. The Orange nine is the hardest of the three, wandering up into more wooded terrain, according to some of the members (it was not played personally). Remember this place is jammed on weekends, meaning it can easily take more than the usual 4½ hours for a round.

Greens fees: $10.50 weekdays, $13.50 weekends. Powered carts: $15 for 18 holes. Orange, 3,219 yards; Blue, 3,191, Yellow, 3,109.

Shawnee Inn.

This is one of the better-known and busier golf resorts in the Poconos, off Route 209, and home in the summer to a big golf school run by pro Dick Farley. Most of the 27 holes are on an island that runs along the western shore of the Delaware River. This is another place that has a well-honed system for churning out the rounds of golf, keeping everyone moving along.

Among the more picturesque and interesting holes are the 185-yard par-3 4th on the White course, where you're shooting straight at the river, and the challenging 8th and 9th holes on the Blue course, as you come back toward the inn. There are plenty of bunkers and water hazards. But this course also is on a flat piece of land, so don't expect a lot of variety or unusual mountain scenery to keep you entertained.

Greens fees: $30 every day. Powered carts, $10 per person. Red, 3,250; White, 3,180; Blue, 3,250.

Fernwood Golf and Tennis Club.

This fairly new course, which sits directly on Route 209 at Bushkill, was carved out of a piece of land that is so rugged even the best of golf architects could not have improved on it much. The course has a big, well-stocked pro shop, is well-maintained and attempts to keep its conditioning up by not allowing carts to drive on the fairways, a good practice that really helps. It has a par-3 course on the same grounds.

Fernwood's terrain, however, simply means it is loaded with holes that clamber up and down steep hills, creating a lot of blind shots and uneven lies for your ball. Time-share condo developments around some holes also press in rather tightly, meaning you may have to look for stray shots on someone's deck.

Greens fees: two for $24 weekdays, two for $30 weekends. Powered carts: $19.50. 6,258 yards.

Water Gap Country Club.

Located off Route 611 in Delaware Water Gap, this is another venerated Poconos course that on weekend mornings usually is reserved for members or for guests staying at the pretty clubhouse. It has a strict "country club attire" dress code, meaning no jeans.

Provided you follow all the rules, you get to play a course that is not terribly long and is in good physical condition, but one that can be torturing because it has virtually no flat holes. There are lots of mountain vistas to look at here.

Greens fees: $13 weekdays, $16 weekends. Powered carts (mandatory before 4 p.m.): $22 for 18 holes, $11 for nine holes. 5,929 yards.

Cherry Valley Golf Course.

On Cherry Valley Road, between Stroudsburg and Delaware Water Gap, this is a fairly short, rough sort of course with few interesting holes. Most of the course is wide open, with fairways adjoining one another. A creek and a lot of hills come into play, but bunkers are no problem. A small modern pro shop with vending machines has been added recently.

Greens fees: $7.50 weekdays, $5 after 3 p.m.; $10 weekends, $7 after 3 p.m. Powered carts: $15. Also on weekdays, there is a special offered: $9.74 for cart and greens fees for two. 5,785 yards.

●

The Poconos also have a number of nine-hole golf courses, including some that offer a surprising challenge.

Cliff Park Golf Course.

This course has a beautiful setting, laid out in front of the handsome, century-old Cliff Park Inn, just outside of Milford and not far from the junctions of Routes 209 and 6. The course itself is not especially hard or varied, with most holes wide open. But the place may have the loveliest setting in the whole area for having refreshments from the bar-restaurant after a round — seated under the huge trees in front of the inn, or on the wide verandah, looking across the course.

Greens fees: $8 weekdays, $13 weekends. Powered carts: $19 for 18 holes, $12 for nine holes. 3,115 yards.

Terra Greens Golf Course.

This little-known course is on Route 447 on the northern side of East Stroudsburg. It is a surprisingly tough and interesting layout, climbing up to a hilly knoll with a grand mountain view to it; you play your way back down. A number of water hazards add to the challenge.

Greens fees: $8 weekdays, $10 weekends. Powered carts, $17 for 18 holes, $8.50 for nine holes.

Cricket Hill Golf Course. Situated near Lake Wallenpaupack at Hawley, just off Route 6, this rolling layout has a variety of challenges, including ample sand traps and water hazards. The most memorable hole is the tough number 6, a 145-yard par-3 with a tee elevated over the green.

Greens fees: $10. Powered carts, $15.90 for 18 holes and $10.60 for nine holes. 3,180 yards.

Pocono Palace Lake and Country Club. This is a Caesars resort geared for couples and honeymooners who don't want to spend all of their time in their heart-shape bathtubs. The nine-hole course is of regulation length and challenge, is in good physical condition and has a nice parklike setting.

Greens fees: $12 every day for 18 holes, $10 for nine holes. Powered carts: $20 for 18 holes. $10 for nine holes. 2,930 yards.

Evergreen Park Golf Course.

Just off Routes 447 and 191 at Analomink, this course is adjacent to the Penn Hills resort. It is shorter than average and over flat terrain, with all nine holes squeezed into a small area. It usually is in good condition. Although it crosses a rushing brook several times, this course will be of interest mostly to the high handicapper.

Greens fees: $9 weekdays, $10 weekends. Powered carts: $16 for 18 holes, $10 for nine holes. 2,578 yards.

Strickland's Wiscasset Golf Course. This short layout, on Route 611 just south of Mount Pocono, bills itself as the "sportiest nine in the Poconos," whatever that means. It goes up and down a number of steep hills and is fairly wide open, with few trees on fairways, but it does have some challenging holes.

Greens fees: $4 for nine holes, $8 for 18 holes.Powered carts: $10 for 18 holes, $7 for nine holes. 2,360 yards.

•

A final note, on a course best suited to adolescents or those just learning the game:

Mount Pocono Golf Course, on top of the hill in Mount Pocono, is quite short, with the first six holes squeezed in a small space. The last three are more normal. Greens fees: $9 for $18 holes, $5.50 for nine holes. Powered carts: $4.50. 2,400 yards.

Saratoga Springs, N.Y.

Grant fought his last battle in this cottage

By Edward Colimore
Inquirer Staff Writer

Grant's Cottage (Mount McGregor)

Saratoga Springs

NEW YORK

Saratoga Lake

Hudson River

Mohawk R.

Schenectady

Troy

Albany

MILES
0   10

Toward the end, each day brought more suffering. But through the haze of drugs and pain, the old soldier sat stoically on the porch, recalling the great battles and faithfully putting them to words.

There was the bloody fighting at Spotsylvania and Vicksburg, the carnage at the Wilderness and Cold Harbor, and the dramatic climax at Appomattox, with the surrender of the Confederate army.

Ulysses S. Grant — the tough, cigar-smoking general and former president — relived all of it in a cottage nine miles north of here at Mount McGregor, fighting one last, heroic battle to finish his memoirs before throat cancer took his life.

Today, the cottage where Grant finished his writing just days before he died remains as it did then — right down to a mantel clock, stopped at the minute of his death.

The cottage is a little-known treasure tucked away in the foothills of the Adirondacks, about a five-hour drive from Philadelphia. It is a perfect diversion for autumn leaf-peepers headed for the Adirondacks or New England.

Visitors can stroll across the wide porch where Grant spent many long hours sitting in his favorite wicker chair and jotting notes on a scratch-pad. In 1885, steady crowds of well-wishers made a pilgrimage to Mount McGregor to catch a glimpse of him there, in his silk top hat, overcoat and white scarf.

"He was a super hero, and people came here with the goal of seeing him," said Cheryl Gold, regional supervisor for the New York state office of Parks, Recreation and Historic Preservation. "So many came that local men who served in the war posted the area so he wouldn't be bothered."

Today's visitors are directed through a rear door of the cottage to a

126

dining room where the Grants had their meals. The room retains the cherry table and cane-seat chairs used by the family, as well as the china that first served them in 1874 at the wedding of the general's only daughter, Nellie, in the East Room of the Executive Mansion.

The adjoining parlor or reception room, probably more than any other, is filled with the ghosts of the past. There, where Grant met friends and fellow Civil War veterans, you can almost sense his presence.

The general's favorite wicker chair sits in a corner, and across from it is the folding bed on which he died. On the nearby mantel rests the blue and white porcelain clock — stopped by one of the general's sons at 8:08 a.m., the time of his father's death on July 23, 1885.

The room also has the same floral print rug, an oil painting of a flower arrangement over the mantel, printed Bible verses on a wall, a print of an allegorical scene and other pieces of furniture "in exceptional condition," state officials said.

Grant came to the mustard-colored, green-shuttered cottage on June 16, 1885, seeking relief from the heat. He had finished much of his memoirs — the first of two volumes had gone to press — but important work lay ahead, and the more comfortable environment of the mountains seemed the best place to do it.

The general and his family originally planned to leave their New York City home for the Catskills, then changed their minds when a New York friend, Joseph W. Drexel, offered them the use of the cottage at Mount McGregor.

From the porch and nearby overlook, Grant and his family enjoyed the peaceful, panoramic view of the Hudson Valley, looking toward the Saratoga battlefield, about 15 miles away, and Vermont, about 40 miles distant.

If you're spending the afternoon at the cottage, you may want to bring a picnic lunch and follow a path to Lookout Point, where you can enjoy the same view Grant did.

There is an eight-foot monument that marks the spot where Grant's chair was placed the last time he went there. "Grant visited the overlook on July 20th, three days before his death," said Laura Gombieski, curator at the cottage.

The general's trips to the overlook, however, were not frequent. His condition confined him mostly to the porch, reception area, dining room and other first-floor rooms, including an office used by his secretary, and the so-called "sick room" where the old man sat for long hours, writing or dozing.

Speaking came with great difficulty, so Grant usually communicated with notes, and rest was only possible while sitting. "He could not lie down because he couldn't breathe, so he was always sitting up in a chair," Gold said.

Grant's black leather armchairs — he sat in one with his feet propped on the other — remain in the sick room along with his top hat, nightshirts and medical supplies. On a side table next to the chairs are Grant's oil lamp, the scissors he used to trim the wick, a water tumbler and a fan presented to him by the Japanese people.

Grant's secretary and a son, Col. Frederick Grant, worked in the office next to the sick room. There, they helped edit the general's writing before it was turned over to the publishing company owned by Samuel Clemens, better known as Mark Twain.

Today, you can see framed prints and photographs of Grant at various times of his life. The room also contains massive floral memorials, now long since dried, that were sent after the death.

The cottage did not have a kitchen because the Drexels had wanted to keep the house as cool as possible. The Grants' meals were brought to them from the Hotel Balmoral a few hundred yards away, and a hotel generator provided electricity to the cottage's few crude ceiling light fixtures, according to Gold.

The second floor of the house is not part of the tour. The six bedrooms there were used by Grant's wife, Julia; his sons, Frederick, Jesse and Ulysses Jr.; his daughter, Nellie, and other family members and friends who spent time with Grant during his six weeks at the New York retreat.

Most of the general's last days, however, were occupied with work, writing and rewriting portions of the second volume despite the effects of cocaine, morphine and brandy used to kill the pain in his throat. His prose was plain and uncomplicated, the words of a common man spun together into one of the great enduring works of American literature.

"The first volume, as well as a portion of the second, was written before I had reason to suppose I was in critical condition of health," Grant said in the preface to his memoirs, written on July 1, 1885. "I would have more hope of satisfying the expectation of the public if I could have allowed myself more time."

Grant saw the end coming in May 1885 while he was still at his New York home. "I said I had been adding to my book and to my coffin," he said in a note to his physician. "I presume every strain of the mind or body is one more nail in the coffin."

In July, death was only days away when Grant wrote another note: "I do not sleep though sometimes doze a little. If up I am talked to and in my efforts to answer cause pain. The fact is I think I am a verb instead of a personal pronoun. A verb is anything that signifies to be; to do; or to suffer. I signify all three."

Grant's life had been a series of highs and lows. He had sold cordwood in St. Louis, worked as a clerk in Galena, Ill., and faced accusations of being a drunkard. But he also had skillfully led great armies, helped restore the Union and served two terms as its president.

His administration had been rocked by political scandals and his business ventures left him virtually penniless, but he was again victorious — even in death — with the completion of his memoirs. Their publication not only immortalized him but also provided financial relief for his family.

The cottage was opened to the public in 1889 and had 10,000 to 15,000 visitors a year. As time passed, however, Mount McGregor's fortune changed: The Hotel Balmoral burned down in 1897, and in more recent years, with a medium-security prison and a sewage-treatment plant nearby, the cottage was being considered for use as state offices.

But the idea was dropped in 1986 when preservationists protested and the Saratoga County Historical Society agreed to take over operation of the cottage.

In 1987 — after years of live-in caretakers and relatively few visitors — the cottage had a curator for the first time.

"I think there is a renewed interest in Grant in the academic community, and we are seeing the number of visitors pick up," said Gombieski, the curator. "We get 30 to 40 a day on the weekends.

"The cottage is a place to contemplate the life and character of Ulysses S. Grant. You can easily imagine him here, enduring great pain as he composed his final thoughts."

Such thoughts are evident in one of Grant's last communications to his physician — on July 16, the day he completed his book, according to Gombieski. "I first wanted so many days to work on my book. ... There is nothing more I should do to it now, and therefore I am not likely to be more ready to go than at this moment."

•

The cottage is about 260 miles from the Philadelphia area. Take the New Jersey Turnpike to the Garden State Parkway, follow that north to Interstate 287 and take Interstate 87 to Saratoga Springs.

From Saratoga Springs, take Route 9 north to Ballard Road and follow that to Parkhurst Road, a bumpy two-lane thoroughfare leading to the cottage.

The cottage is open 10 a.m. to 4 p.m. Wednesday through Sunday from Memorial Day to Oct. 31. After Oct. 31, it is open by appointment. Admission is $2 for adults, $1.75 for senior citizens and $1 for children. For more information, check with the cottage (518-587-8277) or the Saratoga County Historical Society (518-885-4000).

•

Almost 200 years ago, people were coming to Saratoga Springs for their health, fleeing the hot cities and steamy South to enjoy the spring waters and cool mountain air.

Today, visitors still come but the list of attractions has grown considerably in this upstate New York area, five hours from Philadelphia.

During the busy summer season, thousands of people jam the Saratoga Performing Arts Center for performances of the Philadelphia Orchestra, the New York City Ballet and the New York City Opera. They also visit the Saratoga Thoroughbred Race Course, with its charming Victorian-style clubhouse, and Saratoga Raceway, a harness track.

These attractions, along with the nearby resorts and recreation at Lake Placid, Lake George and in the Berkshires, make Saratoga Springs a favorite summer retreat.

But the area has a lot to offer the rest of the year, too. And part of its lure is the preservation of its past. Much of the town, with its ornate structures and large homes, looks as it did more than 100 years ago.

The Canfield Casino, which was built in 1870, is now a museum providing a look back to the time when the town had a lavish gambling establishment and was considered "The Queen of Spas."

The building, in Congress Park, houses the Walworth Memorial Museum, replicas of 19th-century rooms using period furnishings, and the Historical Society Museum, a series of exhibits showing the development of Saratoga Springs from a frontier village into a flamboyant, nationally known resort. Admission is $2 for adults; $1.50 for students and senior citizens.

Other Victorian-era buildings remain in use. The Inn at Saratoga, which was established in 1880, has 40 rooms that have been attractively renovated to provide an English country-inn atmosphere. A portion of the inn's porch has been converted into a glass-enclosed lounge, and an adjacent dining room provides elegant surroundings.

Saratoga Springs also has several fountains, some within picturesque pavilions, and nearby Saratoga Spa State Park has mineral-water springs and bathhouses.

One spring led to the construction in 1792 of Brookside, a Georgian-style mansion and one of the nation's first resort-oriented hotels. Brookside now is a fascinating museum operated by the Saratoga County Historical Society, which has offices there.

The museum displays Victorian-era clothing and furniture and has a room furnished as it would be for a guest during the 1830s. A donation of $1 is requested for adults and 50 cents for children.

Today, the Saratoga Springs area boasts a large variety of accommodations in dozens of inns, motels and hotels, with prices to fit almost any budget. In most cases, rates are highest in August

At the Inn at Saratoga, the rate between Sept. 1 and June 30 ranges from $65 single per day to $150 double, for a suite.

The price at the Ramada Renaissance Hotel between September and Oct. 31 start at $65 for a single single to $75 for a double. Rooms at the stately Gideon Putnam Hotel at Saratoga Spa State Park vary from $75 for a single to $85 for a double from Sept. 1 to Oct. 31. Under the American plan, which includes three meals a day, the rate ranges from $109 for a single to $163 for a double during the same period.

The area has many restaurants — running the gamut from gourmet cuisine to fast food. One of the town's interesting dining experiences can be had at the Court Bistro, which offers an intimate atmosphere and fine food. Its chef, Rob Maranville, was the chef at Philadelphia's Frog for six years before moving to Saratoga Springs.

Tarrytown, N.Y.

The historical and legendary sites of the Hudson River Valley

By Terry Bivens
Inquirer Staff Writer

It's a perfect afternoon for a graveyard — gray and gloomy, with a touch of fog to lap at the headstones. We close our guidebook, turn the car off busy U.S. 9 and slowly enter the massive stone gates of Sleepy Hollow Cemetery.

Let's see now ... here's the old Dutch Reformed Church, its exterior dating to the 1600s ... here's a gravel road leading off to the right and ... ah, yes, here's the sign: Straight ahead.

In a few moments, we are there. We get out of the car and before us, enclosed by a rusted iron fence, is a family plot with about 30 graves. A tiny American flag marks one of them.

Here, under a towering oak, rests author Washington Irving, creator of that angular delight of American fiction, the bachelor Ichabod Crane, and chronicler of a region that fairly shimmers with history and lore.

For us, a trip to Irving's grave site proved to be the ideal beginning to a weekend in the Central Hudson River Valley. In these elegiac environs, hoary legends can grip you like a vise; squint into the fog long enough and you can almost see Irving's headless Prussian soldier rouse himself from the cold ground and gallop off into the mist, in search of the hapless Crane.

But there is plenty of solid history here as well, much of it equal to any author's imagination. Before Sunday evening called us back to Philadelphia, we would visit the Gothic mansion of a 19th-century robber baron, and stand on the spot where Revolutionary War patriots captured Maj. John Andre, the British accomplice of traitor Benedict Arnold.

We would also walk through the estate of a former president, Franklin Delano Roosevelt, and inspect the granite West Point dormitory that the young George S. Patton called home. And there would be no lack of the contemporary, either: Hard-pressed not to drool, we would examine the menus of the Culinary Institute of America, alma mater of some of the nation's finest and most creative chefs.

Through it all, weaving its way through our weekend itinerary like some majestic subplot, was the Hudson itself. Sometimes half-hidden, sometimes revealing itself unexpectedly in a spectacular view, the river captivates now as it did when explorer Henry Hudson, in his vessel the Half Moon, first rode its currents back in 1609.

•

Today the romantic central river valley has something for every season. In autumn its hardwood forests are a visual orgy for leaf watchers. Winter brings good skiing at several resorts off the New York Thruway. And in hot weather, resorts in the Shawangunk and Catskill Mountains offer relief from the simmering funk of the seaboard cities.

During the last decade, thanks in no small measure to its own efforts, the region has soared in popularity. "It's profited from several things," said Bern Rothman, a spokesman for the New York Department of Economic Development. "The river cleanup, lower gasoline prices, the 'I Love New York' campaign. There's no question that the valley is drawing more tourists."

There is plenty for them to explore. From the Hudson's headwaters, gateway to elegant Saratoga Springs and the beautiful Adirondacks, south to Woodstock (yes, Country Joe fans, it's still craftsy and Aquarian) to the Tarrytowns in suburban Westchester County, there are museums, historical landmarks, art galleries, concerts, antiques, wineries, nature walks and festivals celebrating everything from painting to pumpkins.

Indeed, your chief problem may be logistics: selecting a weekend itinerary that entertains without exhausting.

Fortunately much of the central river valley is easily accessible by car from Philadelphia. There are a couple of alternatives, but one approach is the New Jersey Turnpike, to its end, to U.S. 15 to the New York Thruway (Interstate 87). Figure on 3½ hours.

Did I mention money? There are excellent hotels and restaurants scattered throughout the valley — the Culinary Institute of America near Hyde Park, for example, regularly draws internationally known food critics. But if Manhattan is the hub of the universe, the Hudson River Valley is in close orbit. Expect New York prices.

A little homework will be helpful, too. There are several excellent guides to the Hudson River Valley, and some include historical and geographical facts that are worth knowing beforehand.

For example: Did you know that the Hudson River is actually below sea level at several points? It's true, and as a result saltwater tides often flow a long way up the river. The Mohican Indians, in fact, are the "people of the water that flows two ways."

Here's another: Zee, to the Dutch, meant "a widening." Hence the Tappan Zee Bridge, that three-mile span at the Hudson's widest point, northeast of the small town of Tappan, N.Y.

•

Our trip began at the eastern end of that bridge in the Tarrytowns, which include Tarrytown, increasingly the home of new money from Wall Street, and its less affluent neighbor, North Tarrytown. Along with Irvington to the south, these towns make up the legendary Sleepy Hollow country.

Despite the suburban sprawl, the cemetery somehow remains the spiritual center of things. Set on a hill, it boasts some magnificent mausoleums and headstones, many dating to the 1700s. Yes, the Washington Irving site is the draw — who could ever forget Ichabod's terrible fate in the Disney cartoon? But read some of the other inscriptions here; history rises strongly from this ground.

Nearby on U.S. 9 there also are the Washington Irving Memorial and, close to the Tappan Zee, Sunnyside, the author's home from 1835 to 1859. Restored by John D. Rockefeller Jr., the gabled house is a good example of Dutch architecture of the day and contains many of the curios that the author collected during his travels.

Where the Tarrytowns meet, there is Patriot Park. Legend has it that this is where the rebels caught the unlucky British Maj. Andre, whose ship, the Vulture, was hit by rebel fire while he conspired ashore with Arnold.

Stranded, Andre compounded his misfortune by revealing himself to men he took to be loyalists. To his dismay, they were, instead, patriots. And in addition to capturing Andre, they seized the vital defense plans Arnold had provided him.

The Tarrytown area also includes Philipsburg Manor and Lyndhurst. Philipsburg Manor was the home of Frederick Philipse, a carpenter for the Dutch West India Co. who constructed a fortune in the New World. It, too, is a Rockefeller restoration, complete with a grist mill powered by paddle wheel.

Lyndhurst is more modern. Built in 1838 for William Paulding, a hero in the War of 1812 and later mayor of New York, it is billed as one of America's finest Gothic revival mansions. No argument here. From an architectural standpoint, we found its Gothic arches and gargoyle-laden ceilings fascinating.

Even more interesting was one of its tenants, the multimillionaire Jay Gould. Gould, who bought Lyndhurst as a summer home in 1880, was a railroad baron who manipulated the stock market as a cat might play with mice — a kind of 19th-century Ivan Boesky. He is "credited" with engineering the Black Friday market crash of 1867 and was said to be worth $72 million when he died in 1892 of tuberculosis.

The mansion shows his wealth. His heirs lived at Lyndhurst until 1961, when it was passed to the National Trust for Historic Preservation. Lyndhurst now consists of 67 acres of cool green lawns, and the house itself is a treasure chest of Tiffany windows, 19th-century French art and antique furniture. Oh, yes. Out back, Gould had a spectacular view of the river.

•

Enough sightseeing for a day. We hopped back into the car and made for our weekend accommodations, the Mohonk Mountain House near New Paltz. From the Tarrytown area, it is about 90 minutes north up the thruway.

A warning now becomes necessary. The Mohonk can completely frustrate weekend plans to tour the valley. I mean that as a compliment: The Mohonk is *that* good.

It is a weekend unto itself. Perched atop the Shawangunk Mountains, the Mohonk is a 120-year-old inn that gained the status of a National Historic Landmark in 1986. Established by Quakers and still heavily Quaker in spirit, it rises like some medieval stone castle from the rock cliffs of a glacial lake.

The 7,500-acre hotel includes stables, a golf course, formal gardens and miles of nature trails, many of them dotted with wooden gazebos. The ice-green lake waters are good for swimming, fishing and canoeing in warm weather. In the winter, there's cross-country skiing.

The misty weather we encountered in Tarrytown followed us north, but the Mohonk turned it to our advantage: One of my favorite moments of the weekend came as we sat on one of the hotel's grand verandas, staring at the fog-covered lake.

Inside, our weekend's activities included a string quartet concert and, on Saturday night, a dance. But check before you make reservations: The Mohonk hosts many special weekend events, including one of the popular murder-mystery weekends. For a couple, its room rates run from $192 to $238 a night. Three meals daily are included in the rates.

On a drizzly Saturday, we tore ourselves away for an afternoon jaunt. The first stop was New Paltz, home to a branch of the State University of New York. New Paltz is every inch the college town, but there's some history here as well. Try Huguenot Street. Many of its homes were built during the late 1600s.

Across the river is Poughkeepsie, with Vassar College and Locust Grove, the home of Samuel F.B. Morse. We did not stop, however, because the meat of the day's trip lay ahead, up Route 9.

That would be Hyde Park, home of Franklin D. Roosevelt. Normally we are not paying voyeurs at presidents' homes — usually they aren't worth it. But Hyde Park was different.

Over the years, I'd come to think of our war president as fossilized in his familiar caricature — all imperious chin, pince-nez and cigarette holder. Hyde Park made him human.

The Roosevelt home, library and museum are at the end of an orchard-lined drive. The Roosevelts were, of course, rich. FDR's father was a railroad vice president and his mother doted on her only child. He attended Groton, Harvard — he was editor of the Crimson — and Columbia University Law School. In 1920, at the age of 38, he was nominated for vice president on the Democratic Party ticket. He and James M. Cox lost to the Republican ticket of Warren G. Harding and Calvin Coolidge.

The next year, Roosevelt was stricken with polio. Never again would he walk unassisted. Yet he went on to become governor of New York and, in 1932, president.

At Hyde Park, Roosevelt traded his hospital wheelchair for a simple, modified kitchen chair; he found it easier to maneuver. Stairs were impossible, so he pulled himself up to the second floor with ropes, in a special dumbwaiter.

I found FDR's 1936 Ford phaeton especially interesting. The royal blue convertible was engineered to allow Roosevelt to drive using only his hands; it also included a metal box, on the steering column, that dispensed lighted cigarettes. FDR loved to drive the car, and delighted in temporarily giving the Secret Service the slip. (For more information about the mansion, see the Hyde Park story in this book.)

Just south of Hyde Park is the Culinary Institute of America, the prestigious cooking school, which has an enrollment of 1,800. Its students move about like budding artists in the Louvre. As luck would have it, rain canceled an outdoor festival planned for that weekend. So we could only walk the halls and gaze, mouths a-water, at the menus.

On-the-spot reservations are out of the question. The school has four on-campus restaurants, and two of them, American Bounty and Escoffier, are booked three months in advance for Saturday lunch and dinner. If you're planning a gourmet weekend, arrange this stop before anything else.

The Hyde Park area also is home to the Vanderbilt Mansion, the opulent estate of Frederick Vanderbilt, grandson of Cornelius Vanderbilt and former president of the New York Central Railroad. FDR himself sometimes was a guest.

North of Hyde Park on U.S. 9 is Rhinebeck, known for its mushrooms, violets and the Beekman Arms Hotel, which opened in 1766 and bills itself as the oldest continuously operating hotel in America.

If you're really in a driving mood, farther up U.S. 9 lies Kinderhook, a beautiful, tree-lined Hudson Valley Dutch town. And east of there, almost to the Massachusetts border, lies the Shaker Museum, near New Lebanon crammed with the crafts and homely arts of the once-plentiful members of this religious sect.

On Sunday it poured. We had planned a full day at West Point, the 16,000-acre home of the United States Military Academy, but it was not to be.

What cadets we saw were in a glum mood. The previous day, their football team had lost to Holy Cross. In the steady downpour, they moved like wraiths in their gray capes and white hats with gold braid.

Given the weather, we decided to eschew the West Point Military Museum, Fort Putnam, the Cadet Chapel and the other buildings that are open to the public. We settled instead for our own auto tour. But we did not leave shortchanged.

We saw Michie Stadium, home of Army football and, I am told, one of the college game's most beautiful arenas when the fall leaves are ablaze. We also took in the parade ground, deserted then but nonetheless evocative of the long gray line.

The view I still remember, however, was of massive Eisenhower Hall. From our vantage point, directly behind the hall was the Hudson.

Even in the rain, it was stately to the very end.

Washington, D.C.

How to have a capital trip with a pair of teenagers in tow

By John Corr
Inquirer Staff Writer

They sprinted across the mall and raced up and down the steps of the Lincoln Memorial. They stood in line for the privilege of climbing the 859 steps to the top of the Washington Monument. They walked miles along museum corridors and they never got tired.

They were my two teenagers on a family outing in Washington, and they were determined to prove they could do a thousand things in a single weekend. And the nation's capital, its many treasures compactly arrayed, seemed just the place to do it.

I am here to report that, yes, it can be done.

Washington is just three hours away and, once there, you'll find many of the city's major attractions neatly arranged around the huge, rectangular National Mall. The gleaming dome of the Capitol is at one end of the mall, and the dramatic obelisk of the Washington Monument is at the other. In between are the major components of the great national treasure that is the Smithsonian Institution: the National Museum of American History, the National Museum of Natural History, the Hirshhorn Museum, the National Air and Space Museum, the National Gallery of Art, the Freer Gallery of Art, the National Museum of African Art and the Arthur M. Sackler Gallery.

If you are a hardy walker, you can park anywhere around the mall and see just about everything on foot. That should be enough, even for teenagers, in a single weekend. If, however, you are willing to wander a few blocks off the mall, you will find Ford's Theater, the National Museum of American Art and other attractions.

And it's all free.

The museums generally don't get crowded until after lunch time. Because the three of us (Helen, John and me) were getting an early start, we decided to head first for Washington's most popular museum, the National Air and Space Museum. This also was the museum where Helen and John most wanted to spend time, principally because it didn't feel like a museum.

Here you can see everything from the Wright brothers' aircraft and Lindbergh's Spirit of St. Louis to an Apollo lunar lander. Helen and John were most taken by the attractions associated with the space program, particularly the lunar lander.

After a strategy meeting beside the moon rock, we decided to head next to the Museum of American History.

Even though Air and Space will

probably be the first choice for most younger visitors, you can expect to spend more time visiting the Museums of American History and Natural History, simply because they are larger and there is so much more to see. After we had spent three hours in both places, Helen and John concluded that they had been fun to visit, despite the fact that they were "educational."

The exhibits on display in the Museum of American History include the "star-spangled banner" that inspired Francis Scott Key, inventions (such as Edison's light bulb) that changed the course of life in America, antique musical instruments, and material about the armed forces, printing, news reporting, photography and atomic energy.

The attractions that appeared to draw the most attention were the array of first ladies' gowns, the exhibit dealing with the M*A*S*H television show and such examples of Americana as Archie Bunker's armchair, Dorothy's ruby slippers from The Wizard of Oz and the original Kermit the Frog puppet.

The National Museum of Natural History takes quite awhile to get through, even with normally fast-moving teenagers. There are prehistoric creatures ("neat") and an insect zoo ("yuck"), fossils millions of years old, birds of the world, gems and minerals, and a maritime exhibit featuring a full-scale model of a blue whale.

Next, we decided to see the National Gallery of Art. The teenagers did not find the prospect thrilling, but once inside the gallery, they seemed to forget their earlier reluctance.

The gallery, in two adjoining buildings, has one of the world's finest collections of painting and sculpture from Western Europe dating from the 13th century. American art is represented from the colonial era to modern times. Also well represented are Rembrandt and Leonardo da Vinci.

On the mall's south side, you'll find the Smithsonian Institution building itself, a rust-colored castle-like structure that most people call, appropriately enough, the Castle.

But it is the modern art at the Hirshhorn Museum and the adjacent outdoor Sculpture Garden, also located on the south side of the mall, that seemed to hold the strongest fascination for teenagers. I watched quite a number of them walk round and round the large abstract sculptures in the garden, brows furrowed in speculation over the meaning of the forms.

The Hirshhorn concentrates on 19th- and 20th-century art and includes works by Alexander Calder, De Kooning, Eakins, Gorky, Matisse, Moore, Picasso and Rodin. The circular museum has three viewing floors, and it's a good idea to start at the top and work your way down.

Not far from the Hirshhorn is the Freer Gallery, which emphasizes art from the Near and Far East.

New to the mall since our visit are the subterranean Museum of African Art, which specializes in traditional sculpture, musical instruments and textiles, and the Sackler Gallery, dedicated to Asian art.

There are cafeterias in the American History, Natural History and Air and Space Museums. It's a good idea to break for lunch before 12:30 p.m., when the cafeterias become very busy. Even during the busiest periods, however, there generally is not a long wait. Prices are moderate. Teenagers can get all the cheeseburgers they can handle and parents can get a beer or a glass of wine, if you wish.

You might want to consider becoming an associate member of the Smithsonian Institution before making the trip. For $20, you get the Smithsonian's excellent magazine and qualify for admission to the members' dining room in the Museum of Natural History. It, too, is cafeteria-style, but the food is more interesting.

All the museums are open from 10

a.m. to 5:30 p.m., with the exception of the National Gallery, which closes at 5 p.m. During the summer, some of the museums stay open later.

If you're willing to walk four long blocks from the National Mall, you'll find the National Museum of American Art and the National Portrait Gallery, which share a building at Eighth and G Streets.

The Portrait Gallery is not exactly fascinating (even for adults) unless you are intensely interested in what famous Americans looked like. However, the American art collection is captivating (even for teenagers), with the greatest of our nation's painters generously represented.

The Greek revival building that houses the Portrait Gallery and the Museum of American Art is itself worth seeing. It was finished in the 1860s after being under construction for 30 years. It seemed to get increased attention from my teenagers when they learned that it was a Civil War hospital and the scene of Abraham Lincoln's Second Inaugural Ball. (Ford's Theater, where Lincoln was shot, is a short distance away on 10th Street.)

Attached to the National Portrait Gallery is a charming restaurant called Patent Pending. Prices are moderate and the service is relaxed.

You will want to see the dramatic and stirring Vietnam War Memorial. Helen and John were visibly impressed by the understated power of this memorial; they were uncharacteristically quiet.

If you are traveling with younger children, it is probably a good idea to tell them in advance that many of the people who come here are grieving, and this is no place for running, laughing or loud talk.

The beautiful Lincoln Memorial is nearby, and the sweeping view from Lincoln's lofty pedestal — a view that encompasses the reflecting pool, the Washington Monument and the Capitol — is worth climbing the steps to see.

And don't forget to visit the Capitol. The rotunda, with its massive paintings and statuary, is magnificent.

If, by some wild chance, all of this has not exhausted your teenage companions, there is always the National Zoo. Here, you can find a quiet place to rest while the teenagers explore. There are 2,500 animals living at the zoo. If you don't want to drive, you can take the Washington Metro and get off at the Woodley Park-Zoo station.

If overtaken by weariness during all this sightseeing, you can probably talk your teenagers into playing an interesting game that allows everybody to sit down and rest. I call it "What Americans are wearing today."

Take up a position near the entrance to one of the more popular museums and do a fashion inventory. Are boots more popular than shoes, caps more pervasive than hats, jeans more common than skirts?

Tourists in the nation's capital provide an endless source of material for the game. Teens like to play it because it involves clothes and fashion. Their parents like it because it requires no walking, a powerful recommendation during a busy weekend in Washington.

Washington, D.C.

After you've done the Smithsonian, sample the city's little museums

By Tom Belden
Inquirer Staff Writer

At first, I must admit, I was a little disappointed with the introduction I had planned for myself to the world of Washington's small treasures.

The Textile Museum, one of dozens of small, selective repositories tucked away on the side streets of Washington, has space to display only a fraction of its vast and wondrous collection. Yet I was so enthralled that I wanted to see it all, to spend hours looking at all manner of textiles and carpets.

But after wandering happily through only a half-dozen galleries, it was over.

Then Sarah, my wife, pointedly reminded me of exactly what the mission was.

We were exploring only little museums, places devoted to the intense, often eclectic, sometimes eccentric study of a single theme. Washington has an abundance of such spots, ranging from historic homes and buildings to shrinelike structures with storied pasts. And you should celebrate, not bemoan, the fact that no more than an hour is usually needed to get the full flavor of each.

The capital's smaller museums can be especially inviting once you have seen the sprawling arrays of the Smithsonian Institution. The major

Smithsonian museums are important and often delightful places. But they are so full of displays that you can spend a half-day or more in each.

On the other hand, during a two- or three-day weekend journey to Washington, you can easily explore three, four or even a dozen of the little museums, depending on your energy level and attention span.

Here is some guidance about what to see — based mostly on personal whimsy. It is presented in clusters that will enable visitors to see several museums in one trip to a particular part of town. Many of the museums can be reached by using the efficient and clean Metro subway.

•

On the grounds of the Washington Navy Yard, in the city's southeast quadrant, is the Navy Museum, a delightfully informative collection chronicling the history of the Navy.

It's a great place to take children because there are virtually no rules forbidding the touching of the dozens of ships' cannons, guns, bells, anchors and other memorabilia.

The artifacts, including innumerable photographs, excellent model ships and samples of Navy uniforms through the years, are spread throughout a barnlike 1887 building. A Corsair airplane hangs from the ceiling; mockups include the USS Constitution, an early submarine and a

Mercury space capsule, used by astronauts who also were Navy officers.

In front of the museum are Navy ships at anchor. One, the destroyer Barry, is open for tours.

The museum is open from 9 a.m. to 5 p.m. summer weekdays, 10 a.m. to 5 p.m. weekends, and closes at 4 p.m. weekdays after Labor Day. Admission is free.

The Navy Yard entrance is at Ninth and M Streets S.E. The nearest Metro stop is Eastern Market (Blue and Orange lines), about eight blocks away at Eighth Street and Pennsylvania Avenue, so driving or taking a cab is the best way to get there.

On the base, less than a block from the Navy Museum, is the Marine Corps Museum, in the Marine Corps Historical Center. The bulky 19th-century building, overlooking a parade ground, used to be a Marine barracks. Today, much of it is used as space for scholarly research. On the first floor is a chronological history of the Marine Corps. Art work by or about Marines also is on display throughout the center.

The museum is open from 10 a.m to 4 p.m. Monday through Saturday; from noon to 5 p.m. Sunday and holidays; and, on summer evenings, from 6 to 8 p.m. Wednesdays and 6 to 11 p.m. Fridays. Admission is free.

•

The Dupont Circle area and Massachusetts Avenue above the circle are probably the richest places in Washington for small museums, and are full of shops, restaurants and theaters. The area also has numerous embassies and is one of the city's loveliest residential neighborhoods. It is reached from the Dupont Circle stop on the Red Line.

At 2320 S St. N.W., about six blocks from Dupont Circle, is the Textile Museum, housed in two adjoining turn-of-the-century townhouses. The museum is a private endeavor founded in 1925 to house the collection of George Hewitt Myers. It is arguably one of the most important museums in the Western Hemisphere devoted exclusively to the collection, study and preservation of handmade textiles and carpets.

The wealthy Myers was most serious about his collecting, gathering over a half-century works from every major textile and carpet-weaving region. The museum is complemented by a textiles research library with open stacks, plus a gift shop that features the works of contemporary weavers and artisans.

The museum is open from 10 a.m. to 5 p.m. Tuesday through Saturday and from 1 to 5 p.m. Sunday. It is closed on holidays. Admission is a $2 contribution.

Almost next door is the Woodrow Wilson House. This is a National Historic Landmark, where the former President retired in 1921.

The red-brick Georgian Revival townhouse at 2340 S St. N.W. is run by the National Trust for Historic Preservation. Filled with Wilson's mementos and books, it serves as a small monument to upper-middle-class life in the 1920s. Wilson, who died in 1924, is the only president to stay in Washington after his term of office ended.

The house is open from March 1 to Dec. 31 from 10 a.m. to 4 p.m Tuesday through Sunday. It is also open from noon to 4 p.m. Saturday and Sunday in February. Admision is $3.50, $2 over age 65 and students. Children under 7 are admitted free.

A few blocks down Massachusetts Avenue toward Dupont Circle is Anderson House, a home for the nation's oldest patriotic organization. The Society of the Cincinnati was founded by American and French officers of the Continental Army. Membership is open only to the male first-born descendants of the founders.

Larz Anderson, a wealthy career diplomat and member of the Cincinnati, donated his sprawling Washington "great house," built in 1906, to the society when he died in 1937. The building's grand rooms, which give the place the look and feel of a small European palace, contain a museum of the American Revolution and works of art collected by Anderson in his travels.

Anderson House, 2118 Massachusetts Ave. N.W., is open from 1 to 4 p.m. Tuesday through Saturday and is closed on major holidays. Admission is free.

About three blocks from Anderson House and just south of Dupont Circle, at 1307 New Hampshire Ave. N.W., is the Christian Heurich Mansion, headquarters of the Columbia Historical Society, the city's chief historical organization. It houses a research library of more than 75,000 volumes.

The Heurich house was built between 1892 and 1894 in the Richardson Romanesque style as the home of a Washington brewing magnate. The furnishings of many of its 31 rooms, like those of the Anderson House, reflect the tastes and idiosyncrasies of the family that lived there. From personalized German Renaissance-style pieces to gilded French parlor sets, it's eclectic.

The mansion is open from noon to 4 p.m. Wednesday, Friday and Saturday. Admission is $2, $1 for senior citizens, and students enter free.

Not far from Dupont Circle is one of Washington's enduring treasure troves — the collection of the National Geographic Society, in Explorers Hall.

The hall, at 17th and M Streets N.W., certainly qualifies as a small museum, since it occupies only the first floor of the society's headquarters. But it is invariably fascinating because of its changing exhibits. Part of the fun in wandering around is knowing you can come back and find another article that just recently appeared in National Geographic brought to life.

A new feature is a collection of original drawings and paintings that have appeared in the Geographic over the last 25 years. Explorers Hall's permanent exhibits focus on man's physical development over 2½ million years, explorations sponsored by the Geographic Society to the two poles, the Indian cliff-dwellers of the Southwest, a massive Olmec head from the state of Tabasco,

Mexico, and an 11-foot-diameter globe. A visit to this place could easily take longer than an hour, including a rest for your weary feet for a few minutes in front of a television monitor, watching reruns of the society's TV shows.

Explorers Hall is open from 9 a.m. to 5 p.m. Monday through Saturday and holidays, and from 10 a.m. to 5 p.m. Sunday. Admission is free.

•

From the Dupont Circle Metro stop, it is easy to take a Red Line train toward Shady Grove, alighting at the Friendship Heights station and walking less than two blocks to what may be many people's favorite little museum — the Washington Dolls' House and Toy Museum.

This delightful institution is at 5236 44th St. N.W., on a street parallel to and east of Wisconsin Avenue, and is behind a Lord & Taylor department store. This area, too, is loaded with restaurants and shopping.

Just as George Hewitt Myers collected textiles, museum founder Flora Gill Jacobs has made a life's work of collecting antique dolls' houses, toys and games, most of them Victorian. She also is the author of *A History of Dolls' Houses*, the standard work on the subject.

The museum is full of such rare and wondrous miniature settings as a German tin tea party in which, when it is cranked, three ladies raise their teacups and a fourth plays the piano. Plus, there are a 1903 New Jersey seashore hotel, a row of Baltimore townhouses and a fantastic 1890 Mexican mansion complete with a car in the driveway and an open-cage outside elevator. And there's Teddy Roosevelt on safari.

The museum is open from 10 a.m. to 5 p.m. Tuesday through Saturday and from noon to 5 p.m. Sunday. Admission is $2 for adults and $1 for children under 14.

Heading back into the heart of Washington, it is worth a stop in Georgetown for Dumbarton Oaks, which played a key role in world history.

At R and 31st Streets N.W., the restored 1800 Federal-style house and museum is set on a 16-acre estate that includes 10 acres of dramatically beautiful formal gardens.

Although a handsome house, Dumbarton Oaks had no special role until it was acquired in 1920 by Mr. and Mrs. Robert Woods Bliss, both of whom were independently wealthy. They went about creating the house of today. Bliss gave the house to his alma mater, Harvard University, in 1940, but the couple continued to have an interest in it throughout their lives.

The Blisses created the gardens, where you can wander peacefully for an hour or more, and added a monumental music room in 1929. The music room, which has the feel of a Spanish baronial castle of the 18th century, has authentic pieces and reproductions. It was the setting in 1944 of the Dumbarton Oaks Conference, an international meeting that led to the founding of the United Nations.

In more recent years, two modern wings were added to the complex to house the Blisses' outstanding collections of Byzantine and Pre-Columbian art.

The gardens are open from 2 p.m. to 6 p.m. April to October, and from 2 p.m. to 5 p.m. November to March. Admission is $2 for adults, $1 for children and senior citizens. It is closed on holidays and Christmas Eve. Collections are open from 2 p.m. to 5 p.m. daily except Mondays. Admission is free.

Also on the Red Line, directly across F Street N.W. from the Judiciary Square stop, is another little-known yet dramatic building — the National Building Museum — that is being restored with a combination of private and federal money.

The museum, between Fourth and Fifth Streets on F Street, was built in 1885 as the Pension Building.

The Great Hall, an atrium in the center of the building, surrounded by floors where government workers once toiled, is monumental. It contains eight Corinthian columns, each 75 feet tall and 25 feet in circumference. The columns are the tallest in the Corinthian style ever built, made of brick and terra cotta and painted to resemble marble.

Off to one side is a series of interesting galleries, with a good bookstore, a permanent display on the history of the building itself and other changing exhibits.

The museum is open from 10 a.m. to 4 p.m., Monday through Friday, and from noon to 4 p.m. on weekends and holidays. Admission is free.

•

In the area around the White House, there are a couple of unusual museums that could easily take up a whole day. The Farragut West Metro stop is the closest to the two although both are at least several blocks away.

One is the Daughters of the American Revolution Headquarters and Museum at 1776 D St. N.W. (note that address). It does not exactly qualify as small, but it is unusual and somewhat off the beaten track.

Inside a structure that easily qualifies as monumental, a series of galleries display period pieces showing something of the history of the 13 original states. A number of the pieces date from the American Revolution, such as a tea chest from the Boston Tea Party.

The museum is open from 8:30 a.m. to 4 p.m. Monday through Friday, and from 1 p.m. to 5 p.m. Sunday. Admission is free.

The other is the Department of the Interior Museum. Located not far from the DAR building, and inside the headquarters of the agency, on C Street N.W. between 18th and 19th Streets, the museum contains artifacts from the variety of public lands, mostly in the West, that Interior administers. The American Indians are the biggest contributors here, but the national parks, the Bureau of Mines and the map-making Geological Survey also have a place.

The museum is open from 8 a.m. to 4 p.m. Monday through Friday. Admission is free.

Wittenberg Mountain, N.Y.

A breathtaking view makes a rugged hike worthwhile

By Andrew Wallace
Inquirer Staff Writer

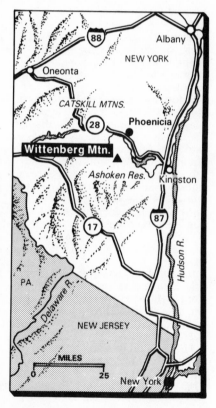

Littered with leaves, studded with rocks and crisscrossed by roots and occasional fallen trees, the path up Wittenberg Mountain, a 3,780-foot peak in the Catskills in southeastern New York, was as rugged and charming a mountain path as you could wish for a fall hike.

From the campground nestled between Woodland Creek and Woodland Valley Road, it was a mere 3.4 miles to the top of the mountain, a distance that should have been a snap for my friend and myself, a pair of sometime runners.

Well, it wasn't. And it left us with a healthy respect for the guidebook notation "strenuous," a word that we had simply skipped over like a dead leaf as we prepared this overnight hike in October. In this book, *Guide to the Catskills*, published by Walking News Inc. (Box 352, New York, N.Y. 10013, $8.95), the word means what it says.

It was worth it. The result was spectacular. After scampering upward for about five hours over two days, we arrived at the summit to be greeted with a breathtaking panorama. Far below, the valley dotted with smaller peaks stretched east toward

141

the Hudson River. A large lake — Ashoken Reservoir — nestled around the foot of the mountain.

At any rate, whether it's an overnight backpacking trip or a day hike, Wittenberg is a spot worth including on a list of weekend back-to-nature getaways — a list that might also include the Highlands of West Virginia, the Shenandoah National Park in Virginia, or the Appalachians of Pennsylvania.

We have barely begun exploring the Catskills. When we set out, we had intended to visit the top of Wittenberg, head for the Cornell peak (3,860 feet) and then the Slide, the highest mountain in the Catskills at 4,180 feet. A couple of factors — a late start and the lack of water — kept us from completing that expedition.

But it was enough. We saved the views from Cornell and Slide for next time.

Before we started up the mountain, we went to our guidebook to find out the origin of the name Catskills. We got no satisfaction. The book relates that the derivation "has proven a conundrum." The end of the word, kill, is the Dutch for small stream. But what about the Cats? The Dutch word for cat is kat, but the plural is katte or katten, not cats. "If Wildcats had been seen on the banks of the Kill it would have been Wildes Katten Kill or Wilde Kat Kill," the book says.

It then makes one other suggestion and drops the subject: Perhaps Henry Hudson, who first explored the area for the Dutch, named it for Jacob Cats, the Dutch national poet (1577 to 1660).

There's a bit of a problem with the other part of the name — mountains. The Catskills are not true mountains. That is, they were not formed by forces pushing the earth's crust up from below. They began a couple of hundred million years ago as the bottom of a shallow inland sea. The sea bottom, covered with material washed out of higher mountains in what is now New England, rose higher and higher.

The floor continued to rise until it formed a plateau about 5,000 feet above sea level and the water drained away. Time and the weather etched valleys, cliffs and ravines into it, leaving the peaks now known as the Catskills. Later, glaciers bulldozed their way through the mountains, wearing them away and softening the edges and leaving the high rounded hills.

In colonial times, the Catskills were the scene of fighting between the French and Dutch and English and Indians for control of the land and the fur trade. By the 1800s, industry was thriving. Roads were built and a variety of industries were started — shipbuilding, brickmaking and ice harvesting were some. Farmers produced tobacco, hops, maple syrup, honey and wool. Catskill creeks provided power for grist mills, sawmills, paper mills and tanneries.

The industry that changed the face of the mountains was tanning. The Catskills were covered with forests of hemlock when the Dutch settlers arrived there in the 17th century, and the bark of the hemlock contained tannin. As the tanning industry grew after the 1840s, the trees disappeared. When the hemlocks were gone, the tanning industry followed. Now most of the trees that cover the hills are hardwoods, although a few hemlocks remain in isolated areas.

Later, naturalists, poets and painters romanticized the region. The Catskills became a tourist mecca where New Yorkers could go to commune with nature. Railroads brought the crowds to great hotels that sprawled across the hills. There the wealthy and the famous came to enjoy the mountains, the ravines and the waterfalls and to breathe fresh air.

But changes in travel habits came again. The grand hotels burned down or were abandoned. The railroads went bankrupt and disappeared. The Catskills became what they are today — a playground for New York, which is about 90 miles to the southeast, northern New Jersey and Pennsylvania.

It also is a playground for Philadelphia-area hikers who don't mind driving 200 miles to hike seven more. When we packed, hopped in the car and headed for the mountains, we found that getting there wasn't so bad. We followed the New Jersey Turnpike to the Garden State Parkway, took that north to Interstate 87 and headed north again until we reached Route 28 in Kingston. It took 4½ hours.

We selected the Wittenberg area on the advice of a hiker at Base Camp, 1730 Chestnut St. in Center City, who pointed out the Wittenberg and Slide Mountains on a map when he sold us the guide to the Catskills. It was, he said, perhaps the most scenic spot in the mountains. But he cautioned that it was a popular area, too, and could be crowded.

We could easily find more isolated spots, he said. Indeed, there were plenty of trails that would not be as heavily traveled. We could, for example, have followed the Mine Hollow, Mink Hollow, Diamond Notch, Devil's Path, Touch-Me-Not, Colonel's Chair, Jimmy Dolen Notch or a score of other trails with equally colorful names. The guide not only describes each trail in some detail, it contains an overall map of the Catskills and small individual maps of the various regions.

The allure of the Catskills was evident soon after we left I-87 and drove west along Route 28 through hills bright with fall colors. Along the way, we stopped at a roadside stand and picked a couple of pounds of apples from gigantic crates brimming over with a dozen varieties. Earlier, along I-87, we had caught a glimpse of apple pickers perched in the treetops. They stood on ladders whose rails were wider at the bottom than the top to provide better stability as they swayed in the branches.

Our final stop before Wittenberg was Phoenicia, a bustling village catering mostly to summer vacationers and tourists, cradled in the mountains beside Route 28. There, we picked up some groceries and flashlight batteries and, following our guidebook, headed for Woodland Valley Road and the start of the Wittenberg-Cornell-Slide trail about four miles away.

Although the guidebook doesn't say so, the trail is easy to find. It begins at a campground run by the state of New York where, for $6 or so, we could have pitched our tent in a sheltered wooded spot, convenient to water and toilets.

But we didn't. Though it was 4 p.m., only 2½ hours until dark, we strapped on our packs, bounced across the springy footbridge that spans rock-strewn Woodland Creek and began the climb to the summit.

Although the path is steep, the climb is pleasant. The light filtered through leaves of green and yellow, orange and red, as we began a steady trek up the moutainside, following the path over rocks and roots and fallen trees. Occasionally, we got a teasing glimpse of the nearby mountains or a bit of blue sky. Occasionally, massive slabs of gray rock were piled against the hill like monumental sculptures.

After walking steadily for nearly two hours, we suddenly realized that the sun had long since disappeared and the light was fading fast. Unfortunately, we found ourselves at one of Wittenberg's less hospitable spots.

Rocks were everywhere and we could find no flat ledge. Although the tent was one of those modern jobs that goes up without much effort, we didn't want to do it in the dark. We quickly chose the best of the bad spots and put up the tent.

By the time we got the stove going to heat up the beans and the water for coffee, an icy wind was sweeping down the mountain. We ate quickly, keeping our hands warm on our plates. Cleaning up the dishes afterward was a finger-numbing chore.

With the chill on the mountains and nothing but a flashlight to hold back the night, we crawled into our sleeping bags to wait for the dawn.

We had chosen the location well. Except for a knobby root that we hacked out with a penknife, the site was actually comfortable. And luckily so. Nights in tents are very long.

Figuring we had a short distance to go to the summit, we got a late start the next morning. We were fooled. It took about 3½ more hours up a path that got steeper all the time. Several lookouts — one of them an idyllic spot on a ledge spongy with fallen needles and sheltered by evergreens — gave us views of the Esopus Valley and adjacent hills.

Except for the chipmunks that rattled occasionally through the dry leaves, there was little wildlife — with one notable exception. A raccoon, apparently accustomed to the hikers who invade its territory, meandered down the trail, and a couple ahead of us froze in their tracks. As the man tried to get the bold animal in focus through his camera, his companion put her finger on her lips to hush us.

She needn't have bothered. The raccoon didn't care if they stood in its path or took its picture. It sauntered along the trail, poking under leaves and sticking its head into a hollow log in search of raccoon goodies. It brushed past us and strolled into the woods, taking no notice of us at all.

(By the way, the path was surprisingly neat. We found only one or two small scraps of paper on our way up Wittenberg.)

The trail, clearly defined by markers tacked onto tree trunks, got more exciting as we neared the top. Sometimes we had to scramble up rock piles on hands and knees or clamber over rock ledges three or four feet high. Sometimes our backpacks got in the way, but we managed. It was like finding a playground for adults on the side of the mountain.

Just after scampering up a steep, rocky slope, I took my first — and I hope my last — fall wearing a backpack. All it took was a second's carelessness. I had paused to take a picture. When I put the camera away and moved quickly to catch up with my friend, who was about to disappear around a rockpile, I tripped over a rock jutting up in the path and fell.

I bruised both knees and got a nasty scrape on one arm, and the shock left me a lot more cautious and slower than I had been. Except for a sore knee that made the descent a little painful, I did no serious damage. But the fall increased my respect for this mountain where, I had begun to suspect, the miles were measured by someone wearing seven-league boots.

But then, at about 2:30, with the sun shining from a hazy sky, we emerged through a forest of shrubs onto the flat top of Wittenberg. There a rocky ledge forms bleachers, where you can sit and cheer the view — and your own efforts at having climbed so far.

When we arrived, we had plenty of company there. The group of teenage boys and girls who had scampered past us as we lurched over the rocks below were there sunning themselves, trading school gossip and eating sandwiches their leader had packed. A European couple in their 60s or more and dressed in Alpine walking togs were resting on the rocks too. Several other couples sat quietly and meditated on the distance.

After basking in the sunshine and enjoying the view for about a half-hour, we had to decide whether to press on to Slide Mountain, which was named for the avalanche scars that mark its side. We wanted to press on and we would have, had we been sure of finding water at the spring near the summit of Slide, a little more than 2½ miles away. But we were not at all sure about that, and we hadn't carried enough water to spend another night and day on the mountain.

We headed back down.

It took a full three hours. We arrived at the Woodland Creek as the path and the trail markers began to grow indistinct in the dusk.

We'll get to Slide next time.

But we don't have to wait until the spring to enjoy the Catskills. The guidebook we used also contains information about skiing, cross-country skiing, snow-mobiling and snow-shoeing. Maybe we'll try that.

A skier sets out on a trail from the Woodstock Inn's Ski Touring Center. Some of the best downhill skiing in the East is also nearby.

Charlottesville, Va.

Jefferson's vision of Monticello is preserved with devotion to detail

By Mike Shoup
Inquirer Travel Editor

Somehow, the pictures I had seen of Monticello since my childhood days had led me to expect something more palatial. But here it was before me, Thomas Jefferson's home, and I was struck not just by its familiar and distinctive architecture, but also by its size: small.

Had it been the pictures in my early history books or the stirrings of my own imagination that caused me to expect something of more substantial proportions? Probably the latter. Both Jefferson and his home are at the core of American history. If his home looms larger than life, well, so did the man.

Jefferson applied himself no less diligently to Monticello than he did to drafting the Declaration of Independence. The home was his creation and his alone, from start to finish of 40 years of construction.

The marvel is that today, Monticello stands pretty much as it was in 1809, when Jefferson finally finished building and enlarging it. Ninety percent of the furnishings are original, also, and more's the marvel for that.

While a visit to Monticello is a walk on historically hallowed ground, it is not without its 20th-century intrusions. Expect crowds if you pick a weekend day in peak tourist season. After you purchase your entrance ticket, you'll be swept up the hill in an 18-passenger Mercedes shuttle bus, and whisked through the home in short order (my tour lasted little more than five minutes). When I confided quietly and in a good-natured way to our college-age tour guide that she was speaking so fast that nobody could understand her, she said with a hint of desperation in her voice, "I try to get it all in; there's so much to tell."

The tours are longer on weekdays, or in off-season when tourists are fewer, and a visit to Monticello might be more pleasant at those times. If that's not possible, unless you're a Jefferson scholar it will help to do some reading about the house ahead of time.

There is nothing static about Monticello and its grounds and gardens. Experts continue to study Jefferson's writings and pore over archaeological and historical evidence in an ongoing attempt to come as close as possible to making Monticello exactly as it was in its owner's day. Most of the work in the last few years has been outside on the grounds, although recent changes in the home itself include restoration of the third-floor Dome Room, and changing the columns on the East Portico from white back to the sandy rust color they were in Jefferson's time.

"The commitment to authenticity is ongoing," says Daniel P. Jordan, director of the Thomas Jefferson Memorial Foundation, which runs Monticello. "The tourist comes and sees a snapshot, but there's a professional staff working every day to enable us to present Monticello to the public in a better way."

Books and academic treatises by the dozen have been written about Monticello and its many unusual features, starting with the location. Jefferson inherited the land from his father, building atop a mountain in a day when his contemporaries were locating their plantations along river banks.

Long a student of architecture, he drew heavily on the works of European architects, particularly the 16th-century Italian genius Andrea Palladio, whose works influence American architecture to this day. Yet what Jefferson created has its own peculiar, almost mystical qualities that sweep the scale from the columned porticoes, dome, skylights and octagonal rooms and bays down to everyday interior features that border on gadgetry.

Here was a genius who could get around obstacles and perhaps laugh a bit at himself in the process. Witness the seven-day calendar clock above the door in the entrance hall when you begin your tour. Thought to be made to Jefferson's design by a Philadelphian, Peter Sprunk, it is run by weights that move almost imperceptibly down the wall and, as the week progresses, also indicate the day by their position on the wall. When it developed that there was no room for Friday afternoon and Saturday, Jefferson simply had a hole cut in the floor and the weights dropped into the basement.

As your first-floor tour progresses, you'll see other contrivances that indicate Jefferson's preoccupation with the mechanical: dumbwaiters, revolving serving doors in the dining room, and single-acting double doors in the parlor (if you pull one, both close).

Unfortunately, the upstairs of Monticello is not open to visitors; the staircases are only 24 inches wide, far too narrow to satisfy today's fire codes. But there is plenty on the first floor to absorb during the tour, especially for those who have familiarized themselves with what to look for.

In the study opposite his bedroom are the revolving chair and revolving table top where Jefferson wrote much of his correspondence. One of his telescopes stands in a south window, and next to a door is a theodolite, one of his surveying instruments. Adjacent is his library, where he kept 6,000 volumes; the books were sold to the federal government and became the nucleus for the Library of Congress. The volumes there today are duplicates.

Nearby is his bedroom, which, like the parlor and dining room, has a higher ceiling and a skylight (there are 14 skylights in the house). Jefferson died here, in this alcove bed, on July 4, 1826, the 50th anniversary of the Declaration of Independence. He was 83.

On your way out to the north terrace, you'll note many other features as you pass through the parlor and dining room and what's called the north octagonal room; the aforementioned mechanical dumbwaiters are on either side of the mantel in the dining room.

While the house tour was brief, the grounds tour was a fascinating 45 minutes of meandering with our guide Frederica Bacher, who wore a wide-brim straw hat to ward off the summer sun and kept a thick volume of Thomas Jefferson's garden book crooked in her left arm.

She reminded us that Jefferson thought of his estate as an "ornamental farm," where he would grow staples like tobacco, corn and wheat while at the same time experimenting in both vegetable and flower gardening and in naturalistic landscaping.

It has taken many years and a lot of

study and archaeological sleuthing, but it seems safe to say that the grounds again reflect Jefferson's vision of Monticello as an agricultural showplace. His 1,000-foot-long terraced vegetable plot is producing the same varieties of herbs, squash, beans and peas (Jefferson's favorite) that it grew 200 years ago — a small percentage of the 250 varieties of vegetables and 150 varieties of fruit that sprouted here.

Mulberry Row, the plantation road that was lined with mulberry trees, has been re-created, as have the orchard and vineyard and grove of shade trees — even Jefferson's "garden temple," a small pavilion midway along the stone-walled terrace, where he sometimes sat and read.

Jefferson is buried here, down the hill from the gardens, in a family plot bordered by an 8-foot-high iron fence that remains the private property of his descendants. You can walk right by it on your way down the hill, and perhaps pause briefly to ponder this great man's legacy — if you decide not to take the Mercedes shuttle bus, that is.

Monticello is open year-round. From March 1 to October 31, the hours are 8 a.m. to 5 p.m., with tours starting every five minutes. From Nov. 1 to March 31, it is open 9 a.m. to 4:30 p.m. Admission is $6 for adults, $4 for senior citizens and $1 for children ages 6 to 11.

Cherry Mills, Pa.

A cold day of snowmobiling yields some warm memories

By Mike Shoup
Inquirer Travel Editor

From the window of Bob and Polly Webster's kitchen, I could see the morning sun just beginning to bathe the stark outline of a tree along the snow-covered ridge.

I had stood there since shortly after dawn, huddled by the century-old cast-iron Seneca Oak stove, chatting with Bob Webster as he fired up the kitchen's two coal stoves and the two wood stoves in the big dining and living rooms of the Cherry Mills Lodge.

I'd brought my teenage children, Rachael and Tim, here for a weekend of snowmobiling in Sullivan County, but they were still asleep upstairs, and neither Webster nor I was in any rush to head outside and start the Arctic Cats snowmobiles. A thermometer on a front-porch post outside the kitchen showed 25 below zero.

"Minnesota weather," I said to Webster.

"Ah, it's not that bad; we've seen 50 below up here," he said.

I knew precisely what my son's first question would be when he finally worked up the courage to emerge from beneath the quilts and blankets in the chilly upstairs and come down for breakfast. And I knew just as precisely what my answer would be.

His shoulders were hunched, and his hands were in his jeans pockets when he joined me beside the kitchen stove. "Hi, Dad," he said. "I'm freezing. When are we going snowmobiling?"

"When it warms up," I said, pointing him in the direction of the thermometer. "It's got to be at least zero."

Soon Polly was in the kitchen, preparing a breakfast of potato cakes, bacon and eggs, helped by Webster's daughter, Tracey Jordan, who had come in from her home nearby. Rachael arrived, not at all eager for anything other than a spot beside the stove. We were the only guests at breakfast, which is served family-style, like all the lodge meals. One family that arrived late at night had already headed for cross-country skiing at nearby World's End State Park. Two other couples were arriving later in the day.

By 10 a.m., Tim had a pleading look in his eyes, and Webster checked the thermometer. It was up to 10 below zero.

"We've got a heat wave going," he announced cheerfully, and we began to bundle up with sweaters and coats over layers of long underwear and street clothes. We donned heavy gloves, ski masks and boots.

It was cold outside, the snow crunching underfoot like cornflakes, the snowmobiles unwilling to start. Webster attached his wife's hair dryer to a long extension cord, and we set about lifting the engine covers to warm the fuel lines. First, one sputtered to life, then another, then the third. While we did this, Webster explained how the machines worked and how to operate them safely.

We listened. Although Webster did not say so, I knew from literature provided by the state Department of Environmental Resources that frostbite was not the only danger. Thirty-nine men and women had been killed in snowmobile accidents over the previous seven seasons in Pennsylvania.

Webster's Arctic Cats were small models, capable of doing 30 or 40 miles an hour, quite sufficient to kill yourself if you bounce off the trail and hit a tree or meet another snowmobile or a four-wheel-drive vehicle at a sharp bend in the trail.

Tim unhappily doubled up with Webster for the trip up to the top of the ridge, Rachael took the middle on her own snowmobile and I trailed behind. It was bitter, bitter cold despite the windshield on the snowmobile and the face shield on my helmet. The wind whipped around the windshield and bit into my hands, which were numb in no time at all.

At the top, we paused, and Rachael now doubled up with Webster and gave her machine over to Tim. Broad smiles shone through their ski masks. Tim hopped up and down a few times, fists clenched tightly. "This is great," he said. "Great. Great."

And it was exhilarating, feeling the engine surge beneath your body, like sitting astride a motorcycle and getting that sudden push of power when you twist the throttle. We were off, then, onto a smaller trail and whipping across an open field with the powdery fresh snow swirling in clouds behind the snowmobiles.

The sun was bright, the sky a perfectly cloudless cerulean, backdropping skeletal hardwoods and snow-draped evergreens along the mountaintop.

We entered the forest again and began our descent, slowly, on a steep and winding trail overhung by spruce and pine boughs heavy with snow. It was tight and touchy, and the machines slewed on the fresh trail as the valley unfurled its wintry sights far below.

Then we were back in the lodge. My hands were bluish when I removed the ski gloves. "Can you and I go out now?" asked Tim, and we did, after a bit of warming. With a warning from Webster to take care, we coursed up the mountain again, pushing the machines harder and feeling them respond to full squeezes of the throttle.

We found another open field laced with snowmobile tracks and ripped across it with wide-open throttles and then paused beside each other at the other side and laughed together, father and son — one of those moments you know you'll recall when the trout are again hitting mayflies in the Little Loyalsock Creek that runs by the lodge.

We were out again for an hour in the late afternoon, but the rest of the time was spent inside the lodge, enjoying its cozy warmth and that of its owners. The inn was once home for a family that ran a sawmill nearby; it later was a rural hotel and then a hunting lodge.

We were joined at dinner Saturday night by Dick and Barbara Brutchey of Maple Shade, N.J., and Dick's younger brother, Bill, and his wife, Denice, acquaintances of the Websters and just as warm and friendly.

The evening featured hunting talk, Scrabble and a rummy board game, and my son and I matched skills at darts on a board beside Bob Webster's collection of rifles and shotguns. I retired early, leaving Tim curled up in an easy chair beside one of the wood stoves, with David Wallechinsky's *The Book of Lists,* and finding Rachael already in bed with her own book. We talked some, about the raptures and frustrations that can visit one in life, then kissed goodnight.

We slept well and arose to a Bob Webster heat wave: The temperature was 20 below.

•

Cherry Mills Lodge, which is now run by Tracey and Pat Jordan, is open year-round. Rates are $55 single and $100 double, on the Modified American Plan, which includes breakfast and dinner. Rates with only a continental breakfast are $35 single and $60 double.

The lodge, a four-hour drive from Center City Philadelphia, is on Route 87, three miles south of Route 220, near Dushore. For more information, write Cherry Mills Lodge, R.D. 1, Dushore, Pa. 18614, or call 717-928-8978.

The lodge does not rent snowmobiles, but visitors are welcome to bring their own. For more information about snowmobiling in Pennsylvania, write to the Snowmobile Unit, Department of Environmental Resources, Box 1467, Harrisburg, Pa. 17120. Or call 717-783-1364. Ask for the current Snowmobile Directory and maps of the snowmobile trails in the area to which you will be traveling.

Chestertown, Md.

This little town is perfect — but don't tell a soul

By Susan Q. Stranahan
Inquirer Staff Writer

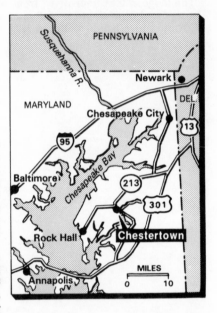

The best way to describe Chestertown, Md., is not to describe it at all. At least that was the consensus of some friends who, after hearing my descriptions of a wonderful weekend visit there, urged me to keep quiet so the delights of this jewel-like town would just be "our little secret" to share.

That's like keeping the name of an intimate restaurant or a charming inn that caters to every whim of its guests under wraps. (By the way, Chestertown has both.) It's like hiding the existence of an enclave of beautifully preserved and restored — or in the process of being restored — examples of colonial and Victorian architecture. (That's Chestertown in a nutshell.) And it's like trusting that nobody will reveal an abundance of diverse, and decidedly un-Philadelphia-type, activities. (Again, that's Chestertown.)

Although it is located about two hours from Philadelphia, on Maryland's upper Eastern Shore, Chestertown might just as well be two days distant.

Things are that different. The subtle flavor of Tidewater gentility is everywhere. So is a delightful mix of the contentment and zest that comes from living amid the natural bounty and beauty of the Chesapeake. Pervading it all is a heritage that traces its roots to the 17th and 18th centuries.

Scattered throughout Chestertown and the surrounding countryside are constant reminders that some things haven't changed much since Lord Baltimore ordered the establishment of a town to serve as a tax collection center in the 1660s. Although that project was delayed a bit — the town was established in 1706 and laid out between 1707 and 1730 — this is old history here. But it's living history. Sunday services are still held in St. Paul's Episcopal Church, built in 1713. (The churchyard, with its box-

152

wood hedges, massive oaks, quiet millpond and moss-covered gravestones, exudes tranquillity.) Maryland's oldest courthouse, built in 1792 in Centreville, is still the seat of Queen Anne's County.

A walk down any number of Chestertown's narrow streets will reveal homes that look exactly as they did when the community served as one of colonial America's foremost trading ports. (Local history buffs proudly note that Chestertown — or Chester Town, as it was known then — had its own revolutionary Tea Party a year and a half before those upstarts in Boston seized on the same idea.) The town was located on the major land route between Virginia and Philadelphia. It's not surprising that George Washington really did sleep there while commuting.

But a fondness for history isn't the only reason to visit Chestertown. A weekend visitor could find more than enough to occupy a couple of days and never even look at a remarkable example of Flemish bond brickwork or an Ionic column. This is, after all, bay country, and that means lots of wonderful things to do and eat, regardless of the time of year. If a weekend of that sounds appealing, Chestertown is the perfect spot.

We had heard intriguing reports about one of Chestertown's newest and most ambitious restoration projects and decided to make the Imperial Hotel our base of operations. The hotel, built in 1902 on Chestertown's main street, had recently been acquired by George and Jane Dean, transplanted Alabamians, who decided to return it to its original Victorian style. It's doubtful the Imperial ever looked as good, or any guest was treated as royally.

The Deans enlisted the assistance of the Victorian Society of America and drew on the talents of Eastern Shore craftspeople to turn an undistinguished hostelry into a jewel. Each room is unique, filled with a dazzling collection of furniture and fixtures, fabrics and prints. But underneath the flowers and chintz, the brass chandeliers and Oriental runners is a modern hotel, with creature comforts a top priority. (In each closet is a thick terry-cloth robe and a large umbrella resplendent with the Imperial Hotel logo. Out of sight, hidden atop the Imperial, is an enormous new heating and air-conditioning system the Deans installed to ensure every guest a pleasant night's sleep even on the hottest or coldest evenings.)

The staff is exceedingly congenial and full of information about the town and the surrounding countryside. They know lots of good places to explore on foot, or by bicycle or car.

Meals at the Imperial are alone worth the trip. The menu draws heavily on the bounty of the bay and, in season, its prosperous produce farms. If you think an Eastern Shore dinner consists only of crabs sizzling with Old Bay Seasoning, washed down with icy beers, think again. The Imperial's dining room is small and elegant, and its offerings in keeping with the ambiance. (For those in quest of a tray full of steamed crabs, however, there are some fine options nearby; just ask for a recommendation.)

There are about a dozen rooms in the hotel, and the room rate (for doubles as well as singles) is $95 a night. In addition, a carriage house (an exact replica of one that had fallen into disrepair) is located behind the hotel, complete with kitchen and living room. There also is a large suite on the top floor of the hotel with kitchen and living room plus a private porch from which one can catch a glimpse of the broad Chester River.

(One amenity available at the Imperial is a dog kennel. Although dogs aren't welcome in the hotel itself, the Deans have provided furry guests with indoor kennel space.)

Those who would like to spend their weekend in surroundings of a different architectural period might choose to check in at the White Swan Tavern, just up High Street from the

Imperial Hotel. (Rooms range from $75 to $100 a night.) Built in 1733, the tavern was beautifully restored in 1978. Guests may find themselves sleeping in the John Lovegrove kitchen, its huge fireplace a welcome asset on a blustery winter day. Even if you don't stay at the White Swan, take a peek at its lobby and fascinating exhibit of artifacts excavated during the renovations.

Although it would be quite possible to spend a weekend doing absolutely nothing taxing in Chestertown, it's also quite possible to find the sun setting Sunday before you have gotten halfway through your activities list. (Maybe that's the measure of a delightful weekend journey.)

We arrived in Chestertown in time for lunch and then set out on a walking tour of the historic section with the affable and knowledgeable George Dean as our guide. At the foot of High Street is the scenic Chester River. It was here that ships docked to trade and taxes were collected in a solid brick customs house.

The riverfront homes of Federal and Georgian architecture are as elegant and beautiful as they were 200 years ago. Glimpses of their formal gardens and antique furnishings through glistening paned windows whet the appetite to see more. Their austerity is pleasantly offset by Victorian homes scattered along the same streets. Many of Chestertown's homes are opened for a candlelight tour conducted on the third Saturday in September. (Check with the Kent County Historical Society in Chestertown for details.)

In spring, summer and fall, Chestertown also is a popular stop for boaters who venture 20 miles upstream from the Chesapeake to explore. Huge old riverfront estates have been carefully preserved, making the cruise to Chestertown a voyage back in time.

Chestertown's proximity to vast expanses of water provides another asset: an abundance of migratory birds that take up winter residence on the bay and its tributaries. Their numbers and the integral part these seasonal visitors play in life on the bay is evident from the names of nearby estates: Featherduster Farm and Hunter's Haven. From late October until early March, the quiet inlets and creeks of the Chester River and the Chesapeake are filled with thousands of magnificent swans, Canada geese and other waterfowl. The Eastern Neck Island National Wildlife Refuge at the mouth of the river is a short drive — or a semi-ambitious bicycle trip over gentle countryside — from Chestertown. Remington (the folks who make the ammunition) Farms is on the way, and well worth a stop if you're in a car (human contact with wildlife is not permitted). The company has established a 3,000-acre wildlife management demonstration area, and its comprehensive self-guided tour offers an interesting introduction to the flora and fauna of Eastern Shore. The farm is open from February 1 to October 31, during the day.

Regardless of your destination, be sure to take binoculars. Even if you've never been a birdwatcher before, the number and beauty of the birds, and the scenic surroundings, are enough to inspire lifetime memberships in the National Audubon Society, Ducks Unlimited and the National Wildlife Federation.

Summers mean fewer birds, but that's certainly not the only thing the bay can offer. The swimming in this part of the Chesapeake is excellent, and a welcome relief from the sometimes oppressive summer heat. Those who would like to see the bay from the water have their choice of boats (a rental stand for rowboats is situated just outside the entrance to Eastern Neck Island refuge); sailboats can be chartered in nearby Rock Hall, which has a number of marinas. There are picnic sites and an abundance of places where you can try your hand at the relatively simple task of catching your own blue crabs. A piece of string, a chicken neck and patience are about all you need.

Corning, N.Y.

Walking a street that changed yet stayed the same

By Mike Shoup
Inquirer Travel Editor

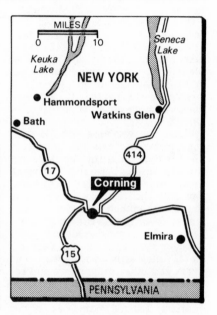

Up to half a million tourists from across America and abroad pour into this company town in rural south-central New York state each year to see the justifiably renowned Corning Museum of Glass. And before dusk falls they are gone, having added, perhaps, a quick look at the Rockwell Museum's first-class art collection of the American West.

Not all, but certainly the majority, give short shrift to Corning's main thoroughfare, Market Street, and for this, one should perhaps give thanks. The street manages to retain its small-town America feel while boasting one of the finest restorations of 19th-century commercial brick architecture you're likely to find anywhere.

Corning, a pleasant little enclave on the edge of the Finger Lakes, has something many other towns have sacrificed on their way to becoming "tourist destinations" in the 1980s: a main street virtually devoid of glitz and fast-food restaurants and chain stores that sell fashionable and overpriced clothing and jewelry to fools easily parted from their money. How long it will last (there are a Crabtree & Evelyn shop and occasional talk of a Rouse-like development along the Chemung River) is anyone's guess, but for now it's a welcome mix of mostly local folk.

Walk into a store — whether it's Jim Iraggi's used-book store, B.J. Smith's cigar shop, Bob Rockwell's department store or Kitty Erlacher's glass boutique or one of the other antique or glass shops that cater to tourists — and you'll likely find the owner.

You don't have to be an architecture buff, in short, to appreciate the feel of Market Street. It starts when you drop a dime into the parking meter and get a half-hour's time. Behind the glass of nearby stores are signs for a country jamboree at Tillotson's Potato Farm in Lowman and a turkey shoot in Cato.

Two blocks west, you can saunter into the Gates Rockwell Department Store and enjoy the Western art, rifles, Indian artifacts and antique toys displayed on the walls above the linens, lingerie and furniture, or the priceless Steuben glass in locked cases. It's part of Bob Rockwell's personal collection, the best of which now rests in the Rockwell Museum.

On the way back to the car to feed the meter, stop at Brown's Cigar Store — that's the one with the ruby-neon Indian in the window. The affable fellow with the white hair is B.J. Smith, the owner, and he's been here — let's see — since 1931. Brown's has been a tobacco store a little longer — since 1889.

When you get back and discover your meter has expired, the likelihood is that you'll find no ticket on the windshield. It wouldn't be right to say they don't write them here; one gets the feeling, though, that they've got enough sense not to make money from their visitors, or their own people, on parking meters.

Perhaps a sign in the Corning Store, which sells Corning ware and Pyrex and other dinnerware and accessories in a building on Pine Street off Market, best sums up the attitude: Tourists Treated Same as Home Folks.

Without doubt, the biggest reason for Corning's success is the Corning Glass Works, which has carefully but steadily bestowed its beneficence on projects deemed proper for the town's well-being. It has been the dominant industry in the region for more than a century. Today the glass works employs 6,000; Corning's 1980 population was 12,953.

Corning's evolution is coincident with three major events in the last two decades: The first was the decision in the late 1960s to restore and rehabilitate historic buildings along Market Street. The second and most significant was Hurricane Agnes and the great flood of 1972, which devastated the region and inundated Corning in the process, thus paving the way for both restoration and urban renewal. The third was the 1980 dedication of a new museum to house the world-famous glass collection. All accelerated Corning's transition from a somewhat drab and desultory one-company industrial town along the Chemung River to what it is today.

Corning's layout is fortuitous in that Route 17 is a block south of Market Street and takes most traffic east and west through town. A block on the other side of Market, and for the most part hidden from view, is the glass works.

Route 17 is where the fast-food restaurants are, along with the service stations and tire dealers and other businesses that are either non-retail or not coincident with the Market Street restoration. If that sounds exclusionary, note this: Although the town has a sign ordinance, it has no zoning law regulating historic structures, so what happens on the main street occurs primarily through jawboning and quiet pressure exerted by the Market Street Restoration Agency.

Market Street has the traditional businesses (banks, drugstores, newsstands, shoe and clothing stores, barrooms, bookstores, a candy store, a department store, camera shops, music store, restaurants), plus those that count more heavily on the tourist trade. The most interesting are antique and glass shops, but these also include a couple of outlet shops: Cannon towels and linens, and Woolrich clothes.

There are two "hot glass" studios, where you can watch glass being shaped and blown and can buy the finished products. One, Brand & Greenberg, is relatively new and came to town under a low-interest loan program designed to attract leading crafts people and artists willing to work in "open" studios and shops on the main street. The financing is from Corning Glass, of course.

After the flood of 1972, the east end of Market Street, the low-income part made up largely of frame dwellings and stores and bars, was bulldozed for urban renewal. Much of that space now is occupied by the civic center, police department and city hall, glassworkers' union hall, public library, plaza and ice-skating rink, along with a Hilton Hotel. The restored Market Street runs west from the Hilton for four long blocks.

If you look up as you walk west, you'll note all sorts of ornamentation, a lot of it brick and terra cotta made at Corning's long-defunct brick and terra-cotta works. Although the architecture is a mix of Victorian, Gothic, Romanesque, Greek Revival, hints of Egyptian and who knows what else, it is understated when compared, say, with the iron ornamentation of post-Civil War towns.

Several buildings have the owners' or architects' names imbedded in stone in their facades. At No. 72, for example, there's Henkel Block, a five-story brick structure, which was the tallest building in the region when it was constructed in 1893. The name block alludes to the multiple uses to which the building was put: a boot-and-shoe store on the first floor, living quarters on the second and third, and warehousing on the fourth and fifth.

As you walk west on Market, if you keep looking up, you'll see all sorts of designs in the brick and a lot of corbeling (stepped ornamental molding) as well as terra-cotta detailing. One might hasten to add that you'll also see "modern" storefronts, as well as a few from the 1920s and 1930s.

At No. 47, Ecker Drug Store, note the square panels of leaded glass in the third-floor windows. The facade, including the windows, was covered with "modern" panels in the 1960s. The panels were removed when the renaissance started to take off in 1978, and Ecker is considered one of the early success stories in the continuing effort to harmonize both the signage and the overall character of the street.

As you stroll on, you'll see griffin heads and lion heads and shell and floral embellishments along the facades, all in terra cotta, with perhaps the most interesting embellishment being a little owl that sits atop the cornice at the Bern Furniture building. It's something of an enigma, although the story goes that it's there for a very practical reason: to scare off pigeons, which are natural prey for owls.

This is a street to explore. At Brown's Cigar Store, the feel is of another era, the same that one occasionally gets while strolling beneath the honey locust trees on the brick sidewalks outside. B.J. Smith has collected tobacco tins, cigar boxes, cigarette and chewing-tobacco signs and memorabilia from a time that substantially precedes the first U.S. surgeon general's report warning of the health dangers of tobacco usage.

"It's fun to lean back and see what's happened on this street," says Smith, who started to work in the store when he was 15 and bought out a partner in the late 1940s.

Farther on, at Erlacher Glass, Kitty Erlacher talks in what seems a perpetually excited voice amid the fine glassware: "I've lived all my life within a five-block radius of where you're sitting right now," she says. "This street has changed, but it's never changed — if that makes sense. It has the same look, smell, taste, feel that it did 20 years ago or 40 years ago or 100 years ago. It's a private place, but it's a welcome place. Everybody says hello, whether they know you or not. It's a funny, strange place, too. You know that Corning Glass feels the warmth and security of this town the same way the longtime neighbors do."

And, unless you ask, you probably won't know that Kitty Erlacher's husband is Max Roland Erlacher, an internationally known master glass engraver, who has his own studio nearby and specializes in cameo relief carving — only custom, commissioned work. "I very seldom have what you would call a shelf item for sale," she says.

157

At the corner of Market and Pine Streets is Baron Steuben Place. A look-in on the Ice Cream Works is a must, just to see the ornate, hand-carved mahogany soda fountain and wooden booths and stools that came from a defunct 19th-century ice cream parlor in Hornell, N.Y. Behind this, from the Pine Street entrance, is the Epicurean Cafe, excellent for an imported coffee and pastry. Through the same side entrance and upstairs are exhibits on New York state wines and winemaking, including a tasting bar. Take a look at the wine bar. It's from a 19th-century Atlanta hotel, complete with colorful leaded glass and a few bullet holes in its pillars.

If you're hungry and don't want a sit-down lunch, try Jim's Texas Hots, next door to the cigar store. Ask for a plain hot dog, and you're likely to face a friendly imprecation from the owner: "Heck, have a Texas Hot. It's our reason for being here." And they taste just fine.

Book lovers will enjoy the Book-mark, for best sellers and current editions, and Jim Iraggi's Book Exchange, for browsing and soaking up that special feeling and aroma that emanate from shelves of second-hand volumes. Iraggi specializes in books on — glass.

A sign above the doorway in his shop sets the mood for an afternoon of meandering on Corning's main drag:

Please Do Disturb. I Like to Talk While I Work.

East Berlin, Pa.

In this small town, it's easy to slide back into another century

By Andrew Cassel
Inquirer Staff Writer

T he shop sign said Buffalo En- terprises, an uncharacteristi- cally woolly name in this tidy Pennsylvania German town. The in- side was even less congruous.

Piles and scraps of heavy cut cloth sat on crowded tables. A counter stretched along one wall displayed three-cornered hats, homespun bon- nets, pewter bowls and candlesticks. Small mysterious items cut from bone or wood filled trays along the counter top. In the middle, mounted on a workbench, was an antique leather saddle, partly unstitched.

"This is the 18th century," an- nounced Raymond Moore, the pro- prietor. "The 19th century starts back by the door." It was unquestion- ably so. Here at Buffalo Enterprises ("Everything for Period Living") there was no visible reason to doubt that we had changed epochs.

Which was true, in a way, of the whole town of East Berlin. The place feels out of time, not so much for what's there, as for what isn't.

On a long, meandering Saturday drive west through the well-worn Pennsylvania Dutch country, we had passed any number of historic mark- ers, old houses and even whole his- toric towns. But the "olde-tyme" gift shops and nearby strip developments always lurking on the fringes gave

them all a self-consciousness that was lacking here, just over the Ad- ams County line about 12 miles west of York.

It looked, at first, an impossibly dull place to spend a weekend. No nightlife, no trinket trade, not even a postcard to be found. But by poking around, we found some unusual charms, and after a while, even the dullness of the place (from a tour- ist's perspective) became part of the attraction. This is the very model of an 18th-century German-immigrant community, the quiet, flat, rectangu- lar kind of place that was eventually duplicated in 10,000 burgs across the United States.

There is one sumptuously Victori- an bed-and-breakfast, a functioning general store/soda fountain/drug- store, and a scattering of crafts and antiques shops, but we had to hunt a bit for these. Most of those who do stop for the night at the Leas-Bechtel Mansion Inn are between other desti- nations or making the antiques cir- cuit. And those who arrive, as we did, late in the day, find they must head back out of town again for dinner; the nearest restaurant with a bar is in Abbottstown, five miles south.

But tucked away down King Street was Buffalo Enterprises, the re-en- actment buff's L.L. Bean. Camping out at Valley Forge this winter? Plan- ning Pickett's Charge? Ray Moore's your man. For about $500, he'll outfit you and your horse; specify length, width and decade.

Moore himself makes a pretty good period piece, with his wispy, Dickensian beard and chiseled features. With a red stocking cap, he looked that day like a department-store Santa between shifts. For that matter, he could have been the real thing.

Moore, a blacksmith, tinker and jack-of-all-trades, will restore or duplicate anything down to the buttons on a British redcoat's coat; partner Carole Roberson makes the coat itself, from wool specially ordered and dyed to the original specifications. They're sticklers for detail; when I asked Moore if he'd done much work at Williamsburg, Va., he fixed me with a baleful look and asked if I realized that the costumes at Williamsburg contained (shudder) polyester.

Because the bulk of their business consists of catalogue sales, Moore and Roberson don't need the kind of walk-in trade they would get in a more magnetic town. That suits them fine. "My biggest problem is keeping the business from growing too fast," Moore confided on my visit. The kind of life he'd have in, say, Gettysburg, is pretty much what he moved out of Bucks County to escape.

East Berlin was once the western frontier for Pennsylvania's German settlers, and their stolid character is still on the town and the gently rolling farmland that surrounds it. But without the flash and high visibility of the Lancaster area, few outlanders realize it.

"We consider ourselves just as much Pennsylvania Dutch as the Amish. We just haven't been promoted as much," said Charles Bechtel, a Washingtonian who returned to his boyhood home several years ago to buy the old Leas mansion on West King Street. Transformed into a working bed-and-breakfast, the extensively restored Victorian building stands out among the generally older, plainer buildings in town.

Bechtel and his innkeeper, Ruth Spangler, can accommodate up to 18 guests with lodging and light breakfast. The downstairs rooms are heavy with brass, mahogany and porcelain; lush, dark Oriental rugs and local quilts accent many of the bedrooms. But it's a deliberately quiet place, without the parlor life that, to my mind at least, is the main draw of a country inn.

Bechtel opened an adjacent crafts and antiques shop when he first started the inn in 1983; he has also added a combination ski package with the Round Top ski area 18 miles northeast, including lift tickets, lodging and breakfast.

When there's no snow, you can take a walk down to Sweigart's Mill, built in 1794 on Beaver Creek, or visit the Studebaker House, once owned by the forebears of the automakers and now a private museum. Bicycling is good here, with virtually all the roads leading out to farm country within a mile or two.

All along King Street, on which the inn sits, are restored 18th- and early 19th-century buildings laid out in neat rows. The properties remain as they were laid out originally: long and narrow, to accommodate the barns in which citizens kept their cows and chickens. The barns are still there, but cattle and poultry are frowned on, as witness the tale of Joe and Joy Mailey's goose.

When the Maileys, who are in their 20s, were preparing to move up from Annapolis, Md., a couple of years ago, they let it be known that along with their antiques and other household treasures was Anniebelle, their pet goose.

"Before anyone had seen her, we had 11 complaints filed against us," said Joy Mailey. Being of Pennsylvania German heritage herself, and no pushover, she went to court, and won. Anniebelle is now a neighborhood celebrity and takes her swims in Conewago Creek.

But if East Berlin wasn't somewhat resistant to change, the Maileys probably wouldn't have chosen it for their home and business. Joy Mailey, who learned woodworking in her father's basement near Hanover, Pa., specializes in primitives ("not the ruffly stuff," she cautions, but hand-hewn, rustic furniture and accessories).

Their house at 412 W. King St., built in 1790 by John Fox, is classic Pennsylvania German: vertically divided, with two rooms downstairs and four up. One half is Mailey's Pennsylvania Primitive. The other half is their home. On the front is an unusually large date stone, which matches two found on area homes built in 1788 and 1789. The Maileys adapted the style in their own logos and catalogue.

"We don't do reproductions, in that we don't copy anything in particular," she said. "We just make what we like." The stock is unusual: rough, solid chairs, rockers and cabinets, finished in a mustard-color milk-based paint, and redware pottery, along with practical German household devices, such as blanket warmers.

In town, however, the emphasis is on crafts. Besides Buffalo Enterprises and the Maileys, there are Stan Hollenbaugh's gunsmithing studio and Cora Melchers' doll museum. All of this comes together the second Saturday in September when East Berlin stages its Colonial Day crafts show; in 1986 the juried exhibit drew 1,000 applicants.

East Berlin could become a refuge for the over-microchipped. "A nice, quiet town" is what everyone most likes to call it; an exciting evening might consist of a walk down to Beaver Creek or a summer stroll around the back alleys to talk with the old folks. "They tell us how in the old days, they could make a party out of making apple-butter," Joy says.

Lakeville, Pa.

Champagne-glass Jacuzzi in the 'Land of Love'

By Judi Dash
Special to The Inquirer

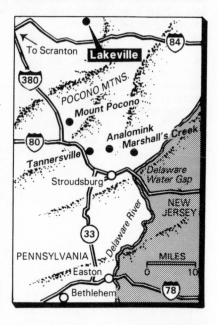

The brochure shows a man and woman sitting in a champagne glass, bubbles foaming up around them.

Trick photography, we think. Silly idea.

Two weeks later we are sitting in a champagne glass, bubbles foaming up around us.

No trick. Very silly — and yet . . .

We have ventured into a world where seven-foot-champagne-glass Jacuzzis, mirror-backed beds and rooms with multiple baths but no windows are standard issue.

"You are entering the land of love," a heart-shaped signpost says, and, indeed, there is no point in attempting to adjust the picture. We have just crossed over into The Erotic Zone — Pennsylvania's Pocono-no's.

We are at Cove Haven, the sine qua non of sentiment gone shtick. It was at this very resort 24 years ago that one Morris Wilkins created the first heart-shaped tub, and it was that same Morris, now 61, who recently fathered the double-occupancy champagne glass.

Morris' stemware has been installed in Cove Haven's top-of-the-line Champagne Tower suites, 16 trilevel chambers that also are equipped with heart-shaped pools, redwood saunas and large, round beds encircled by mirrors. (No, there are none on the ceiling.)

But before you get into the champagne glass or any of the resort's other aquatic playpens, you must first pass registration — and pay up to $525. "You folks married or is this a business trip?" a clerk says, winking, to the couple next to us, as he hands them the keys to a Garden of Eden suite — one of the few accommodations with no heart-shaped facilities.

We are seated on swivel stools facing semicircular counters in a large hall that resembles the waiting room of an upscale beauty salon. The walls are covered with red cardboard cupids and hearts.

A snowmobile in the center of the room stands testament to the availability of outdoor recreation. But most people congregate at a corner booth, examining an album filled with photographs of couples in heart-shaped tubs and round beds.

Some photographs are framed by giant keyholes. Guests pay staff photographers $7 a photograph for a "memory album" of their stay. They don't get the negatives.

We are processed into Cove Haven life by a chirpy man who relieves us of our charge card — debit $525 a couple for two nights and six meals for the champagne-glass suites (lesser lodgings start at $325).

He gives us two keys, a parking pass, a large cardboard key proving that we are guests and labeled "Your Personal Key to Pocono Pleasure," and a list of activities in which we are urged to participate — the volleyball game, the bingo game, the X-rated newlywed game (more on the latter later).

The adjacent couple's registration clerk is funnier than ours, so we eavesdrop on his briefing.

"This here's your dining room — ya gotta eat, kids — your health spa, your ice skatin' rink, your nightclub ... you'll see how ya feel, right?" he says, circling color-coded shapes on a Cove Haven map. Then he sends the two off in the Love Machine, a white van that shuttles guests around the resort, sparing them the need to expend precious energy driving cars.

On the narrow road to the Champagne Tower suites, we pass a cluster of Garden of Eden buildings — brown, saucer-shaped structures that look like they just flew over from a Steven Spielberg set. The pie-wedge rooms have a triangular pool at the point and a round, mirror-backed bed at the base.

There are no windows.

"Those are basically isolation units," we are told by the Love Machine driver. "Nobody cares what time of day it is."

Our quarters have a full complement of portholes. Guests are encouraged to keep their blinds drawn, however — particularly in the Champagne Tower suites, where passers-by tend to stop by for a glimpse of the towering tub.

From the outside, the rooms that Cove Haven calls the "ultimate fantasy" seem ho-hum. Grouped in a row of cheerless brown barracks, they look like places from which you'd request a parole, not room service.

But you can't judge a nook by its cover.

Behind the brown door is a hedonist's heaven, a veritable ode to excess. Enter and behold the seven-foot plexiglass goblet, soaring from the ground-floor living room to the second-floor bathroom, from which you descend into the bowl.

The ground level also contains a color television, a large modular couch and a wood-burning fireplace, above which hangs a print of a woman wearing only a come-hither expression and a black cat draped across her chest.

Sliding doors lead to a glass-enclosed, heart-shaped pool. Down a few steps, a redwood sauna and rubdown table glow red under a heat lamp.

The round bed upstairs overlooks the pool, and is semicircled by a six-paned mirror that reflects everything in sextuplicate.

In the bathroom, one wall switch turns the shower into a steam room, another makes the champagne glass a Jacuzzi. A sign above the Jacuzzi switch requests that guests refrain from the use of bubble bath — but management assures us that it doesn't mean it; we may bubble at will.

There's a small refrigerator for stocking subsistence foods — champagne, strawberries, Brie.

Throughout, floors and walls are carpeted in thick, red shag (partly for posh, mostly for soundproofing); recessed bulbs provide the palest pink glow, no matter how many switches are flicked; and mirrored walls reflect every surface on which a couple conceivably could camp.

We are tempted to call it a night. Alas, it is only 5 p.m. We are still tempted to call it a night.

But we go to dinner.

By getting to the dining room early, we hope to nab a cozy corner booth for two.

"You are numbers 198 and 199," the hostess shouts over the din of clattering dishes and what looks like the cast of a Cecil B. DeMille epic, minus the horses.

It is the biggest dining room that we have ever seen.

People stand in long lines at a buffet table that stretches halfway across the hall, piling their plates high with slabs of beef and chicken, sausage and pates, salads, cheeses, cakes, puddings.

About 250 couples are called, in groups of 20, to sit at tables for 10. "We're only up to 120," the hostess yells. "Go sit in the lounge."

After waiting in that heart-shaped chamber for 30 minutes, our number is boomed across the room.

We eat and run, hoping for greater intimacy at the nightclub. But the red-plush amphitheater is even more immense than the dining room, with the ubiquitous tables for 10.

The cocktail waitresses wear white and gold mini-togas with plunging necklines. They bend low over the tables to take orders and accept tips.

On stage, a man who introduces himself as Honest Phil and claims to be our social director warms up the crowd with jokes. His vocabulary is drawn from potty training.

He goes into the audience to track down honeymooners. "You've been married since Sunday, huh?" he says to a couple in the front row. "Nice to see you up and around. Have any kids yet?"

Phil introduces the big act, Thea and Le Clique. Le Clique sings "All Night Long," which seems to last that amount of time, before bringing on Thea, a woman in a silver lame dress.

After a few torch songs, Thea bounds off the stage and onto a succession of front-row male laps for an extended version of "Big Spender" — at least it extends beyond our stay.

We pay the waitress leaning closest to us, then catch the Love Machine

back to our room, detouring to the registration center. Couples line the check-in counter, waiting to rent video-cassette recorders.

We select from a list of 77 movies. The left column contains titles such as *Vietnam: A Documentary*. The right side includes *Debbie Does Dallas*. We choose the Southwest over the Far East.

●

In the morning, so little light filters through the drawn blinds that we do not know it is daytime.

That is why we miss breakfast.

Lunch isn't that crowded, either.

At the 2 p.m. X-rated newlywed game in the nightclub, Honest Phil asks five couples explicit questions about their sexual activities.

"Do you want to whisper it to me?" Phil asks a woman who appears to be gagging on an answer. When she nods and leans toward him, he sticks his microphone up to his ear.

We drop by the gift shop for a memento of our stay. Among the items we pass up are a crucifix with "Cove Haven in the Poconos" inscribed at the base, a wood-block print of The Last Supper bearing the same inscription, a red garter with the Cove Haven logo and "Land of Love" playing cards.

And so it goes here in the heart of the Poconos, "the honeymoon capital of the world," where, incidentally, an impromptu poll by Honest Phil determines that a substantial portion of the guests are not honeymooners — nor are they married.

All in all, the experience is a light-hearted pairing of levity and lust — with the latter in the lead.

But lest you think Cove Haven is just a one-track find, be advised that the resort also has snowmobiling and skiing, video games, an ice-skating rink, a shooting gallery, indoor miniature golf, an Olympic-size pool, a weight room, saunas and horseback riding nearby. Perhaps you'd like to hear about those activities now.

I didn't think so.

Judi Dash is travel editor of The Record in Hackensack, N.J.

Morristown, N.J.

A place where Washington slept is now a most exclusive address

By Regina Schrambling
Special to The Inquirer

When George Washington and his ragged troops needed a winter shelter for two seasons of the Revolutionary War, they found the perfect location in this little North Jersey town. Shielded by the Watchung Mountains, lookouts posted along the ridges could spot any threats, particularly from the Redcoats 30 miles away in New York City.

Today, the settlement that Washington knew as a couple of churches, a courthouse and a tavern, arranged around the town green, has evolved into a bustling small city in one of the most exclusive enclaves in the country. Like Washington, the area's wealthy new settlers chose Morris County for its location, less than an hour from Manhattan.

Morris County is not a bad drive from Philadelphia — about 3½ hours — and it has more than proximity to offer for a weekend journey. Morristown leaders boast that their community has history to rival Valley Forge's. Within the city limits are two private homes that Washington's men converted into headquarters, the Jockey Hollow encampment and the embankment known as Fort Nonsense.

For more modern tastes, the area also has surprisingly sophisticated restaurants, antiques shops, crafts galleries and more. And for the outdoors-oriented, some of the historical parks are lined with hiking trails and, for warm weather, picnic sites.

The more modern amenities might be lures for visitors, but they sprang up to serve the well-heeled locals. On a Friday night, the clogged exits off the Garden State Parkway look like a Mercedes-Benz lot. Houses here are not just big, but mansion-size, especially on the outskirts of the New England-pretty towns strung out along the commuter tracks like a northern Main Line. And the liquor stores (many restaurants have bring-your-own policies) are stocked with more $20 California Chardonnays than $5 Italian jugs.

Rumors of highly rated restaurants ostensibly in the middle of nowhere first lured me to Morris County, but friends and I soon went back twice more to explore along Route 24, the state highway that winds from the Garden State Parkway to the antiques center of Chester.

In spring or summer, we might have been tempted to try the trails and spend more time strolling through Jockey Hollow. But we soon realized that one of the best times to see Morristown might be in the cold months, when one gets a discomfortingly real understanding of what the

Continental Army went through, huddled in tents and huts on the hillsides through 28 blizzards, with little food and fewer clothes. Only a few of the 1,000 huts thrown up in the winter of 1780 remain at Jockey Hollow, but with the wind whistling over the snow, the misery seems tangible.

Even at the Ford Mansion, Washington's headquarters for those two winters, the sense of deprivation and difficulty dominates. Late on a cold afternoon, the two-story house is unheated and lighted by candles.

Mrs. Jacob Ford Jr., the widow and mother of four who turned over her home to Washington, moved her family into two rooms for the duration. They're not big rooms, and the family couldn't have been very comfortable all those months. The spare parlor and bedroom are preserved as they were when the Fords lived there, while the kitchen is as primitive and bare as any of that era. Upstairs is even bleaker, with unheated rooms where Washington's aides slept on bare floors on pallets or tentlike camp cots.

At the well-maintained museum below the main house, exhibits and a film recount the Washington era. He first came to Morristown in 1777, leading 5,000 ragtag soldiers after their victories at Trenton and Princeton. That first winter was spent rebuilding and training his army, with veterans and recruits sleeping anywhere they could: in private homes, public buildings, barns, sheds, even tents.

Along with an army dwindling because of death and desertion, icy weather and constant shortages, Washington had to combat an outbreak of smallpox. Low morale was also a problem. In May 1777, Washington ordered his men to dig trenches and build embankments on the highest hill in the area. Today, the site is known as Fort Nonsense, since legend has it that the general was only giving his men busy work.

By that spring, though, Washington's army was ready to fight again.

For the next two years, he was away from Morristown. In the interval, British forces surrendered at Saratoga, Philadelphia was captured and then abandoned by the enemy, and the Continental Army survived the winter at Valley Forge.

In December 1779, Washington returned to Morristown in a driving snowstorm and moved in with the Fords. Over the winter, the troops worked to build huts from the chestnut, maple and oak trees growing nearby. Because of the continuing blizzards, food shipments were delayed and the men often had nothing to eat for days. But once again, spring brought good news. The young Marquis de Lafayette arrived to say that France was sending six warships and 6,000 troops to help the American cause.

Besides the tale of those two winters, the museum gives more insights into the era. Intelligently arranged displays contain Revolutionary War rifles and weapons, 18th-century housewares, clothing, furniture and other items.

Through the year, the center also stages "living history" events such as a weekend encampment in Jockey Hollow, with a drill and tactical demonstrations, to mark the one holiday — St. Patrick's Day — granted Washington's troops. (For more details, call 201-539-2085.)

The museum on Washington Place is open from 9 a.m. to 5 p.m. daily (except Thanksgiving, Christmas and New Year's Day). It provides a small map and guide for exploring Jockey Hollow, Fort Nonsense and the Wick Farm, a comfortable private home on 1,400 acres that was converted to Gen. Arthur St. Clair's headquarters in 1780.

Near the Ford Mansion, at 68 Morris Ave., a glimpse of a more luxurious age can be had at Acorn Hall, a Victorian house supposedly named for the biggest and oldest black oak tree in New Jersey. The hours here are limited (the hall is closed January and February; after that, it is open from 11 a.m. to 3 p.m. Thursdays and 1:30 to 4 p.m. Sundays), but it's worth a look inside at the rococo revival parlor furniture, the 1800s carpets and the bedroom set decorated with trompe l'oeil effects, brought from Kentucky more than a century ago. The Morris County Historical Society also maintains a Victorian-style garden outside and a Victorian gift shop.

While Washington gets most of the glory, Morristown also has been home to other significant names. Bret Harte once lived here, as did cartoonist Thomas Nast, who developed the Santa Claus character as he's depicted today.

At Historic Speedwell, displays commemorate Stephen Vail, who manufactured the first steamship engine to cross the Atlantic, and his son, Alfred, who with Samuel F.B. Morse perfected the telegraph here. (The restoration is open by appointment from November to March; from May 1 to Oct. 31, it is open on Thursday and Friday from noon to 4 p.m. and Saturday and Sunday from 1 to 5 p.m. Phone: 201-540-0211.)

History of a different sort can be found with a stop for lunch around Morristown. Right in town, there's always Society Hill with its period decor — a North Jersey branch of the Philadelphia watering hole at the Society Hill Hotel — with good food on that crosswire between trendy and traditional, nachos and club sandwiches.

But for a real taste of history, an even better choice is the Black Horse Inn in the sedate little town of Mendham. A sign on the highway reads: "I'll Mend 'Em, 1742." A waitress informed us that the town name — "fer sure" — was drawn from that blacksmith's slogan at the old inn.

The Black Horse serves lunch and drinks in its pub, a multi-room affair crammed with antiques and pseudo-antiques, and dinner in a separate building with a more romantic decor (red tablecloths, flowers, candles) and a pricier menu. For lunch, nothing could top the pub's generous crab cakes and fresh grilled salmon steak, accompanied by crisp, skinny French fries and garlic bread. Since the bar also pours real wine (Raymond Chardonnay) at jug prices, lunch for two with drinks should come to about $30.

Mendham, home as well to some tasteful shops and galleries, is a good stop between Morristown and Chester. Route 24 here meanders through some of the most soothing scenery in New Jersey; this is horse country, with hills as rolling and fields as green as in the Kentucky bluegrass.

While winding past white fences and beautiful houses, pulling over occasionally to let drivers more immune to the scenery pass, it's easy to forget what state you're in.

Chester, however, is a town with a split personality. At one end of the main street is a row of antiques and gift "shoppes"; a little farther and the road forks into the 20th century, with fast food, gas stations and even a little strip mall.

On our trip, we doubled back for a closer look at the antiques stores and spent a good 15 minutes perusing Woodcock's Gourmet and Aunt Pittypat's Porch and the Chester Carousel. A little quaintness goes a long way. The rest of the hordes out shopping, however, were apparently blissful among the armoires and tea cozies.

Taylor's Ice Cream Parlor looked more appealing, with its turn-of-the-century decor, but the blue Smurf ice cream was a bit jarring.

When it comes to food, though, Morris County isn't always so anachronistic. With so many wealthy locals reluctant to battle Meadowlands traffic into the city on a weekend night, good restaurants are thriving. Naturally, prices are anything but small-town. Anyone not inured to $10 tuna sandwiches in Manhattan might suffer from sticker-price shock from some menus.

But this is not New York, and so the emphasis is often on quantity, stupefying quantity in some cases. The $35 fixed-price menu at Cook Plaza Cafe in Madison, for instance, is a downright bargain. Every day the menu at Cook Plaza changes, with a new blurry mimeographed sheet listing the options. Keeping that handy through the meal is a good idea, since the sheer quantity and variety of food on each plate can be confusing. Only when we were stuffed did we read the fine print and learn that Cook Plaza will serve a lighter meal — salad, entree and vegetable — for $21.95, but only to those who ask in advance when making reservations (201-377-1420).

A second noteworthy stop in Madison is Joie de Vivre, a nice small-town restaurant that has already seized on the bistro tag to compensate for a rather blurred culinary identity. Along with lace curtains, big windows and ceiling fans, it has a huge claw-foot table in the middle of the dining room arrayed with a dozen or so desserts in all their sugary splendor, from three-layer cakes to Grand Marnier tortes.

Entree prices at Joie de Vivre are in the $13 to $18 range, but bringing wine from the store down the block keeps the total tab at bargain levels, around $25 to $30 a person for three courses. (For reservations, call 201-822-1917.)

We explored further and found Rod's 1890 at the Madison Hotel, a few miles out Route 24 in Convent Station. From the outside, the place looks like a huge amusement park. Inside, the bar has been decked out like an 1800s bordello; some dining rooms are housed in restored velvet-lined railroad cars. Besides its oddly enticing ambiance, though, Rod's is worth a stop for cognac at brown-bag brandy prices.

The Madison Hotel, with 195 rooms, is also a lucky find for overnighters, since lodgings are in fairly short supply. In Morristown and farther away in Parsippany, where there are more corporate offices, there are also large motels.

The best way to get to Morris County from Philadelphia is to drive north on the New Jersey Turnpike to Route 287 and then west and north to Route 24, the main road winding through Chatham, Madison, Morristown and on to Chester.

Oakland, Md.

Finding a bit of the Old West in the western corner of the state

By Peter J. Ognibene
Special to The Inquirer

There are buffalo on the range, bear and bobcat in the mountains, cattle and sheep roaming rural pastures. A hike through the forests will flush deer, beaver, muskrats and other four-legged critters, but hours might pass before you encounter another human being. If you'd rather ride than walk, there's a dude ranch where you can saddle up.

If that sounds a bit like the Wild West, it is. There's just one difference: This is Garrett County, the westernmost part of Maryland, a rugged land where newcomers consult topographical charts rather than road maps to figure their way from A to B.

Like most Marylanders, I live in the congested corridor between Baltimore and Washington. Though

I am well-acquainted with Chesapeake Bay and the resort towns that line the Atlantic shore, Garrett County was new to me. But in the time my wife and I spent there, I found one thing after another that reminded me of Colorado, where I once lived.

The Rocky Mountains are, of course, more majestic than the Alleghenies, and the distances between settlements in Colorado are far greater. Yet their farms, ranches and small towns have much in common. The people in both places have a direct friendliness that makes travelers feel welcome.

Bordered by Pennsylvania on the Mason-Dixon Line to the north and a similarly straight line with West Virginia to the west, the rough right-triangle that forms Garrett encompasses 662 square miles, mak-

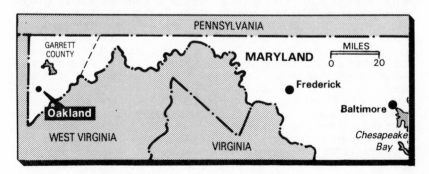

ing it the largest of Maryland's 23 counties. It has a population of 28,400, and its county seat and largest town, Oakland, has 2,000 residents. Backbone Mountain, at 3,360 feet, is the highest point in the county and the state. Farming dominates the economy; there are also coal mining and logging. Of late, as more and more people rediscover the region, tourism has become important.

I say "rediscover" for a reason. At the turn of the century, Western Maryland was among the nation's most popular summer destinations, thanks to the Baltimore & Ohio Railroad, which extended its rails to the region in 1851. Four presidents vacationed there and one, Grover Cleveland, spent his honeymoon in a three-story, 14-room "cottage" in Deer Park.

In 1918, Henry Ford, Thomas A. Edison and Harvey Firestone drove to Garrett County and camped beside Muddy Falls to convince skeptics that motor travel might have an impact on tourism. Ironically, it was the automobile, followed by the airliner, that led to the county's decline as a vacation mecca.

The B&O no longer carries passengers to the county, but the Queen Anne-style station in Oakland, built in 1884, still stands, an architectural monument to the elegance of rail travel. In 1912 Mountain Lake Park had 28 hotels and boarding houses and an amphitheater that could seat 5,000 for uplifting declamations from William Jennings Bryan, Billy Sunday and other speakers popular on the Chautauqua circuit. Though a few of the grand Victorian houses have been restored, others remain boarded up and plastered with danger signs. Today, the principal form of passive entertainment is drawn from backyard satellite dishes that pull down distant TV signals.

For the traveler, the pull of Garrett County is the outdoors. About 60 percent of the land is forest; the area is remote, and the fall colors are spectacular. The appropriately named Savage River has five miles of some of the most challenging white water on earth. In 1989, it will host the White Water World Championships, the first time these events will have been held in the United States.

In winter, Alpine skiers take to the slopes of Wisp Mountain and cross-country buffs hit the wooded trails. There are five state parks and more than 70,000 acres of state forests in Garrett County. Two of the parks — Herrington Manor and New Germany — have marked trails devoted exclusively to Nordic skiers in the winter and hikers during the warmer months. Other tracks, totaling 35 miles, are reserved for snowmobiles.

Roughly centered in the county, Deep Creek Lake was created in 1925 to provide hydroelectric power. The largest freshwater lake in Maryland, its many arms spread over six square miles amid hills and mountains.

With an average depth of 26 feet, it attracts sailors as well as power-boaters from late spring through much of the fall. In winter, the ice averages 18 inches, thick enough for skating, iceboating and ice fishing. Fishermen prize the lake in any season for large-and small-mouthed bass, yellow perch and walleye.

Paralleling the Pennsylvania border is the venerable National Road. Originally an Indian path called the Nemacolin Trail, the route was broadened in 1755 during the French and Indian War by troops under British Gen. Edward Braddock and remained the Braddock Trail until the 19th century, when Congress financed the nation's first interstate road to promote commerce between the East and the Ohio River Valley.

You can still see white-painted iron mileposts along U.S. 40, but the best relic of the old National Road is the Casselman River Bridge, a single-arch, stone span of 80 feet that was the largest of its type when built in 1813. Reinforced in 1911, it carried traffic until 1953 and became a Registered Historical Landmark in 1964.

Abutting the eastern approach to the bridge is Penn Alps, a fine Pennsylvania Dutch-style restaurant. A typical dinner might include Dutch sausage or another meat, potatoes, corn, homemade breads and dessert. The tariff for two typically runs about $15.

Also at Penn Alps are a string of cottages devoted to weaving, pottery, stained glass, wood carving and other traditional handicrafts. You can stroll through, watch an artisan at work and learn the basics, say, of transforming raw wool into a strong and even yarn.

A mile farther west in the town of Grantsville is the Casselman Hotel, which opened in 1824 as the Drover's Inn and took in travelers on the National Pike. Still open and run by Mennonites, the Casselman rents out five rooms in the old building and 40 more in a modern motor inn close by. The kitchen turns out hearty fare at prices that are at least 20 years out of date.

Also in Grantsville is Yoder's Country Market, an old-fashioned grocery that has superb meats and sausages, homemade breads and jams and anything else you might need to set up temporary housekeeping.

The more expensive restaurants and lodges are located on Deep Creek Lake. A room for two at the Will O' the Wisp ranges from $62 to $86 a night. Dinner for two at the Silver Tree, which specializes in steaks and Italian food, will set you back $30 or more.

If you can ignore the decor, which is old-time motel, the Oak-Mar in Oakland is a good place for homemade soups, inexpensive sandwiches and a $9 T-bone.

Though a black bear was once sighted at Swallow Falls State Park, you are unlikely to meet any of his ursine cousins. Local wildlife specialists have recorded (but wisely kept secret) the location of two bobcat dens. The buffalo, however, are in plain view on fenced-in rangeland adjacent to Herrington Manor Road, just south of the state park of that name.

If you like the rustic life, you can rent a cabin at Herrington Manor or New Germany state parks. All have electricity, refrigerators, stoves and the like. The state supplies sheets, pillowcases and blankets; you have to bring soap and towels. Each cabin has its own wood pile and a long, heavy ax that's perfect for splitting wood. You'll probably need it. (I did.) With average temperatures of 66 degrees in summer and 28 in winter, a fire is often necessary in the unheated cabins.

Because the cabins are so popular, the state conducts a lottery in January to assign weekly rentals for the summer. Winter vacationers can reserve heated cabins on a nightly basis (two-night minimum) by calling the parks directly.

Though Garrett County has no central reservations number, the office of tourism in Oakland tries hard to match people and places.

•

To participate in the lottery for summer weekly rentals of state park cabins, write or phone Maryland Forest and Park Service, Tawes State Office Building, Annapolis, Md. 21401, phone 301-269-3771. For nightly rentals of winterized cabins, contact Herrington Manor State Park, Route 5, Box 122, Oakland, Md. 21550, phone: 301-334-9180 (no reservations for winter will be taken until the second Tuesday in August), or New Germany State Park, Route 2, Box A-63, Grantsville, Md. 21536, phone: 301-895-5453.

The Double G dude ranch in McHenry can be reached at 301-387-5481. Additional phone numbers for obtaining information or lodging: Garrett County Promotion Council, 301-334-1948; The Casselman Hotel, 301-895-5055, and Will O' the Wisp, 301-387-5503.

Pittsburgh, Pa.

The former industrial heartland sparkles with new developments

By Don Clippinger
Special to The Inquirer

The images, now more than three decades out of date, are as indelible as W.C. Fields' slander of his native Philadelphia.

Pittsburgh. The smoky city.

The place where the wash is white when it goes on the clothesline and gray when it comes off.

The city of iron and steel. A shot-and-a-beer town.

Those stereotypes of western Pennsylvania's metropolitan center were seriously challenged when Pittsburgh was rated as America's most livable city — yes, first in the nation — by the 1985 edition of Rand McNally's Places Rated Almanac.

The book quickly became a best seller here. Pittsburghers take pride in their city and region, and always have. By and large, they consider it a good place to grow up and a moderately paced (and priced) place to live and work.

Today, the former industrial heartland sparkles with new, architecturally interesting buildings and commercial developments that preserve the structures of the past. The physical changes have accompanied a metamorphosis in the core of Pittsburgh's economic life. At the same time, the city's cultural life — which always has been active — has expanded.

It is now a good place to visit as well as to live. Three hundred miles from Philadelphia, the city is six hours by the Pennsylvania Turnpike, a comparable time by Amtrak train, and an hour away by plane.

Pittsburgh has many similarities to Philadelphia. It is a city of neighborhoods, some of them retaining their ethnicity, and some of them, like Philadelphia's Manayunk, hanging on hillsides. And, like Philadelphia, it is a city that cannot be fully appreciated in a one-day visit. A weekend of wandering is definitely in order.

One of the most stunning vistas of Pittsburgh's glowing downtown area greets air travelers when they traverse the 13 miles from Greater Pittsburgh Airport to the city by car or cab. Traveling on the Parkway — Pittsburgh's equivalent of the Schuylkill Expressway — they pass under Mount Washington and emerge from the tunnel with the city immediately ahead.

A focus of the city is its Point, where the Monongahela and Allegheny Rivers join to form the Ohio. The Point was the predominant characteristic of the city in 18th-century drawings — from the time that the British seized Fort Duquesne from the French in 1758 and renamed it Fort Pitt.

It remains a frequently photographed panorama, and most of

those photos are taken from Mount Washington, where the city has built overlooks on the face of a cliff.

The overlooks are the best places to get a view of Pittsburgh, and getting there is half the fun. A brief walk from the downtown area leads across the Smithfield Street Bridge — one of many in a city with three rivers — to the Station Square retail development on the city's South Side. Station Square was built entirely with private money more than a decade ago, and it preserved the under-utilized Pittsburgh and Lake Erie Railroad terminal.

The Grand Concourse, which houses a full-menu restaurant, was formerly the passenger terminal. The railway's freight shops have been converted into a mall containing many shops.

The freight shops' restaurants are quite diverse. Japanese, Chinese and Mexican restaurants offer full specialty menus, and a quick kielbasa sandwich is available from a fastfood outlet in the central portion of the two-level mall.

The railroad tracks remain, and parked on them are early 20th-century rail passenger cars that now house small, narrow shops selling crafts items.

Also on display within the Station Square development is a Bessemer Converter, the towering steelmaking cauldron that turned Pittsburgh into a city of steel in the 19th and early 20th centuries.

At the edge of Station Square is the terminal for the commercial Gateway Clipper river tours. The company's three passenger ships provide a river-level look at Pittsburgh's sites and a commentary on important events in its history.

Another sort of rail car leads to the top of Mount Washington. Across Carson Street from Station Square is the entrance to the Monongahela Incline ($1.20 round trip), one of the city's two remaining cable cars that carry passengers up and down the mountainside.

First put into operation in 1870 to carry German immigrants to and from Coal Hill (Mount Washington's former name), the incline now is operated by the region's transit authority, the Port Authority of Allegheny County. The other incline, the Duquesne Incline ($1.50 round trip), about a mile to the west, is privately maintained, and the cars' Victorian-era appointments have been restored.

Looking north from atop Mount Washington, the sweep of Pittsburgh lies below. With new construction going on, the skyline changes regularly. Only one thing is missing now.

Smoke.

Indeed, the smoke is gone — most certainly for the better, but not without its price. The demise of heavy industry in America has hit Pittsburgh hard. On a recent afternoon, only one plume of smoke punctuated the horizon, and that was from an electrical power plant.

The Pittsburgh region could have been devastated by the graying of its industrial base, but it was not. The city rebuilt its downtown area in the 1950s and 1960s, a process known as the Pittsburgh Renaissance.

It transformed a mass of warehouses and railway lines at the Point into the Gateway Center office plaza and a park. Point State Park contains the original Fort Pitt blockhouse and a large fountain marking the confluence of the Monongahela and Allegheny.

Just to the left of the Point, across the Allegheny on the city's North Side, is Three Rivers Stadium, the home of the Pittsburgh Steelers professional football team and the Pirates, the city's baseball franchise.

Also on the North Side is Buhl Planetarium, which has given decades of Pittsburgh youngsters an introduction to the universe. The county's community college also is located there, not far from the forbidding Western Penitentiary.

Today, Pittsburgh is going through another renewal of its

downtown district — called Renaissance II. Not far from the rust-brown U.S. Steel Building is the new Mellon Bank Building. PPG Industries' new glass, cathedral-like headquarters dominates the lower downtown area. The PPG complex abuts Market Square, a once-dingy collection of shops and bars and nightspots that have become increasingly upscale.

Several families have built enormous fortunes out of Pittsburgh, and placed their names on (and a great deal of money into) the city's cultural and educational institutions.

The Heinz family, descendants of H.J. Heinz, provided the funds for Heinz Hall, a spectacular renovation of an old theater that is now the home of the Pittsburgh Symphony and other performing arts. Heinz Hall, although not clearly visible from atop Mount Washington, is located in the downtown area, northeast of the Point.

Steel magnate Andrew Carnegie endowed libraries throughout the region, and the main Carnegie Library is located in the city's Oakland section.

From Mount Washington, Oakland is visible to the right on the horizon, beyond Duquesne University, a college built upon a steep hill known as the Bluff. The height of the University of Pittsburgh's Cathedral of Learning marks the location of the Oakland district, which is the city's educational and medical center.

Across Forbes Avenue from the Cathedral of Learning is Carnegie Institute. In addition to Carnegie Library, the institute houses two museums. The older portion contains the Carnegie Museum of Natural History, whose dinosaur hall has fascinated generations of Pittsburgh children. The newer part of the structure houses the institute's Museum of Art. The Carnegie Institute museums are open from 10 a.m. to 5 p.m. Tuesday through Thursday, 10 a.m. to 9 p.m. Friday, 9 a.m. to 5 p.m. Saturday and 1 to 5 p.m. Sunday.

North of Fifth Avenue is the Shadyside community, one of Pittsburgh's most interesting and diverse. Over the decades, it has been the home of many business, legal and educational leaders who have chosen to live in the city, and it remains a desirable area.

But it also has been the center of just about every avant-garde movement. The city's beatniks inhabited Shadyside in the '50s, and they were succeeded by the folkniks of the early '60s. The area was a focus of anti-Vietnam War sentiment in the late '60s and early '70s.

Today, you can see an occasional punk rocker on roller skates, but the Walnut Street shops cater more to the yuppie trade, the sidewalks are rolled up early, and Shadyside seems to be returning to its quieter carriage-trade beginnings.

Two large parks dominate the eastern end of the city. Schenley Park, beginning at Carnegie Institute, runs above Carnegie-Mellon and extends to the Squirrel Hill neighborhood. Beyond Squirrel Hill is Frick Park, named for Carnegie's partner, Henry Clay Frick. The park, at the city's eastern border, contains a remnant of the past, grass bowling greens.

The Frick Museum, located across Reynolds Street from the bowling greens, contains a collection of artworks from the early Renaissance through the 18th century. It is open from 10 a.m. to 5:30 p.m. Tuesday through Saturday, and noon to 6 p.m. Sunday.

The University of Pittsburgh has two art galleries that are open to the public. The University Art Gallery is in the Frick Fine Arts Building, located across from Carnegie Library. The UP Gallery, operated by the school's studio arts department, is located on Forbes Avenue at Bouquet Street.

Both galleries are open from 10 a.m. to 4 p.m. Tuesday through Saturday and 2 to 5 p.m. Sunday.

Rehoboth Beach, Del.

The deepest thoughts surface on a winter's day by the sea

Yes, as everyone knows, meditation and water are wedded forever.
— *Moby Dick* by Herman Melville

By Mike Shoup
Inquirer Travel Editor

Is there a better time to take to the seaside than in the dead of winter, or in the first breath of spring? I think not, at least when you are talking of the heavily developed New Jersey coastline, or those stretches of vacation beaches to the south known as Rehoboth Beach, Del., and Ocean City, Md.

The mood must fit, of course, for it is not a time to frolic in the surf with your children, but rather one to pause, listen and ponder, to watch the sea roll inexorably to shore and sweep out again in its timeless ritual.

And so, I went south to explore that stretch of ocean that lies between the quaint, historic town of Lewes, Del., and the roaring, high-rise wonderland of Ocean City. And to let the ocean talk.

My companion was not Melville, nor the usual Follett, Forsythe or Ludlum. Instead it was a thin volume written in 1922 by a German named Hermann Hesse and titled *Siddhartha*, short to read and long to ponder, the story of one man's spiritual quest and how he finds peace and wisdom by listening to the river he plies as a ferryman.

Heady stuff, indeed, and while my goals were not so lofty, if the ocean talked like Siddhartha's river, I was more than willing to listen.

No three towns contrast more sharply than these: Lewes, founded as a Dutch whaling colony in 1631 and home today to riverboat pilots and a relatively sparse vacationing crowd. Rehoboth Beach, once a Methodist seaside resort, today a clean, attractive shore community with a boardwalk big enough for walking but too small for honky-tonking. Ocean City, a summer mecca and year-round retreat for Washington-weary politicians and bureaucrats, its beach now lined with high-rise hotels and condominiums, Miami Beach fashion.

I took a boardwalk room at the Atlantic Sands Motel in Rehoboth, between the two extremes, with a window and balcony looking out to sea. It was night when I arrived, and falling asleep with the waves crashing down below was a respite from the normal nighttime noises.

The day dawned not as the February winter one it was, but spring-like. Strollers were upon the boardwalk and along the beach, masters walked their dogs, bikers pedaled swiftly by the shuttered shops, and children tagged along with their parents, rushing off to settle down into the sand and clutch and sift it through their hands, with the fascination that only the very young can muster for something as mundane as silica.

A run on the boardwalk found it absolutely spotless, not a piece of paper or debris to be seen. (And surprisingly little appeared later in the day.) By 11 a.m., some of the shops along Rehoboth Avenue, the main street that runs down to the boardwalk, were open for business. The temperature went into the 50s.

This is Rehoboth at its best, but even in summer the town maintains a more sedate posture than many shore communities, due in some degree to its Methodist origins. The name itself is biblical, from the Book of Genesis. The Israelites wander the desert in search of a home, finally settling in a place they call Rehoboth, a word that means "room for all."

Lewes, a few miles north of Rehoboth, is more a place to explore, not without its beaches, but definitely without a boardwalk. I headed there in the afternoon, to stop at Zwaanendael Museum and stroll past antiques shops and historic homes and old church graveyards.

The museum is a replica of the Town Hall in Hoorn, the Netherlands, and named for the Dutch colony established at Lewes in 1631. Zwaanendael means "Valley of the Swans." The displays here are not overwhelming, but nicely tell the town's story.

There's a flag said to have flown over Lewes in 1813, when the British navy bombarded the town in an unsuccessful attempt to take it; a portrait of Col. Samuel Boyer Davis, who commanded the U.S. troop garrison at that time; reproductions of clothing worn by the early Dutch settlers; an 1818 wooden grave marker, hand-carved in memory of one William Wolf.

The upstairs, which is closed on Sunday, contains antiques and memorabilia from the early days in Sussex County. (The museum is free and open Tuesday through Saturday from 10:30 a.m. to 4:30 p.m., and on Sunday from 1:30 to 4:30 p.m. It is closed Mondays.)

Just behind the museum is Joshua Fisher's house, a simple structure where once lived "one of the wealthiest men in the new world," according to a Lewes walking-tour booklet picked up in the museum. Fisher, a merchant, shipper, surveyor, navigator and chartmaker, died in 1783. (The house, which is also home to the Lewes Chamber of Commerce, is open Monday through Saturday 10 a.m. to 3 p.m.; during the winter, these hours may change so it is advisable to call ahead: 302-645-8073.)

Wandering about looking at this and other historic homes, I chanced into an antiques shop a few blocks away on Second Street, called Memories, where the door stood open and the talk was of spring, Feb. 19 or not. The proprietor said he'd seen his first robin, and yes, said a friend, his crocuses were in bloom.

I took leave of Lewes, knowing I would return the next day to take the ferry across the mouth of Delaware Bay to Cape May. Evening found me an hour's drive away in Ocean City, dining on grilled swordfish in a fine seafood restaurant called Fager's Island, at 60th Street and the bay, which I'd heard of by word of mouth. That was as much of Ocean City as I wanted.

That night I read *Siddhartha* and pondered (not too deeply) on the phases of his life: his early years of extreme asceticism, his middle years of rampant hedonism, his final search for Om — ultimate wisdom, perfection. Were not the first two phases comparable to winter and summer outside on the boardwalk? And, if so, where did the final third fit? Or, perhaps paramount, did it really matter? Can the ocean or a river really talk?

I was waiting for the ferry in Lewes the next day when an ebullient middle-aged woman with bright lipstick bounded from her car and exclaimed "This is like *The Rapture*. Where are all the people?"

Her name, she said, was Seagull,

but she was thinking about changing it to Barnaby Watergate. She'd lost her job recently, she said, and was aimlessly wandering about, considering taking the ferry to Cape May, or heading west to visit a son in college. She'd swum in the ocean at Rehoboth the day before, she said, and the crazy people laughed at her.

She wandered on, quite madly, like a character from a John Irving novel, making sense but no sense and slashing her cheeks with lipstick and rubbing the color into her skin. She wanted champagne, she said. Where could she find some?

Perhaps in town, I suggested. She rambled some more, then jumped in her car and drove off after the champagne, promising to come back, which I knew she never would. She'd probably forgotten the conversation before her car left the parking lot.

It was onto the car ferry then, and a wonderful hour's journey across to Cape May. Back home that night, my old Smith-Corona portable, a constant companion of 22 years, beckoned from a corner.

The ocean had indeed spoken: Back to work. It was time to begin again, and to end. Om was still a long way off.

•

The Cape May-Lewes Ferry is worth a trip in itself. The ferry, which started service in 1964, maintains five vessels, each of which holds 800 passengers and 100 cars. All have snack bars. There is free parking at both terminals.

For a schedule and fares, write the Cape May-Lewes Ferry, Box 827, North Cape May, N.J. 08204. Phones: Cape May Terminal 609-886-2718, Lewes Terminal 302-645-6313.

For more information on Lewes, contact the Lewes Chamber of Commerce, Box 1, Lewes, Del. 19958. Phone 302-645-8073.

For more information on Rehoboth or Ocean City, contact the Rehoboth Beach Chamber of Commerce, Box 216, Rehoboth Beach, Del. 19971, phone 302-227-2233, or the Ocean City Chamber of Commerce, Route 1, Box 310-A, Ocean City, Md. 21842, phone 301-289-8559.

Sturbridge, Mass.

Old Sturbridge Village is built on the love of a simpler time

By Karen Heller
Inquirer Staff Writer

On a cool, crisp Saturday afternoon, two broad and sandy horses pull a wooden sleigh across the glistening common, freshly covered with a thick blanket of milky powder. There are no cars, no sirens, no radios blasting — just the sounds of kids laughing and families chatting as they trudge from house to historic house.

Old Sturbridge Village is a historic Brigadoon, a place built on dreams and love of a simpler time. The town never quite existed as it does now, clean and orderly. Through the miracle of preservation, on the south side of the common is the 1748 Richardson Parsonage, which stood for two centuries in East Brookfield, Mass.; a 1796 law office originally constructed in Woodstock, Conn., and the 1810 Knight store, which long graced Dummerston, Vt.

Old Sturbridge Village, an hour southwest of Boston and 4½ hours northeast of Philadelphia, is 42 or 158 years old, depending on how you look at it. The new old town was established in the 1940s by the Wells family, avid collectors of early Americana and owners of American Optical Co. in nearby Southbridge. After its establishment, the town's board of trustees began acquiring and moving buildings from throughout New England to re-create a Massachusetts town of 1830. Old Sturbridge continues to experience growth; the Bixby House was under reconstruction when we visited, the roof missing so that it gave the amusing appearance of a 19th-century, white-clapboard trailer.

The town is lovely, a small jewel in south central Massachusetts, but it is not for everyone. It is best suited to families with well-behaved children ages 5 to 14. It is useful, if you plan to stay overnight, to possess a certain amount of discretionary income — though there are some bargains to be found. Old Sturbridge is fine for those with a passionate love of history and a particular interest in the origins of craftsmanship. It is not, however, the place to spend an idyllic romantic weekend or a rustic weekend or any kind of weekend for cynical adults whose tolerance of corn or hoke is almost nil.

The admission fee ($9.50 for adults, $4 for children ages 6 to 15, free for children under 6) allows visitors to peruse at their leisure 40 restored buildings situated on 200 acres and to watch a variety of planned demonstrations each day.

The attitude is relaxed and informal, and the village is fully staffed by knowledgeable personnel in period costumes who, like ski slopes, come in varying degrees of difficul-

178

ty. Some of the docents are as friendly and agreeable as beauty pageant contestants, while others have enough attitude to humble even the most ardent downtown New Yorkers. (That this visit was made on a cold Saturday afternoon may have been a key factor in this.) Perhaps the winner in this latter category was a tinsmith who referred to his 19th-century predecessors not once, not twice, but three times as "dumb and stupid."

So much for cherishing the past.

Some of the Old Sturbridge structures are graced with a stark simplicity of timeless design. The 1796 white-clapboard Friends Meetinghouse, originally located in Bolton, Mass., is a far more severe building than the Center Meetinghouse located just south of it, an 1832 steepled Greek Revival building, a classic New England postcard Congregational church.

The Center Meetinghouse, incidentally, is one of the few buildings that was situated in Sturbridge proper. In the early 19th century, Congregationalists, the most direct religious descendants of the Puritans, were prevalent in New England. In this, as in other such churches, wealthy parishioners had their own pews and decorated them as they pleased. A variety of colorful carpet remnants and fancy cushions adorn the floor. Many of the moneyed parishioners brought portable foot stoves, heated with coal from home, that helped keep them comfortable during winter services in the large, frigid hall.

The town is filled with fascinating souvenirs of 19th-century life. The Freeman farmhouse contains a precursor of the Murphy bed, a vertical — though by no means hidden — bed that was raised during the day to allow more room in the house. The Towne house, Old Sturbridge's grandest residential structure, has a serving pass-through so that kitchen servants didn't have to enter the grand dining room. Even though early 19th-century New England was an age of modesty, window treatments (drapes or curtains) were considered such a luxury that the Towne house master bedroom is the sole sleeping quarters that has them.

The Towne house also features a brave use of print upon print upon print, a kind of visual overload that would make Ralph Lauren feel perfectly at home. The palette is a bit off to the contemporary eye; yellow was mixed into almost everything. The top floor of the house was used at various times as a Masonic Lodge (there are stars painted on the ceiling), ballroom and sleeping quarters for some of the family's seven children. And the multiplicity of uses is evidence of a lesson about the resourceful economy of our ancestors that is prevalent throughout Old Sturbridge Village: Whatever existed was used again and again; there appears to have been almost no waste.

The village is also home to the J. Cheney Wells Clock Gallery, a first-rate collection of antique timepieces. There are coopers, blacksmiths, cobblers and potters toiling away and willing to talk about the 19th-century state of their trades. Some of the docents speak in character ("I've been working the field all day") and some do not. The banker readily admitted that he doubled as the lawyer across the common.

When visiting Old Sturbridge, it is best to ask questions, and plenty of them, because many of the docents have given their speeches more times than a presidential hopeful. (Of course if you have outgoing kids, asking questions won't be a problem.) Perhaps the best guide working one recent day was the schoolteacher, a blond ringer for Molly Ringwald, who had all the visitors sit in her tiny schoolroom and then proceeded to give a wonderful talk, not only about schools, teaching and children, but also about women's lives during the period. For example, a woman could make a great deal more in the mills than by teaching. Perhaps the most startling fact was that the literacy rate in Massachusetts was 95 percent in 1830 and has actually decreased over time.

Old Sturbridge is rightfully proud of the fact that it is entirely restored as opposed to Williamsburg, Va., which contains many reproductions. But Old Sturbridge is also much smaller. How long does it take to visit? Well, with kids it may take a full day. With a lot of kids, it could possibly be a weekend. But for a couple of adults with a good though not voracious interest in historical minutiae, an afternoon would do it.

Old Sturbridge can cost, too. It is, after all, a business. Bullard Tavern, the only restaurant on the common, is a lot less quaint than it appears — and a good deal more expensive. The only lunch being served that day in the village was a full buffet, $9.95 for adults, $5.75 for children. The museum gift shop may be the single largest building in the village, teeming with costly souvenirs and four-figure reproductions.

And lodging and food can be dear. When we were there, the Publick House in Sturbridge, the main lodging in the area, offered only a two-night, five-meal package for $175 or $185 a person, which included taxes, gratuities and entrance to the village on Saturday. The charge for children ages 6 to 15 was $94.50.

The New York company that owns the Publick House also owns the Chamberlain House, the Colonel Ebenezer Crafts Inn and the Country Motor Lodge. During the winter season, many of those rooms are reserved for the spillover from the special weekend packages offered by the Publick House.

Fortunately, during the winter, the lovely Oliver Wight House (c. 1789) on Route 20 right next to the village has rooms with canopied beds available by the evening for $75. The adjacent Old Sturbridge Village Motor Lodge, not to be confused with the Country Motor Lodge, has rooms for $58. Both lodgings are owned by the village. It is advisable to call ahead as rates vary according to season.

The Publick House is the place to eat and drink. There is a cozy downstairs bar with an inviting fireplace. But be warned: There is a piano bar, and the sound of a less-than-gentle songbird crooning "New York, New York" in such surroundings can be off-putting.

Upstairs there is an enormous restaurant split into two sections, a cozy dining area and one as large as a barn, handsomely decorated with quilts and sleds. Entrees are in the $10.95-to-$19.95 range and are of the meat-and-potatoes, scrod and stuffed sole variety. The restaurant has gone so far as to put a Chateau Lafite Rothschild-Pauillac on its wine list at $145; but the vintage is not cited, an omission worthy of capital punishment in the World Court of enology. And the sartorial attitude is definitely New England rustic, which means people do dress for dinner. Many of the men wore ties and jackets, a good number of the women were in skirts and heels.

Though the people at Old Sturbridge Village, and their friends at the Publick House, would be happy if you never left the premises, there are other places to dine.

The Whistling Swan at 502 Main St., Sturbridge, is a popular establishment with people in town; the continental menu features entrees from $8.95 to $18.95. Upstairs is the Ugly Duckling Loft, an enormous room with good bar food for under $9. The loft also has fishbowl-size margaritas for $3.50. New England may not be noted for margaritas, but these were splendid.

Past the Publick House on Route 131 in Sturbridge is Rom's, offering reasonably priced Italian fare; entrees run from $7.95 to $13.50. For those truly conserving, there is Burger King, a McDonald's and a Friendly all within yards of each other on Route 20. The low prices are appreciated, though the brash architecture hardly helps in making a journey into the past. (The sole complaint about the Oliver Wight House is that it is next-door neighbor to the Friendly — preservation cannot always be achieved in the face of commerce and competition.)

The best deal found all weekend, one that successfully combined quaint with thrift, was Annie's Country Kitchen, located a bit farther up Route 131 from Rom's. (It took almost the equivalent of a tooth extraction to get the people at Oliver Wight to recommend something that was not operated by Publick House.) This glorious diner offers a Lumberjack Special with three eggs, toast, bacon, juice and coffee for $3.25, and it's worth paying an extra 35 cents to get the wonderful home-baked blueberry muffins. For those less hungry, two eggs, toast and home fries are a whopping $1.25. To a city person, this is history.

If you have kids and are interested in learning more about 19th-century American life, by all means go to Old Sturbridge and stay overnight in the area. If you don't have kids and a grand passion for the past, try this: Visit Boston for the weekend and make a day trip to the village.

•

The village is open Tuesday through Sunday through the winter. From April through October, it is open on Mondays, too. One suggestion: If you plan to make the trip in winter or spring, wear waterproof boots — the unpaved walkways are often thick with mud.

You can reach Sturbridge by taking the New Jersey Turnpike to the George Washington Bridge and following I-95 to New Haven, Conn. Take the exit for I- 91 north and, in Hartford, Conn., take the exit for I-84 east and proceed to the Sturbridge exit just over the Massachusetts state line.

For information on Old Sturbridge Village and area accommodations and restaurants, write Old Sturbridge Village, 1 Old Sturbridge Village Rd., Sturbridge, Mass. 01566; or phone 617-347-3362.

Williamsburg, Va.

History lives through an artful mix of architecture, costumes and crafts

By Janet Ruth Falon
Special to The Inquirer

Colonial Williamsburg is like new white sneakers before their first scuff: a little too nearly perfect, a little too clean, almost off-putting in its purity.

After all, the Williamsburg that's being preserved here was a living, breathing colonial town, the capital of 18th-century Virginia, a town in which dramatic events that helped lead to the Revolutionary War took place against a backdrop of the ordinary lives of normal, imperfect men, women and children.

For this reason, the horses that clip-clop around the historic district today, towing carriages with photograph-snapping visitors, are a welcome sight. Their earthy smells and uncontrollable deposits in the street are a reminder that this well-done, well-run popular tourist spot was once dusty and dirty and wonderfully alive.

Similarly welcome are the demonstrations, on the village green, of mustering militiamen, of costumed fun-seekers playing an old form of cricket and of other manifestations of life as it might have been. For me, such scenes provided a measure of relief from a host of jarring 20th-century intrusions: the constant stream of buses that circle the historic district, the costumed "wenches" with digital watches up their sleeves.

But although the purist in us might wish for a more authentically colonial experience, Colonial Williamsburg is still worth visiting, particularly its famous historic district adorned with preserved and restored homes, shops, taverns, public buildings and gardens (and famous oatmeal cookies at the Raleigh Tavern bake shop). Williamsburg offers visitors a substantial hunk of American history through an artful mix of architecture, costumes, furniture and crafts and a wonderful introductory movie (on a huge-screen, space-age theater in the Visitors Center) that sets the tone for your stay and helps you know what to look for.

Yet a slight warning: You shouldn't plan to build your entire visit around the historic district, an attraction that seems more appropriate as an educational interlude. Luckily, there are in or near Williamsburg other attractions that are perhaps more fun, such as the Busch Gardens theme park (closed between October and April) and the incredible bargain-shopper's heaven that is the Williamsburg Pottery Factory.

It all adds up to a more balanced visit, especially for families with children.

To distill the best from Colonial Williamsburg, you should start with the Visitors Center film, *Williamsburg: The Story of a Patriot*. It's here, too, that you can purchase the Patriot's pass ($24.50 for adults, $12.25 for children 6 to 12), which provides unlimited admission to all major exhibits and is good for one year.

From the Visitors Center, take a bus to the historic district, a five-minute ride. Be aware that the buses may be filled, so you might be passed by during the busy opening and closing hours of the day.

The mile-long historic district covers 173 acres of the original town, using the still-existing street plan devised in 1699. Its main artery is Duke of Gloucester Street, on which many of the buildings open to the public are situated. What is surprising is the number of buildings on this street that are private residences, some of which are rented to the public or to visitors.

At one end of Duke of Gloucester Street is the Wren Building, the substantial brick main structure of the College of William and Mary. It has an exquisite campus that blends in nicely with the historic district, and you can't help wondering how it feels to go to school next to a tourist attraction.

Some of the most popular buildings in the historic district are the 20 craft shops in which costumed artisans use hand methods and 18th-century tools to fashion articles similar to those made here by their colonial predecessors. The wheelwright, in particular, is fascinating in his no-nails, no-glue craft.

The buildings that appear in the introductory movie are, because of their historic or architectural significance, big draws: the Capitol, in which Patrick Henry defiantly protested the Stamp Act until accused of treason; the octagonal magazine and guardhouse; the Bruton Parish Church, with a lovely shaded cemetery (and gravestones with such inscriptions as a daughter of the Confederacy, reminding you that you are in the South);the Governor's Palace, which was the official residence of seven royal governors, including Lord Dunmore, who fled in 1775,

thus ending British rule in Virginia.

The streets come alive, of course, when visitors walk them, taking the requisite photographs of the children in the stocks or on an ox-drawn wagon, looking appropriately silly in tricorn hats or tootling on fifes bought in one of the many Williamsburg shops. A wide variety of other goodies can be purchased in those shops: traditional souvenirs and an eclectic assortment of books, records, silver, pewter and china.

Merchants Square, at one end of the historic district, is a complex of stores that, with its outdoor eateries and chic shops, is quite similar to the Cape May, N.J., mall. There's a first-run movie theater there, too.

There are two recent additions to Colonial Williamsburg. One is the DeWitt Wallace Decorative Arts Gallery, containing 8,000 English and American decorative objects from the late 17th, 18th and early 19th centuries: furniture, ceramics, textiles, paintings, prints, clocks, scientific instruments, mechanical devices and weapons. The other, adjacent to the gallery, is a reconstruction of the Public Hospital, the first American institution devoted exclusively to treating the mentally ill when it was completed in 1773.

With the help of audio-visual presentations and re-creations of inmates' quarters, the exhibit in the hospital documents three distinct eras of patient-care philosophy: the age of restraint, from 1773 to 1835, when mental illness was regarded as a physical disease and treated in a setting that was part jail, part infirmary; moral management, from 1836 to 1862, when kindness was combined with physical labor, leisure activities and quack treatment plans, such as phrenology, and custodial care, from 1862 to 1885, during which mental institutions were regarded as long-term homes for the chronically ill.

Cage-like cells, straitjackets and other paraphernalia are as disturbing as the narrative, as is a quotation, from a patient to her sister at the very end of the exhibit: "I wish you would come and see me."

During your Williamsburg visit, be sure to go to Carter's Grove Plantation, one of several plantations in the area. Run by the Colonial Williamsburg organization, the mansion and grounds will make you think of Tara, and you'll no doubt be humming the theme from the movie *Gone With the Wind* sometime during your visit.

Plantations are an inescapable indication that this is truly the South. There are other signs: You might overhear women calling each other "Miss Ginnie" and "Miss Agnes," and there will be many reminders of the highly touted Virginia country hams.

What's strange, and perhaps a bit disappointing, about the Carter's Grove mansion is that it has been restored to look like the home of its last owners, Archibald and Molly McCrea, who purchased it in 1927. Even though the house echoes with history, dating to its construction in 1750, it is filled with modern furniture and contains none of the pieces of the time when, for example, both George Washington and Thomas Jefferson proposed marriage to early loves in the southwest parlor. (The room has since been called the "refusal room.")

On the banks of the James River, on Carter's Grove property, is the site of the archaeological excavation of Wolstenholme Towne, an early English settlement (1619 to 1622, when it was destroyed in an Indian attack). The site is fascinating, with dramatic wood-frame outlines of buildings that provide a bare-bones hint of what once existed here. Only a watchtower has been reconstructed; a short tape provides a nice explanation of the site.

As for food, be sure to try the Old Chickahominy House, on the road to Jamestown, for great breakfasts. The Cascades restaurant in Colonial Williamsburg, at the same complex of buildings as the Visitors Center, is famous for its lavish brunch. Excellent cider is sold on the streets of the historic district, too, and peanuts (remember, this is the South) are a common snack.

The Colonial Williamsburg Foundation runs several inns and lodges, and there's also a huge strip of motels on U.S. Route 60.

Five miles out of Williamsburg on Route 60, in Lightfoot, is the Williamsburg Pottery Factory, known as the Pottery. It is an enormous complex of factory-outlet shops at which it's not inconceivable to find anything you want, need or dream of.

The best way to attack the Pottery is with your shopping list in hand, because aimless wandering will drive even the most avid shopper nuts. The Pottery even has its own campground, water slide and miniature golf course.

Williamsburg is close to Virginia Beach; the naval shipyard and harbor cruises of Newport News; the quiet capital city of Richmond; Yorktown, site of the surrender of Lord Cornwallis, ending the Revolutionary War; Jamestown, site of the first permanent English settlement and the story of Capt. John Smith and the Indian princess Pocahontas; and the modern city of Norfolk.

•

Christmas is a special time at Colonial Williamsburg.

For Christmas time, beginning the first weekend in December, the place comes alive with a huge range of Christmas festivities. Among them is the dramatic Grand Illumination: At the sound of a cannon's firing, occupants of the historic area light candles in their windows.

Other seasonal events usually include caroling, concerts, special exhibits and tours, and the chance to make Christmas ornaments based on colonial designs.

It's all based on the 18th-century tradition of "raising joyful noises" to celebrate the birthdays of queens and kings.

For more information about Williamsburg, contact the Colonial Williamsburg Foundation, Williamsburg, Va. 23187 or call 804-229-1000.

Woodstock, Vt.

A ski weekend based in a village that eludes time

By Rob Buchanan
Special to The Inquirer

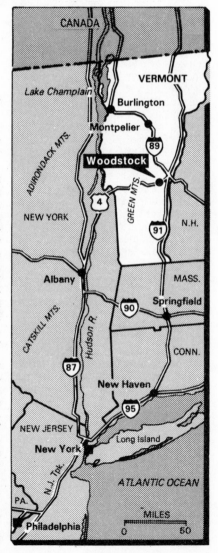

Tourist: Do you think it'll ever stop snowing?

Vermonter: It always has.

Something in the Vermont spirit seems opposed to the very idea of a winter vacation. After all, a vacation is a frivolous, hedonistic affair, a temporary abdication of responsibility. A Vermont winter, on the other hand, is a season to be endured. One stays in one's white box of a house, even if it means risking "shacky wacky," or cabin fever. One represses furious passions; one reads *Ethan Frome*. Yet, somehow, this colonial austerity, this puritanical tidiness, has been made into a tourist attraction. Woodstock.

It's not unusual, especially in New England, to find town names repeating themselves across state lines. There are, in fact, seven Woodstocks in the United States. When most people hear the name, they think of Woodstock, N.Y., supposed site of the 1969 rock festival. (The concert was moved down the road to Bethel after uneasy citizens changed their minds.) Or they think of the comic-strip bird invented by Charles Schulz.

Of all the Woodstocks, however, the Vermont version is the most precious. Set at a confluence of rivers in the

185

foothills of the Green Mountains, this village looks like — and in large part is — a Rockefeller's tasteful idea of what America should be. Much of the village has been designated a National Historic District, and its inhabitants, a chamber of commerce pamphlet notes, "have zealously guided its development and growth past hazards of change that overtook much of the country."

A walk through Woodstock is a stroll through the colonial era. Bells cast by Paul Revere ring in its church belfries, maple syrup flows from its hillsides, and, yes, roofs cover its bridges. Many of the town's original houses have been preserved, not so much for their tourist potential or historic interest, one suspects, as for their innate value as well-built homes. If Woodstock has the appearance of another country, it's because, as William Least Heat Moon noted in *Blue Highways*, "it was not a restoration or renovation, but rather a town — like the best English villages — with a continuous and evident past."

The country around Woodstock is calendar-perfect, even in the wintertime. It is a landscape of twisting river valleys, wide meadows and dense forest. Decades ago, its west-running brooks, birch groves and stone fences inspired Robert Frost. Today they help boost real estate prices to the point where only gentlemen can farm.

There are fewer than a half-dozen farmers left in Woodstock who actually make their living through agriculture. Nevertheless, the hills are alive with people who believe in the Jeffersonian model of a nation of independent farmers, or at least in a Vermontish combination of self-sufficiency and democracy. Exiled Soviet novelists seek out these soft hills, drawn by their resemblance to Mother Russia's, and so do hippies who plow with draft horses, Republican decentralists and survivalists. The eccentric rich live cheek by jowl with the tar-paper poor. What results is a sort of cacophony of voices, almost all of which seem to enjoy, to borrow the motto of nearby Dartmouth College, "crying in the wilderness."

Like Aspen and Newport, Woodstock toes the line between legitimate city and resort. In any case, long before it became a summer colony, it was a fashionable wintertime retreat. America's first ski lift was built two miles out of town, in 1934, and some of the best downhill skiing in the East lies within a 20-minute drive. If you don't ski, it's still worth a weekend.

There's plenty to look at and photograph and mull, and if all else fails, the shopping is good, too.

Historic Woodstock begins on the Green, a 600-foot-long ellipse planted with tall maples. They almost make up for the elms that have disappeared here, as they have elsewhere in New England. In the old days, the Green was the center of business.

Today, the Green is as quiet as a postcard. It's encircled by the town's oldest houses, prosperous-looking wood and brick structures with white picket fences and carved porch railings. Their architecture is that of the young republic, a sort of modified Georgian style that has come to be known as Federal. Most of it dates from the early part of the 19th century. Many of the houses are made of the distinctive tawny-colored local brick, and their plain New England lines are spruced up with scrolling cornices and Ionic columns. Others are of frame construction, with narrow clapboarding. Not one of them seems to need painting.

The Ottauquechee River flows past the northern side of the green, the quality of its water somewhat suspect. (Killington, the East's largest ski area, only 13 miles upstream, has been accused by some public officials of having sewage-treatment facilities that are unequal to its ambitious development scheme.) The river is crossed by a covered bridge — not one of the quaint 19th-century bridges, like those found four miles upstream, at Lincoln, and four miles downstream, at Taftsville, but a relatively new one, built in 1969.

The village elders weren't always so enlightened. In 1830, according to a story in the Vermont Standard, a boy whose brother had recently died of consumption was stricken with the same disease. On disinterring the body of the first brother, several "sound-minded fathers among the community" found the heart curiously undecayed and, adjudging it "a case of assured vampirism," put the offending organ in an iron pot and burned it in the middle of the Green.

"A hole ten feet square and fifteen feet deep," the article continued, "was dug right in the center of the park where the fire had been built, the pot with the ashes was placed in the bottom, and then on top of that was laid a block of solid granite weighing seven tons, cut out of Knox Ledge. The hole was then filled up with dirt, the blood of a bullock was sprinkled on the fresh earth, and the fathers then felt that vampirism was extinguished forever in Woodstock."

A few alarmist Woodstockers, however, feel the vampirism issue was reopened for debate in 1967. In that year, Laurence Rockefeller bought the Woodstock Inn, a rambling fire hazard whose front porch stretched all the way to the edge of the Green. He bulldozed it and built the present inn, which, while handsome, is too large to go by that name.

A few years before, Rockefeller had purchased two nearby ski areas as well as the local golf course, which he promptly had Robert Trent Jones redesign. He also began to buy up the town's oldest houses as they came onto the market. Today, his company continues to pour money into Woodstock, which has become the flagship of the RockResorts fleet.

The wave of investment has, over the years, prompted grumbling around town about monopoly capitalism, and triggered fears that Rockefeller would turn Woodstock into "a little Williamsburg." The fact is, though, that Woodstock was already as close to Williamsburg as you could get without charging admission.

Tourists had been flocking up from Boston and New York since 1875, when the Woodstock railway was built. This spur connected Woodstock to the main Montreal-New York line at White River Junction, 14 miles east on the Connecticut River. Until the Depression forced the railway out of business, the casual weekender could leave Penn Station in New York at 9 p.m. and find himself in Woodstock the next morning at 7:05, all without leaving his Pullman.

Even before the train, Woodstock was known as a winter sports mecca. City folk loved skating and sleighing in a setting as quaint as a Currier and Ives print. Tobogganing became the rage when the management of the old Woodstock Inn built a course on a bluff overlooking the golf course and supplied a team of horses to haul the tobogganers back to the top after each run. Downhill skiing took place for the few and the hardy.

"It's almost impossible nowadays to conceive of what the skiing world was in the early 1930s . . . ," Rockwell Stevens, an early visitor, once told a Woodstock ski-club gathering. "Those early trails were pretty rugged, and no wider than a table top. We'd walk up on our skis, and then we'd come down. But two or three runs a day was a man's work. Every once in a while we'd get discouraged. If we could just find a place where we could get pulled up, and save our legs, and then ski down over some open ground — without the menace of trees at our elbows — that would be paradise."

Three New York businessmen saw the light and hired a Yankee inventor named David Dodd from South Newbury, Vt., to attach a Model T Ford to an 1,800-foot rope loop. In January 1934, on the treeless hill behind Clinton Gilbert's sheep farm, paradise materialized. It was America's first ski lift, and, after all those years of trudging uphill, it was a gas. An operator sat in the Model T, watching the rope spin around a tireless wheel. "When we'd say, 'Hey, step on it,' " Stevens recalled, "he'd step on the accelerator pedal."

By 1936, Woodstock had 12 rope tows operating on four hills. One of the areas was founded by a daredevil skier from Dartmouth named Wallace "Bunny" Bertram, at a spot that was marked on the local topographical map as Hill No. 6.

"I remembered something from high school English about alliteration," Bertram would later say, "so I called the area Suicide Six." Today, it's Woodstock's only remaining downhill ski area, a small (two chairlifts; 600 feet vertical) but meticulously groomed hill that's owned by the Woodstock Inn. Nearby are bigger ski areas like Mount Ascutney and Okemo, and Killington, a Los Angeles-size ski complex (18 lifts; 107 trails; 3,160 vertical feet).

Although the venerable institution of riding uphill only to slide back down began in Woodstock, the town's winter-sports reputation today rests on its Nordic, or cross-country, ski facilities. Vermont is quite popular among cross-country skiers because of its terrain, which is steep but not too abrupt, and its many-centuries-old forest roads, now unused, which were laid out with gentle turns and slopes for horses. They make perfect ski touring trails.

The countryside around Woodstock is still better-suited to the sport. As the town is still an equestrian center in the summer, its upland roads are kept clear of brush and branches by summer horse traffic. The rolling pasture land common to the Woodstock area provides abundant open slopes for downhill running, and the gladed maple woods that fringe the fields are clear enough to negotiate even by moonlight. The sheer number of absentee landowners, most of whom are "summer people," affords the skier a sense of solitude in a landscape that has a settled feel and look.

Winter in Vermont is trespassing season. It's a good time to quote Frost to oneself:

Whose woods these are I think I know.
His house is in the village though.
He will not see me stopping here
To watch his woods fill up with snow.

A good place to stop by if you've never done any cross-country before is the Woodstock Inn's Ski Touring Center, which is what the golf course becomes as soon as it begins to snow in the late fall. It's an extremely spacious and pleasant place for learning the stride-and-glide technique favored by all but elite racers.

Once at ease on skinny skis, the traveler can set out to explore the organized networks of trails on Mounts Tom and Peg, the two high hills that bracket the dell in which Woodstock lies. The trail head for Mount Tom is behind the River Street cemetery, just across the covered bridge from the Green; you can ski up to Mount Peg from the golf course. Trails are well-marked with arrows whose color indicates their difficulty, and they are, like those at the Ski Touring Center, regularly groomed by a tracking machine.

Another road leads out of town and up Kedron Brook for five miles, to South Woodstock. This is perfect riding country in the summer, and sweet country to live in, too: a narrow valley of clear brooks and wild back roads, rambling country houses and barns painted red as if by governmental decree.

South Woodstock's institutions include a volunteer fire department, an old schoolhouse that was once home to the Green Mountain Liberal Institute and to a "Social Library", a general store and the Kedron Valley Inn. The KVI, as it's known, is the genuine article: Built in the 19th century, it has antique quilts on the beds, sleighs tugged around by shaggy-hoofed horses and skating on the pond out back.

Just in case it was your dream to own and operate a place like KVI, you should know that it was sold in 1985, for $1.1 million, to a New Yorker who'd worked as an options trader for eight years specifically with the goal of retiring to an authentic country inn. He and his wife found the place through a broker in Brattleboro who specializes in country inns.

Yes, indeed, there's green in them thar mountains.

Index

HOURS ON THE ROAD

THINGS TO SEE